INTERNATIONAL
CHILDREN'S
BIBLE®
DICTIONARY

A Fun and Easy-to-Use Guide to the
Words, People, and Places in the Bible

To my dear Gabrielle,
Above all get understanding. 1/29/07
I hope you'll use this to get
to know God better.
I love you and so does Jesus!
Denise

INTERNATIONAL
CHILDREN'S
BIBLE®
DICTIONARY

A Fun and Easy-to-Use Guide to the Words, People, and Places in the Bible

RONALD F. YOUNGBLOOD, F. F. BRUCE, and R. K. HARRISON

Tommy nelson®
A Division of Thomas Nelson Publishers
Since 1798

International Children's Bible® Dictionary

Copyright © 2006 by Tommy Nelson®, a Division of Thomas Nelson, Inc., P.O. Box 141000, Nashville, Tennessee 37214

Cover Design: Funnypages Productions, Inc.
Cover illustration: John Pomeroy

Tommy Nelson books may be purchased in bulk for educational, business, fund-raising, or sales promotional use. For information, please email SpecialMarkets@ThomasNelson.com.

Unless otherwise indicated, all Scripture quotations are from the *International Children's Bible®, New Century Version* (NCV), copyright 1986, 1988, 1999 by Tommy Nelson®, a Division of Thomas Nelson, Inc. The New King James Version (NKJV), © 1979, 1980, 1982, Thomas Nelson, Inc., Publishers.

The King James Version (KJV).

New American Standard Bible (NASB), © 1960, 1977 by the Lockman Foundation.

The Holy Bible, New International Version (NIV), © 1973, 1978, 1984, International Bible Society. Used by permission of Zondervan Bible Publishers.

The New Revised Standard Version Bible (NRSV), © 1989 by the Division of Christian Education of the National Council of the Churches of Christ in the USA.

Library of Congress Cataloging-in-Publication Data

Youngblood, Ronald F.
  International children's Bible dictionary : a fun and easy-to-use
guide to the words, people, and places in the Bible / Ronald F.
Youngblood, F.F. Bruce, and R.K. Harrison.
     p. cm.
  ISBN 1-4003-0809-7
  1. Bible—Dictionaries. I. Bruce, F. F. (Frederick Fyvie), 1910– II.
Harrison, R. K. (Roland Kenneth) III. Title.
  BS440.Y67 2006
  220.3—dc22   2005037687

Printed in The United States of America
06 07 08 09 10 QUE 9 8 7 6 5 4 3 2 1

Contents

Charts, Tables, and Maps

Contents

Introduction

What did Lazarus's tomb look like?

Who was Jehosophat?

How do you spell Nebuh . . . Nebbi . . . Nebucka . . . you know, that really means king of Babylon?!

Stumped? Well, you've picked up the right book! From *Aaron* to *Zipporah, The International Children's Bible® Dictionary* will help you to understand the tough terms in your Bible.

If you're reading the *International Children's Bible®,* you already know that it was written just for you, in a language that you can understand. A team of scholars worked very hard to accurately translate the original Hebrew and Greek text into short sentences, simple phrases, and modern expressions. But still, there are weird words, interesting customs, and faraway places that most of us have never seen—or even heard of—before. That's where this handy, little book comes in.

Flipping through these pages, you'll find:

- Simple explanations of the Bible's most important words
- An easy-to-read, color-coded timeline of Bible history
- Over 200 colorful photos, maps, and charts
- Lists of the miracles of Jesus, different kinds of money in the Bible, and many other interesting facts!

You've probably already discovered that the Bible is an amazing book. With the help of this dictionary, we pray you will be able to fully understand its God-given message and apply its guiding truths to your life.

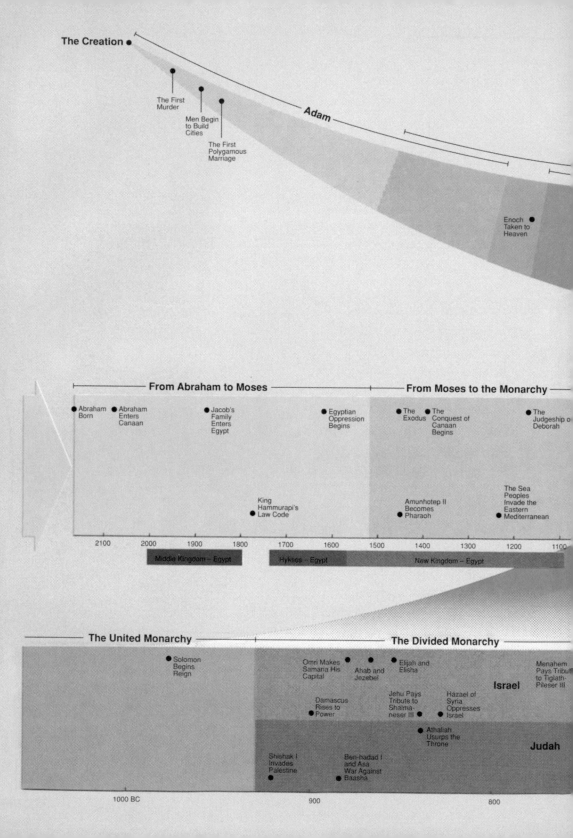

The Creation ●

The First
Murder ●

Men Begin
to Build
Cities ●

● The First
Polygamous
Marriage

Adam

Enoch ●
Taken to
Heaven

―――――――― From Abraham to Moses ――――――――   ―――――― From Moses to the Monarchy ――

● Abraham   ● Abraham   ● Jacob's   ● Egyptian   ● The   ● The   ● The
Born   Enters   Family   Oppression   Exodus   Conquest of   Judgeship o
               Canaan   Enters   Begins   Canaan   Deborah
                                   Egypt   Begins

                                          King   The Sea
                                          Hammurapi's   Amunhotep II Peoples
                                          Law Code   Becomes   Invade the
                                        ● Law Code   ● Pharaoh   Eastern
                                                                             Mediterranean
                                                                           ●

   2100   2000   1900   1800   1700   1600   1500   1400   1300   1200   1100

        ▐ Middle Kingdom ~ Egypt ▌   ▐ Hyksos ~ Egypt ▌   ▐ New Kingdom ~ Egypt ▌

―――――― The United Monarchy ――――――   ―――――――――― The Divided Monarchy ――――――――

              ● Solomon   Menahem
                Begins   Omri Makes   ●   ●   ● Elijah and   Pays Tribu
                Reign   Samaria His   Ahab and   Elisha   to Tiglath-
                                    Capital   Jezebel   **Israel** Pileser III

                                          Damascus   Jehu Pays   Hazael of
                                          Rises to   Tribute to   Syria
                                        ● Power   Shalma-   Oppresses
                                                             neser III   ● Israel
                                                           ●
                                                                      ● Athaliah
                                                                        Usurps the   **Judah**
                                                                        Throne
                                    Shishak I   Ben-hadad I
                                    Invades   and Asa
                                    Palestine   War Against
                                  ●   ● Baasha

   1000 BC   900   800

Bible history

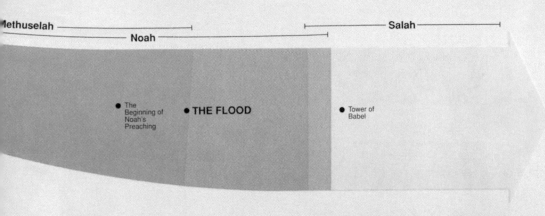

Methuselah ——————————— Salah ———————————

Noah ———————————

- The Beginning of Noah's Preaching
- **THE FLOOD**
- Tower of Babel

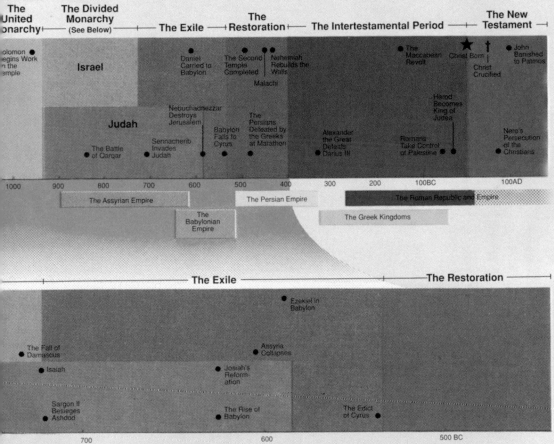

| The United Monarchy | The Divided Monarchy (See Below) | The Exile | The Restoration | The Intertestamental Period | The New Testament |

- Solomon Begins Work on the Temple

Israel

- Daniel Carried to Babylon
- The Second Temple Completed
- Nehemiah Rebuilds the Walls
- The Maccabean Revolt
- ★ Christ Born
- † Christ Crucified
- John Banished to Patmos

Malachi

Judah

Nebuchadnezzar Destroys Jerusalem

- The Battle of Qarqar
- Sennacherib Invades Judah
- Babylon Falls to Cyrus
- The Persians Defeated by the Greeks at Marathon
- Alexander the Great Defeats Darius III
- Romans Take Control of Palestine

Herod Becomes King of Judea

- Nero's Persecution of the Christians

| 1000 | 900 | 800 | 700 | 600 | 500 | 400 | 300 | 200 | 100BC | 100AD |

- The Assyrian Empire
- The Persian Empire
- The Roman Republic and Empire
- The Babylonian Empire
- The Greek Kingdoms

The Exile ——————————— The Restoration ———————————

- Ezekiel in Babylon
- The Fall of Damascus
- Assyria Collapses
- Isaiah
- Josiah's Reformation
- Sargon II Besieges Ashdod
- The Rise of Babylon
- The Edict of Cyrus

| 700 | 600 | 500 BC |

A

AARON [a´-ur-un] — the older brother of Moses and the first high priest of the Hebrew nation.

When God told Moses to lead the Hebrew people out of slavery in Egypt, Moses argued with God because he did not believe that he would be able to talk in a way that would make Pharaoh understand and do what God wanted. God listened to Moses and had Aaron speak for Moses (Exod. 4:14–16).

AARON'S ROD — a rod used by Aaron to perform miracles.

When Moses and Aaron stood in front of Pharaoh, Aaron threw down his rod and it turned into a serpent (snake). When the magicians of Egypt did the same thing, "Aaron's rod swallowed up their rods" (Exod. 7:12).

ABADDON [ab-ad´-dun] *(destruction)* — comes from a Hebrew word that usually means destruction (Job 26:6; 28:22).

In the Book of Revelation, Abaddon is an evil angel who is the ruler of the bottomless pit.

ABASE — realizing that we have needs that only God can take care of (Phil. 4:12, NKJV).

ABATE — pull away from (Gen. 8:8, NKJV; Lev. 27:18, NKJV).

ABBA [ab´-bah] *(father)* — a word in the Aramaic language that is like the English word "Daddy" (Mark 14:36).

ABEDNEGO [ab-ed´-ne-go] *(servant of Nebo)* — the Chaldean name given to Azariah in King Nebuchadnezzar's court when he was chosen to be one of the king's servants (Dan. 1:7–2:49). Abednego was thrown into the fiery furnace, along with Shadrach and Meshach, because he would not bow down and worship a golden image. A miracle happened, and God protected them from the fire (Dan. 3:12–30).

ABEL [a´-bel] *(breath, vapor)* — the second son of Adam and Eve (Gen. 4:2) killed by his jealous brother, Cain (Gen. 4:4–8).

ABHOR — to hate something or someone (Rom. 12:9, NKJV).

ABIATHAR [ab-i´-uth-ur] *(father of abundance)* — the son of Ahimelech and a priest in the royal court of King David.

When Saul destroyed the village of Nob for helping David, Abiathar was the only one to escape (1 Sam. 22:6–23). When David became king he made Abiathar a priest in the royal court (2 Sam. 8:17; 1 Chron. 18:16).

ABIDE — stay; continue (1 Sam. 1:22, NKJV).

ABIGAIL [ab´-e-gul] *(father of joy)* — the wife of Nabal the Carmelite. After Nabal died, she became the wife of David (1 Sam. 25:3, 14–42; 2 Sam. 2:2; 1 Chron. 3:1).

ABIHU [a-bi´-hcw] *(he is my father)* — the

second son of Aaron and Elisheba (Exod. 6:23). Abihu and his brother Nadab were killed in the Wilderness of Sinai for making a bad offering (Lev. 10:1) to the Lord.

ABIMELECH [a-bim´-e-lek] *(my father is king)* — the name of five men in the Old Testament:

1. The king of Gerar in the time of Abraham (Gen. 20:1–18; 21:22–34).

2. The king of Gerar in the time of Isaac (Gen. 26:1–31).

3. The son of Gideon and the ruler of the city of Shechem (Judg. 8:30–10:1; 2 Sam. 11:21). His mother was a slave from Shechem.

4. A priest in the time of David (1 Chron. 18:16).

5. Abimelech was probably the royal title of Achish, the king of Gath (1 Sam. 21:10–15). He was a Philistine king who met David while David was running from King Saul (Ps. 34).

ABLUTION — the ceremonial washing of your body, clothing, and other personal items to make them pure (Heb. 9:10, RSV).

ABNER [ab´-nur] *(the father is a lamp)* — the commander-in-chief of Saul's army (1 Sam. 14:50–51; 17:55).

After Saul died (1 Sam. 31:1–6), Abner tried to make Saul's son Ishbosheth become king. There was a war between David and Ishbosheth. During this war, Abner killed Joab's brother in self-defense. Joab was one of David's military officers (2 Sam. 2:12–3:1). Joab killed Abner for murdering his brother (2 Sam. 3:22–30).

ABODE — the place where you stay; home (John 14:23, NKJV).

ABOLISH — to make something end; destroy completely (2 Tim. 1:10, NKJV).

ABOMINABLE, ABOMINATION — anything that upsets you so much that you feel really disgusted, or makes you feel like you hate something or someone.

Sacrificing weak or sick animals to God was abominable (Deut. 17:1, NKJV). The carved images of pagan gods were an abomination (Deut. 7:25–26, NKJV).

ABOMINATION OF DESOLATION — using the temple of the Lord for something so horrible that it would make the people stop coming to the temple. The prophet Daniel predicted this would happen.

The phrase is found in Matthew 24:15 and Mark 13:14 as a quotation from Daniel 11:31 and 12:11 (NKJV).

ABOUND — to increase; to grow (Prov. 28:20, NKJV).

ABRAHAM [a´-bra-ham] *(father of a multitude)* — the first great Patriarch of ancient Israel and a good example of faithfulness for Christians. The stories about Abraham are found in the Book of Genesis 11:26–25:11.

ABRAHAM'S BOSOM — a phrase that means life after death. In the Old Testament, when a person died, he went to "be with his fathers" (Gen. 15:15, NKJV; 47:30, NKJV; Deut. 31:16, NKJV; Judg. 2:10, NKJV).

ABRAM [a´-brum] *(exalted father)* — the original name of Abraham (Gen. 17:5).

ABSALOM [ab´-sal-um] *(father of peace)*

— the selfish, greedy son of David who tried to take the kingship from his father (2 Sam. 15–2 Sam. 18).

ABSTAIN, ABSTINENCE — to do without something, or to not do something because you think it is the right thing to do (Acts 15:20, 29, NKJV; 1 Thess. 4:3, NKJV; 5:22, NKJV; 1 Tim. 4:3, NKJV; 1 Pet. 1:11, NKJV).

ABUNDANCE — much more than is needed (John 10:10, NKJV).

ABUSE — when used as a noun it means very bad treatment; when used as a verb it means to hurt someone on purpose (Heb. 10:33, NKJV).

ABYSS [a-biss] — the bottomless pit. This word is used in the Bible to describe the prison of disobedient spirits, or the world of the dead (Luke 8:31, NKJV; Rom. 10:7, NKJV; Rev. 20:1–3). "The pit" and "bottomless pit" represent the place where the wicked go when they die.

ACACIA [a-cay´-shih] — a large tree that was an excellent source of wood. The Ark of the Covenant was made from the wood of this tree (Deut. 10:3).

ACCEPT — to receive; to treat with favor. In the Bible, a person is accepted by the grace, mercy, or covenant love of God through faith and repentance (Eph. 1:6, NKJV).

ACCESS — being allowed to go to someone, especially a person who holds a position of authority. We have access to God through Jesus (Heb. 10:20, NKJV).

ACCOMPLISH — to succeed; to finish; to complete (Isa. 55:11, NKJV).

Photo by Howard Vos

Traditional well of Abraham in the plains of Mamre (Gen. 21:22–32).

ACCORD — agreement; conformity; harmony (Acts 2:46, NKJV; 7:57, NKJV; 15:25, NKJV).

ACCOUNT, ACCOUNTABILITY — the biblical truth that says we have to answer to God for our thoughts, words, and actions. The Bible plainly teaches that "the whole world [is] accountable to God" (Rom. 3:19, NASB).

ACCURSED — under a curse; doomed; anything that a curse has been placed on (Josh. 6:17–18, NKJV; Gal. 1: 8–9, NKJV).

ACCUSE — to blame; to say that someone did something (Luke 11:54, NKJV).

ACHAIA [ak-ah´-yah] — the name for all of Greece, except Thessaly (Acts 19:21, NKJV). The Romans gave the region this name when they captured Corinth and destroyed the Achaian League in 146 B.C. Later it included several Greek cities, including Athens.

ACHAN [a´-kan] — the son of Carmi of the tribe of Judah. He accidentally caused the Israelites to lose the battle at Ai (Josh. 7:1, 18–24; 1 Chron. 2:7).

ACHOR [a´-kor] *(trouble)* — a valley near Jericho where Achan was stoned to death. Also called the Valley of Trouble (Josh. 7:24, 26).

ACKNOWLEDGE — to recognize; to agree with (Deut. 21:17, NKJV; 1 Cor. 14:37, NKJV).

ACTS OF THE APOSTLES — the only historical book of the New Testament. It tells about the growth of the early church after the ascension of Jesus.

A doctor named Luke who traveled with Paul wrote it. The Book of Acts tells how Peter and Paul taught people how to become Christians.

A.D. — abbreviation for *Anno Domini,* which is Latin for "in the year of our Lord."

ADAM [ad´-um] *(red, ground)* — the name of the first man. He was created by God on the sixth day of creation and placed in the Garden of Eden (Gen. 2:19–23; 3:8–9, 17, 20–21; 4:1, 25; 5:1–5). His wife Eve was created from one of his ribs (Gen. 2:21–22). Adam and Eve are the ancestors of all people.

ADAR — the Babylonian name of the twelfth month of the Jewish year (Ezra 6:15; Esther 3:7, 13; 8:12; 9:1, 15–21).

ADDAR [a´-dar] *(cloudy)* — the name of a town in southern Judah (Josh. 15:3).

ADDER — a snake; a serpent (Gen. 49:17, NKJV).

ADHERE — to stick to; to obey; to show loyalty (2 Kings 17:34, NIV).

ADJURE, ADJURATION — to ask for something or tell something with strong feelings (Matt. 26:63, NKJV). Adjuration is the power (authority) that makes one person keep a promise to another (1 Sam. 14:24, NKJV; 1 Kings 22:16, NKJV; Mark 5:7, NKJV; Acts 19:13, NKJV).

ADMONISH — to suggest; to encourage; to inspire; to motivate (Col. 3:16, NKJV; 2 Thess. 3:15, NKJV).

ADONIJAH [ad-on-i´-jah] *(the Lord is my Lord)* — the name of three men in the Old

This Greek inscription at Athens contains the text of Paul's speech which he delivered at the Areopagus (Acts 17:22–31).

Testament, but it usually refers to David's fourth son (2 Sam. 3:4).

When David was old, Adonijah tried to become king even though he knew his father wanted Solomon to become king (1 Kings 1:13).

ADULTERY — breaking marriage vows by having sexual relations with someone you are not married to. Jesus said the act of adultery also included wrong thoughts (Exod, 20:14; Mark 10:11, 12; John 8:3–5). This can also mean breaking vows (not necessarily by sexual relations). The Bible states that the nation of Israel committed adultery (Jer. 3:8–9; Ezek. 23–37).

ADVERSARY — a person who fights you or holds you back; an enemy. In the Bible, this word is used when talking about Satan. Satan is the adversary of God and His perfect plan for the world (1 Pet. 5:8, NKJV; 1 John 2:1, NKJV).

ADVERSITY — a difficult situation (Prov. 24:10, NKJV).

ADVOCATE — a person who tells another person's side of the story before a court, like an attorney. The Bible refers to Jesus (1 John 2:1, NKJV) and the Holy Spirit as a "Helper" (John 14:16, 26; 15:26; 16:7).

AFFECTION — a feeling; liking (Rom. 1:26, NKJV).

AFFLICTION — any condition or problem that causes suffering or pain. The Bible says affliction can be caused by sin (Isa. 53:4, NKJV; Matt. 24:29, NKJV; Rom. 2:9, NKJV), but sometimes affliction can help people trust Jesus (Rom. 5:3–5, NKJV; 2 Thess. 1:4–7, NKJV).

AGABUS [ag´-ab-us] — a Christian prophet of Jerusalem who went to Antioch of Syria while Paul and Barnabas were there. The Holy Spirit told him to tell the people about a great famine that was going to happen (Acts 11:28).

AGAPE [a-gah´-pay] — a Greek word that means love that is used in the New Testament (John 13:35, NKJV; 1 Cor. 13, NKJV; 1 John 4:7–18, NKJV).

AGE — a certain period of time during which certain things will happen. In the New Testament, age generally refers to now instead of the future (Col. 1:26, NKJV).

AGRIPPA I [a-grip´-pah] — a Roman ruler of Galilee. He eventually ruled over the same territory that his grandfather, Herod the Great, used to rule. Agrippa was very mean. He tortured and killed many of the Christians in Jerusalem (Acts 12:1–23).

AGRIPPA II [a-grip´-pah] — the son of Agrippa I and the great-grandson of Herod the Great. Shortly before the apostle Paul was taken prisoner in Rome, he had to appear before Agrippa II (Acts 25:13–26:32).

AGUE — fever (Lev. 26:16, NKJV; Deut. 28:22, NKJV).

AHAB [a´-hab] *(father is brother)* — the seventh king of Israel (1 Kings 16:30).

Ahab was a wicked king who was married to Jezebel. She was evil and worshiped Baal, a false god. Jezebel asked Ahab not to worship the Lord anymore. He listened to her and decided to destroy the altars to God and kill the prophets of God.

AHASUERUS [a-has-u-e´-rus] *(mighty man)* — the name of two kings in the Old Testament:

1. A king of Persia and the husband of Esther. Ahasuerus is the same person as Xerxes I (485–464 B.C.).

2. A king of the Medes and the father of Darius (Dan. 9:1).

AHAZ [a´-haz] — the name of two men in the Old Testament:

1. A son of Jotham and the eleventh king of Judah (2 Kings 15:38; 16:1–20; Achaz, KJV).

2. A Benjaminite and descendant of King Saul. Ahaz was a son of Micah and the father of Jehoaddah (1 Chron. 8:35–36; 9:42).

Photo by Howard Vos

Remains of a palace from Ahab's time, uncovered in an excavation at the site of ancient Samaria.

AHAZIAH [a-haz-i´-ah] *(the Lord sustains)* — the name of two kings in the Old Testament:

1. The son of Ahab and the ninth king of Israel (1 Kings 22:40, 49, 51). He reigned from 853 to 852 B.C.

2. The son of Jehoram and the nephew of the first Ahaziah (2 Kings 8:24–26; 2 Chron. 21:17). He is also called Jehoash (2 Chron. 25:23), and Joram (2 Chron. 22:6). He was the sixth king of Judah, and he reigned for only one year (841 B.C.).

AI [a´-i] *(the ruin)* — a Canaanite city (Josh. 10:1) located east of Bethel (Gen. 12:8). Many years before Joshua's time, Abraham set up his tent at Ai before traveling to Egypt (Gen. 12:8). Ai is also an Ammonite city in Moab (Jer. 49:3).

ALABASTER — a smooth stone used to make containers for perfumes and ointments (Matt. 26:7; Mark 14:3; Luke 7:37).

ALAS — an expression of sadness or grief; can also be used in a warning (Josh. 7:7, NKJV).

ALEXANDER [al-ex-an´-dur] *(defender of men)* — the name of five or six men in the Bible, but usually referring to Alexander the Great, the founder of the Greek Empire.

ALIEN — a "foreigner," "traveler," or "stranger" from a country other than Israel. Aliens were not allowed to have the same rights as the Israelites (Deut. 14:21; Job 19:15; Ps. 69:8).

ALLEGORY — a symbolic explanation of a truth about human behavior.

The apostle Paul used allegories in his writing. In Ephesians 6:11–17, he urges his readers to "wear the full armor of God" and then gives the symbolic explanation for each item worn by the Christian soldier.

ALLELUIA [al-e-loo´-yah] *(praise the Lord)* — a Greek form of the Hebrew word *Hallelujah,* used to express joy, praise, and thanksgiving (Ps. 104:35; 116:19; 147:1, NKJV).

ALLOTMENT — a system of land management in the Old Testament. Israel used this system to distribute the land to the tribes, clans, and families (Josh. 13–19).

ALMIGHTY — all powerful; having total control (Gen. 17:1, NKJV).

Photo by Howard Vos

Bust of Alexander the Great, Greek military conqueror.

Alexander's Greek Empire
(Daniel 2, 7, 8, 11)

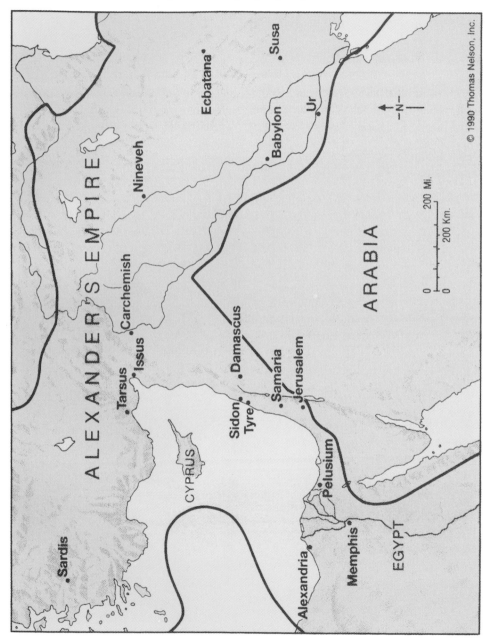

ALMS — money given to the poor (Deut. 15:11, NKJV).

ALPHA AND OMEGA [al´-fah, oh-may´-guh] — the first and last letters of the Greek alphabet.

This title is given to God the Father and God the Son (Rev. 1:8; 21:6). Jesus says, "I am the Alpha and the Omega, the First and the Last, the Beginning and the End" (Rev. 22:13). The writer of the Book of Revelation called Jesus the "Alpha and Omega," because he knew and understood that Jesus is the Creator, the Redeemer, and the Final Judge of all things.

ALPHAEUS [al-fe´-us] *(leader or chief)* — the name of two men in the New Testament:

1. The father of the apostle James (Matt. 10:3; Acts 1:13).

2. The father of Levi (or Matthew), the apostle and writer of the first gospel (Mark 2:14).

ALTAR — a table, platform, or elevated place on which a priest placed a sacrifice as an offering to God (Gen. 8:20).

AMALEK [am´-al-ek] — a grandson of Esau (Gen. 36:12; 1 Chron. 1:36) and a chief of an Edomite tribe (Gen. 36:16). The Amalekites got their name from Amalek.

AMBASSADOR — a representative (Eph. 6:19–20, NKJV).

AMEN *(so be it)* — a solemn word spoken by a person who agrees with a statement, an oath, or a covenant (Neh. 5:13). In worship it is said to agree with a sermon, a psalm, or a prayer.

Photo by Gustav Jeeninga

Excavations at ancient Megiddo, showing the ancient round altar used for pagan sacrifices.

AMOS [a´-mos] *(burden bearer)* — the famous shepherd and prophet of the Old Testament who told the people of the northern kingdom of Israel that they were sinners. His prophecies and the few facts known about his life are found in the Book of Amos.

AMOS, BOOK OF — a prophetic book of the Old Testament. The book is named for its author, the prophet Amos, whose name means "burden bearer." Amos had the burden of sharing God's message of coming judgment to a sinful and disobedient people.

Amos was a humble shepherd who was brave enough to tell God's message to the proud rich people of his day. He begged the people to return to a life of justice and righteousness. The message of Amos is also right for us today because God still places a higher value on justice and righteousness than on all the things that money will buy.

ANANIAS [an-an-i´-as] *(the Lord is gracious)* — the name of three men in the New Testament:

1. A Christian in the early church at Jerusalem (Acts 5:1–11). He and his wife, Sapphira, sold a piece of property and gave only part of the money made from its sale to Peter. When Peter scolded him for lying about the money, Ananias died. Later, his wife Sapphira told the same lie, and she also died.

2. A Christian disciple living in Damascus at the time of Paul's conversion (Acts 9:10–18; 22:12–16). In a vision, the Lord told Ananias about Paul and told him to go welcome Paul into the church. Ananias was scared but when the Lord told him, "I have chosen [Paul] for an important work" (Acts 9:15), he went to Paul

and laid his hands upon him. Paul was able to see again and he was baptized (Acts 9:18).

3. The Jewish high priest who spoke against Paul to the Roman governor Felix (Acts 24:1).

ANATHEMA [a-nath´-em-ah] *(accursed)* — a Greek word that means "accursed" or "separated" (Rom. 9:3, NKJV; Gal. 1:8–9, NKJV).

ANCIENT OF DAYS — a name the prophet Daniel called God (Dan. 7:9, 13, 22, NKJV).

ANDREW [an´-drew] *(manly)* — the brother of Simon Peter and one of Jesus' first disciples. Andrew and Peter were fishermen (Matt. 4:18; Mark 1:16–18) from Bethsaida (John 1:44).

At the feeding of the 5,000, Andrew told Jesus about the boy with five barley loaves and two fish (John 6:5–9).

ANGEL — a spiritual being (Heb. 1:14). Angels are stronger and smarter than human beings (2 Sam. 14:17, 20; 2 Pet. 2:11). God uses angels to deliver messages and help people. They are not like God, though; they are not all-powerful and all-knowing (Ps. 103:20; 2 Thess. 1:7).

ANGER — a strong feeling of frustration. God and humans can both feel anger. God feels anger when people sin. People feel anger because of their own sins or the sins of another person (Ps. 37:8).

ANNA [an´-nah] *(favor)* — the daughter of Phanuel (Luke 2:36), a widow, and a prophetess. She was at the temple in Jerusalem when Mary and Joseph brought Jesus to be dedicated (Luke 2:27). Anna knew Jesus was the Messiah (Luke 2:37–38).

ANNAS [an´-nas] *(grace of the Lord)* — a high priest at Jerusalem when John the Baptist began his ministry, about A.D. 26 (Luke 3:2).

ANNIHILATE — to completely destroy; to eliminate; to "wipe out" (Esther 3:13).

ANNUNCIATION — the announcement made by the angel Gabriel (Luke 1:26–38) to the Virgin Mary about the forthcoming birth of Jesus. The angel told Mary that the Holy Spirit would cause her to become pregnant and that the child would be called the Son of God (Luke 1:35).

ANOINT, ANOINTING — to give a person the authority to do a particular job (Isa. 61:1, NKJV). In the New Testament, everyone who was a disciple of Christ was anointed. This meant that they had the power and the authority to serve God and do His will (2 Cor. 1:21, NKJV).

ANTICHRIST, THE — a false prophet and evil being who will try to stand up against Christ and the people of God in the last days before the Second Coming (1 John 2:18, 22; 4:3; 2 John 7).

ANTIOCH OF PISIDIA [an´-te-ok, pih-sid´-e-uh] — a city of southern Asia Minor, located just north of Pisidia. Antioch was a busy commercial area and an important place for the teaching of the gospel. It was founded by Seleucus I Nicator around 300 B.C. and named for his father Antiochus.

ANTIOCH OF SYRIA [an´-te-ok, sihr´-e-uh] — the capital of the Roman province of Syria that played an important part in the early growth of the church. Antioch was located about 16.5 miles from the Mediterranean Sea and three hundred miles north of Jerusalem. Seleucus I Nicator founded this city around 300 B.C.

APOCRYPHA, THE [a-pock´-rih-fuh] — a group of books written during a difficult time in the history of the Jewish people. These books have two main divisions, Old Testament apocryphal books and New Testament apocryphal books.

APOLLOS [a-pol´-os] *(destroyer)* — a Jewish teacher from Alexandria and a leader in the early church. Apollos was a disciple of John the Baptist (Acts 18:25).

APOSTLE — a person who Jesus picked to

The Order of the Books of the Apocrypha

1. First Esdras
2. Second Esdras
3. Tobit
4. Judith
5. The Additions to Esther
6. The Wisdom of Solomon
7. Ecclesiasticus, or the Wisdom of Jesus, the Son of Sirach
8. Baruch
9. The Letter of Jeremiah
10. The Prayer of Azariah and the Song of the Three Young Men
11. Susanna
12. Bel and the Dragon
13. The Prayer of Manasseh
14. First Maccabees
15. Second Maccabees

do special jobs and help spread the gospel. The word "apostle" is the title given to the twelve disciples of Jesus (Mark 3:14; 6:30).

APOSTOLIC COUNCIL — a group of apostles and elders of the New Testament church in Jerusalem. This council had to decide if Gentiles had to be circumcised and follow other laws of the Jewish faith in order to be members of the church (Acts 15). They decided that a Gentile does not have to become a Jew in order to be a Christian.

APPAREL — clothes (1 Tim. 2:9).

APT — likely (Prov. 15:23, NKJV).

AQUILA [ac´-quil-ah] *(eagle)* — a Jewish Christian living in Corinth when Paul arrived there from Athens (Acts 18:2). Aquila and his wife Priscilla lived in Rome until Claudius ordered all the Jewish people to leave the city. They moved to Corinth and began making tents.

ARCHANGEL — a spiritual being that is the leader of God's angels.

The word "archangel" is found several times in the Bible. In the Old Testament, Michael is

The Twelve Apostles
(in the order in which they are mentioned)

Matthew 10:2–4	Mark 3:16–19	Luke 6:14–16	Acts 1:13
Simon Peter	Simon Peter	Simon Peter	Peter
Andrew	James	Andrew	John
James	John	James	James
John	Andrew	John	Andrew
Philip	Philip	Philip	Philip
Bartholomew	Bartholomew	Bartholomew	Thomas
Thomas	Matthew	Matthew	Bartholomew
Matthew	Thomas	Thomas	Matthew
James	James	James	James
(of Alphaeus)	(of Alphaeus)	(of Alphaeus)	(of Alphaeus)
Thaddaeus	Thaddaeus	Simon (the Zealot)	Simon (the Zealot)
Simon	Simon	Judas	Judas
(the Zealot)	(the Zealot)	(of James)	(of James)
Judas Iscariot	Judas Iscariot	Judas Iscariot	....

Matthew and Mark have the name Thaddaeus while Luke, in his two lists (Luke 6 and Acts 1), has Judas (of James). Some think Judas may have been his original name and that it was changed later to Thaddaeus (meaning perhaps "warm-hearted") in order to distinguish him from Judas Iscariot.

It is interesting that all four lists begin with Simon Peter and end with Judas Iscariot (except the Acts 1 list, for Judas had already killed himself). Also, the names would appear to be in groups of four. Peter, Andrew, James, and John are always in the first group—though not always in that order—and Philip, Bartholomew, Thomas, and Matthew are in the second group in all four lists.

In all four lists, Peter's name heads the first group, Philip heads the second, and James (of Alphaeus) heads the third.

Photo by Gustav Jeeninga

The Areopagus (Mars' Hill) is a little hill near the acropolis in Athens where Paul may have been brought before the philosophers of this city (Acts 17:16–34).

described as "one of the most important angels" (Dan. 10:13) and is the ruling angel (Dan. 10:21), especially in the "time of much trouble" in the last days (Dan. 12:1).

In the New Testament the voice of an archangel and the sounding of the trumpet of God will signal the coming of Jesus for His people (1 Thess. 4:16). Michael the archangel argued with the devil about the body of Moses (Jude 9).

AREOPAGUS [a-re-op´-a-gus] *(hill of the god Ares)* — a limestone hill in Athens between the Acropolis and the Agora. Areopagus is also the name of the council that met near the hill (Acts 17:16–34).

ARIMATHEA [ar-im-ath-e´-ah] *(height)* — a city in the hills of Judea, northwest of Jerusalem. A member of the Jewish Sanhedrin

named Joseph lived there. Joseph placed the body of Jesus in the tomb at Arimathea (Luke 23:50).

ARK OF THE COVENANT — a sacred portable chest that—along with the Mercy Seat and Cherubim—was the most important sacred object of the Israelites while they wandered in the wilderness.

ARK OF MOSES — a small basketlike container that Moses' mother hid him in to save him from the slaughter of Hebrew children by the Egyptian Pharaoh (Exod. 2:3–6). The basket was made of woven bulrushes and sealed with a tarlike substance called pitch. The lid on the basket kept insects and the sun off of Moses so he could sleep. The Pharaoh's daughter found the ark when she came to the river to take a bath.

ARK, NOAH'S — a giant boat built by Noah to save him, his family, and the animals from the Flood (Gen. 6:14–9:18).

ARMAGEDDON [ar-mag-ed´-don] *(mountain of Megiddo)* — the place of the final battle between God and Satan. God will destroy the armies of Satan and throw Satan into the bottomless pit (Rev. 16:16).

ART — the use of skill and creativity to create beautiful objects. Not much is known about the art of the Hebrew people. Except for the descriptions of the tabernacle and the temple in the Bible, art is really not mentioned in the Scriptures. Most of the information that is known about art comes from archaeologists.

ASCENSION OF CHRIST — the rising of Jesus into heaven forty days after His resurrection (Mark 16:19; Luke 24:50–51; Acts 1:9–11).

ASHER [ash´-ur] *(happy)* — the eighth son of Jacob (Gen. 30:13), and the name of a city located east of Shechem (Josh. 17:7).

ASHERAH [ash-er´-ah] — a pagan goddess (Judg. 3:7).

ASHTORETH [ash´-ta-roth] — many pagan goddesses. The Philistines had a temple to the Ashtoreth (1 Sam. 31:10). The Ashtoreth were often worshiped with the male god Baal (Judg. 2:13). A pagan goddess worshiped by the Sidonians (1 Kings 11:5).

ASLEEP — in the state of sleep (Matt. 8:24), and also a reference to death (1 Thess. 4:13, NKJV).

ASP — a snake or a serpent. A cobra-like snake (Isa. 11:8).

ASS — a donkey (Num. 22:21, NKJV).

ASSEMBLY — a group of people with a common cause or purpose (Joel 1:14, NKJV).

ASSURANCE — being sure; without doubt. Assurance is the believers' confidence that their sins have been paid for and they will go to heaven. They know this because of Christ's death and resurrection (1 John 5:12, NKJV).

ASSYRIA [as-sir´-e-ah] — a kingdom between the Tigris and Euphrates rivers. Assyria often controlled many of the smaller countries around it. After defeating the northern kingdom of Israel in 722 B.C., the Assyrians sent away thousands of Israelites and made them live in other parts of the Assyrian Empire. This was a terrible situation that the nation of Israel never recovered from.

ASTROLOGER — a person who looked for answers about life by studying the sun, moon, planets, and stars (Isa. 47:13).

Photo by Levant Photo Service

A stone carving that may represent the Ark of the Covenant, discovered at the excavation of a synagogue in Capernaum.

A fine example of mosaic art, this map shows Palestine in the sixth century A.D. Note the city of Jericho in the lower part of the mosaic.

Photo by Gustav Jenringa

ASUNDER — a division or separation, usually a bad thing (Acts 15:39, NKJV).

ATONEMENT — the act of God's atoning grace and forgiveness that restores a relationship of harmony and unity between God and humans. The word can be broken into three parts to show this great truth in simple terms: "at-one-ment."

ATONEMENT, DAY OF — a Jewish holy day. Its modern name is its Hebrew name, Yom Kippur. The Day of Cleansing (Lev. 16). On this day the nation of Israel asked for forgiveness of its sins (Lev. 23:27; Num. 29:7). The Day of Atonement was the only time fasting was required by the law (Lev. 16:29, 23:31). It was a solemn, holy day with many ceremonies.

AUGUSTUS [aw-gus´-tus] *(consecrated, holy, sacred)* — a title of honor given to the first Roman emperor, Octavian (27 B.C.–A.D. 14). Luke refers to him as "Caesar Augustus" (Luke 2:1). Octavian eventually became the ruler of Rome and ruled for more than forty-four years, until he died in A.D. 14. Jesus was born during the time Octavian ruled (Luke 2:1).

AUTHORITIES — those who hold a position of power (Luke 12:11, NKJV; Eph. 3:10, NKJV). This position of power can be physical, spiritual, or both.

AUTHORITY — the power or right to do something, especially to give orders and make sure they are followed (Rom. 13:1, NKJV).

15

Bust of Augustus Caesar, first emperor of the Roman Empire.

AVENGE — to provide full justice (Jer. 46:10, NKJV).

AWAKE — to revive (Dan. 12:2).

AWE — admiration; amazement (Ps. 33:8, NKJV).

AZARIAH [az-a-ri´-ah] *(the Lord has helped)* — the Hebrew name of Abednego. Nebuchadnezzar placed him, Shadrach, and Meshach in the fiery furnace because they refused to worship his golden idols (Dan. 1:6–7, 11, 19; 2:17).

AZAZEL [az´-a-zel] — a word that means scapegoat (Lev. 16:8, 10, NKJV).

B

BAAL [ba´-al] *(lord, master)* — the name of a false god of the Canaanites (Jer. 11:13), a city (1 Chron. 4:33), and two men in the Bible (1 Chron. 5:5–6; 1 Chron. 8:30; 9:36).

BABEL, TOWER OF [ba´-bel] — a very tall tower built after the Flood.

The people were selfish and greedy and thought they could build a tower so high in the sky that it would let them reach God. God did not like their attitude and changed their languages so they could not understand each other. Since they could not work together any more, they stopped building the tower (Gen. 11:1–9).

BABYLON, CITY OF [bab´-i-lun] — a city built between the Tigris and Euphrates rivers and capital of the Babylonian Empire.

BABYLONIA [bab-i-low´-nih-uh] — a pagan empire in southern Mesopotamia. The Babylonians were always fighting with the Assyrians for control of the entire area.

BACKBITE — to say things about a person with the purpose of hurting them or causing trouble (Ps. 15:3, NKJV; Rom. 1:30, NKJV).

BACKSLIDE — to go back to a sinful life (Jer. 2:19, NKJV; 31:22, NKJV; 49:4, NKJV).

BALAAM [ba´-la-am] — a magician (Josh. 13:22) who was called by Balak, the Moabite king, to place a curse on the Israelites before they went to Canaan (Num. 22:5–24:25; Deut. 23:4–5). God told Balaam to go and then used a donkey to make him understand that he should only say what God told him to and not curse the Israelites.

BALANCES — a tool used to measure weight. In the Bible, talking about balances is often done to teach a lesson (Lev. 19:36).

BALM — a plant-based ointment used for medical purposes (Jer. 51:8).

This drawing of Babylon shows the main avenue of the city, passing through the Gate of Ishtar in the city wall.

17

BAPTISM — a ceremony used in the New Testament church (Rom. 6:1–4) that is still used in churches today. A lot of churches have different ideas about baptism. They have different views on who should be baptized, and also on how to be baptized.

BAPTISM OF FIRE — a phrase used by John the Baptist to describe the work of Jesus Christ: "He [Christ] will baptize you with the Holy Spirit and with fire" (Matt. 3:11; Luke 3:16).

BAPTIST — a person who baptizes, like John the Baptist (Mark 1:4–5); also the name of a Christian denomination.

BARABBAS [ba-rab´-bas] — a "robber" (John 18:40) and notorious prisoner (Matt. 27:16) who was chosen by the mob in Jerusalem to be set free instead of Jesus.

BARBARIAN — a person who is different from most of society. Originally, the Greeks used the word to describe anyone who did not speak the Greek language (Rom. 1:14, NKJV). Later, when Rome conquered Greece, "barbarian" was the word for people who didn't take part in Greco–Roman culture.

BAR–JESUS [bar-je´-sus] *(son of Jesus)* — a false prophet who stood against Barnabas and Paul at Paphos, a town on the island of Cyprus (Acts 13:4–12). He is also called Elymas, which means "magician" or "sorcerer." Bar–Jesus lost his sight for a short time because of his stand against the gospel.

BARNABAS [bar´-na-bus] *(son of encouragement)* — an apostle in the early church (Acts 4:36–37; 11:19–26) and a partner to Paul during his first missionary journey (Acts

A baptistry, or bath, used for purification ceremonies in the Essene community at Qumran.

Photo by Gustav Jeeninga

Photo by Howard Vos

A baptistry shaped like a cross in the Church of St. John at Ephesus.

13:1–15:41). Barnabas was a Levite from the island of Cyprus. His birth name was Joseph, or Joses (Acts 4:36). When he became a Christian, he sold his land and gave the money to the apostles in Jerusalem (Acts 4:36–37).

BARREN — the condition of being unable to produce. This word could be used to speak of a woman who couldn't have children, or it could be used to talk about land (2 Kings 2:19, NKJV). Sometimes it even meant a whole nation (Isa. 54:1, NKJV).

BARTHOLOMEW [bar-thol´-o-mew] *(son of Tolmai)* — one of the twelve apostles of Jesus (Matt. 10:3; Mark 3:18; Luke 6:14; Acts 1:13). He might have also been called Nathanael (John 1:45–49).

BASE — when used as an adjective, it means humble or lowly (Ezek. 29:15, NKJV); when used as a noun, it is a pedestal (Ezra 3:3, NKJV).

BASHAN [ba´-shan] — a territory east of the Jordan River and the Sea of Galilee (Deut. 32:14).

BATH — a liquid measurement that equals about 5.8 gallons (1 Kings 7:38, NKJV).

BATHSHEBA [bath-she´-buh] *(daughter of oath)* — a wife of Uriah the Hittite. After Uriah died, she became a wife of King David (2 Sam. 11; 12:24).

David had Uriah killed so he could marry Bathsheba. David and Bathsheba had a child together, but because of the sin involved in their relationship, the child died (2 Sam. 11:26–27).

B.C. — a time reference that means *"Before Christ."*

Photo by Gustav Jenninga

The tomb of Barnabas on the island of Cyprus in the Mediterranean Sea.

BEATITUDES, THE — Spoken by Jesus at the beginning of the Sermon on the Mount (Matt. 5:3–12).

BEELZEBUB [be-el´-ze-bub] — the Greek name of Baal–Zebub, a false god of the Philistines (Matt. 12:24).

BEERSHEBA [be-ur´-she-ba] *(well of the seven or well of the oath)* — a main city located in the territory of Simeon (Josh. 19:1–2) and the most southern city in the land of Judah (Josh. 15:21, 28).

BEGET — to make happen; in the Bible, it usually means "fathered" (1 Cor. 4:15, NKJV).

BEGOTTEN, ONLY — a New Testament phrase that describes Jesus Christ as the special, only Son of His heavenly Father (John 1:14, 18, NKJV; 3:16–18, NKJV; 1 John 4:9, NKJV; one and only, NIV). As the special, sinless Son

of God, Jesus provided the way to our salvation by dying on the cross.

BELIAL [be´-le-al] *(worthlessness)* — an Old Testament word used to describe a bad person. Belial is sometimes used as a name for a demon or Satan (2 Cor. 6:15).

BELIEVE, BELIEVER — to trust in God's truth; a person who knows that what God says is true and trusts Him for salvation (John 14:1; 20:31).

BELSHAZZAR [bel-shaz´-ar] *(Bel, protect the king)* — the oldest son of Nabonidus and the last king of the Neo–Babylonian Empire (Dan. 5:1–2; 7:1; 8:1).

BELTESHAZZAR [bel-te-shaz´-ar] — the name given to Daniel by King Nebuchadnezzar (Dan. 1:7; 5:12). This name is not the same as Belshazzar.

Photo by Levant Photo Service

Chapel on the Mount of Beatitudes, the site where Jesus delivered His Sermon on the Mount, according to many scholars.

BENJAMIN [ben´-jam-min] *(son of the right hand or son of the south)* — the name of three men in the Old Testament, but usually refers to the youngest son of Jacob and his favorite wife, Rachel (Gen. 35:18, 24).

BEREA [be-re´-ah] — a city in Macedonia about forty-five miles west of Thessalonica. On his first missionary journey, the apostle Paul preached there (Acts 17:10). The Bereans were praised for the way they studied the Scriptures to make sure what Paul taught them was the truth (Acts 17:11).

BERYL — a stone that was usually green or bluish-green (Ezek. 1:16, NKJV; 10:9, NKJV).

BESEECH — to beg; to ask (Rom. 12:1, NKJV).

BESIEGE — a military word that means surround (Deut. 20:19, NKJV).

BETHANY [beth´-a-ny] — the name of two villages in the New Testament:

1. A village located at the base of the Mount of Olives (Mark 11:1).

2. A village where John the Baptist ministered (John 1:28).

BETHEL [beth´-el] *(house of God)* — the name of two cities in the Old Testament but usually refers to a city of Canaan about twelve miles north of Jerusalem. Bethel is mentioned more often in the Bible than any other city except for Jerusalem.

BETHLEHEM [beth´-le-hem] *(house of bread or house of [the god] Lahmu)* — the birthplace of Jesus Christ (Matt. 2:1) and the hometown of King David (1 Sam. 16:4).

Bethlehem was located about five miles south of Jerusalem in the area known as Ephrathah in Judah (Mic. 5:2). This region was

Photo by Levant Photo Service

Abraham's Well at the ancient city of Beersheba.

Photo by Gustav Jenninga

Bethlehem, in the hill country of Judah—the home of David and the birthplace of Jesus (1 Sam. 16:1, 4; Luke 2:11).

known for its fertile hills and valleys. It was also a town in the land of Zebulun (Josh. 19:15).

BETHSAIDA [beth-sa´-da] *(house of fishing)* — Bethsaida, which was later called Julias, was located two miles north of the Sea of Galilee and east of the Jordan River. The gospels of Mark, Luke, and John seem to refer to another Bethsaida which was the home of Philip, Andrew, and Peter (John 1:44), and maybe of James and John (Luke 5:10). That town was located northwest of the Sea of Galilee (Mark 6:45, 53) near Capernaum (John 6:17) in the city of Galilee (John 12:21).

BETROTHAL, BETROTHED — a promise or contract for marriage; engaged (Deut. 20:7, NKJV; Jer. 2:2, NKJV; Luke 1:27, NKJV).

BEWRAY — to give information in order to cause trouble (Matt. 26:73, NKJV).

BIBLE, THE — a collection of books inspired by God. The Christian church uses the Bible to provide guidelines for belief and behavior.

The Bible contains two major sections known as the Old Testament and the New Testament. The books of the Old Testament were written over a period of about one thousand years in the Hebrew language, except for a few passages that were written in Aramaic. The Old Testament tells what happened before Christ came.

The New Testament was written in Greek over a period of about sixty years. This section of the Bible tells about Christ's birth, His life and ministry, and the growth of the early church.

BIBLE VERSIONS AND TRANSLATIONS — The Bible was written over a period of several centuries in the languages of Hebrew and Aramaic (Old Testament) and Greek (New Testament). Because nations and cultures change over time, these original writings have been translated many times to make the Bible available in different languages.

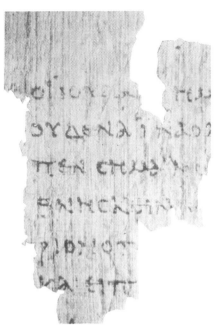

Photo by Howard Vos

Parts of John 18 can be seen on these papyrus fragments which date from about A.D. 125–150.

BILDAD [bil´-dad] — one of Job's friends. The three times he spoke to Job (Job 8:1–22; 18:1–21; 25:1–6), Bildad said he believed that all suffering is a direct result of a person's sin. He wasn't very kind or patient with Job.

BIRTHRIGHT — a right, privilege, or a property given to a person, especially the firstborn son, in Bible times (Deut. 21:17, NKJV; Gen. 27:27, NKJV; Gen. 43:33, NKJV).

BISHOP — an "elder" or pastor who was responsible for the spiritual leadership of a local church in New Testament times (Acts 20:17; Titus 1:5–7).

BISHOPRIC — the office and the responsibilities of a bishop (Acts 1:20, KJV).

BITTER HERBS — herbs eaten by the Israelites during the celebration of Passover. The herbs helped them remember their bitter experience as slaves in Egypt (Exod. 1:14; 12:8; Num. 9:11). Those herbs were probably plants like dandelions and horseradish.

BLASPHEME, BLASPHEMY — the act of cursing God or saying bad things about God. In the Old Testament, blaspheming God was a serious crime and the punishment for that crime was death (Matt. 9:3; 26:65). If a person committed blasphemy, they were guilty of breaking the Third Commandment (Exod. 20:7).

BLESS, BLESSING — the act of saying or wishing good for others. A blessing from God is the act of God saying, doing, or giving something good to His children.

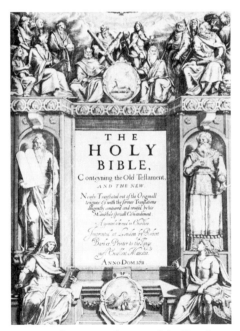

Title page from an early copy of the King James Version of the Bible, first published in 1611.

23

The fields of Boaz, near the city of Bethlehem (Ruth 2:1–4).

BLOOD — the red fluid that circulates in the body. It provides nourishment to the body and carries away waste. The word "blood" is used a lot in Scripture. Sometimes the word means the blood of animals (Gen. 37:31). Other times it means human blood (1 Kings 22:35).

BLOODGUILTINESS — guilt felt by a person who commits murder (Ps. 51:14).

BOAST — as a word with a positive meaning, it means to praise something or someone (Ps. 44:8, NKJV). As a word with a negative meaning, it means to "brag" about sin and to have false pride (Ps. 52:1).

BOAZ [bo´-az] *(in him is strength)* — the name of a wealthy, honorable man from Bethlehem. He was a relative of Naomi's husband, Elimilech, and he married Naomi's daughter-in-law, Ruth (Ruth 2–4).

Boaz was also the name of one of the two

bronze pillars that stood in front of King Solomon's temple (2 Chron. 3:17, NKJV). The name of the other pillar was Jachin.

BODY — the physical part of a person. The Bible teaches that the body is a gift from God. In the Old Testament the word "body" sometimes means "corpse" (Num. 6:6). The word "body" is also used as a symbol for the church (Rom. 12:4–5; 1 Cor. 12:12–14; Col. 1:18).

BOND, BONDS — something that holds an object or person still or holds an object or person back. In the Bible, the word is used to describe the chains of prisoners (Judg. 15:14, NKJV). It is also used to describe the way sin has a hold on a person (Isa. 58:6, NKJV). The word can also speak of good things like a covenant or "agreement" (Ezek. 20:37), or "peace" and love (Eph. 4:3).

BONDAGE — physical slavery or bondage in sin. Bondage in sin is a reference to life before knowing Jesus Christ (Rom. 8:15, NKJV; Gal. 4:7–9, NKJV).

BONES — the skeleton of the human body. The Israelites thought the bones of Joseph were special (Exod. 13:19). The prophet Ezekiel had a vision of the valley of dry bones. In his vision the dead bones came to life. The meaning of this vision was that the Jews would some day be a nation again after years of being held in captivity in Babylon (Ezek. 37:1–14).

BOOK — a group of words written on a "scroll," a roll of papyrus, leather, or parchment (Jer. 36:2).

BOOK OF LIFE — a heavenly book where the names of righteous (saved) people are written. Moses was the first to speak of the "Book of Life." He prayed that God would black out his name in the book rather than cause trouble for the other Israelites (Exod. 32:32–33). This idea probably came from the practice of registering people by genealogy (Jer. 22:30; Neh. 7:5, 64) and keeping a record of priests and Levites (Neh. 12:22–23).

At the end of time (Rev. 20:11–15), the people whose names are not written in the Book of Life will be "cast into the lake of fire" (Rev. 20:15). But the people whose names are written there (Rev. 21:27) will be allowed to enter the New Jerusalem.

BOOTHS, FEAST OF — also called the Feast of Tabernacles (Lev. 23:34–36).

BOOTY — the name used to describe all the valuable items taken from an enemy in battle. Things like gold and silver, clothing, food, household items, weapons, tools, animals, and even people to be used as slaves were all considered booty (Gen. 14:11–12, NKJV; Jer. 49:32, NKJV).

BORN AGAIN — a spiritual birth (John 3:3).

BORNE — carried (Matt. 23:4, NKJV).

BOSOM — a word for the chest of the human body. This word is used in the Bible as a symbol of closeness. To take something into the bosom means to accept it completely (Isa. 40:11, NKJV). The word "bosom" can also mean a person's inner thoughts (Ps. 35:13, KJV; heart, NKJV). "Abraham's bosom" is a term that means a place of honor (Luke 16:22–23, NKJV).

BOUNTY — abundance (more than is needed); blessing (2 Cor. 9:5, NKJV).

BOWELS — the internal parts of a person's body. The bowels were considered a deep place where emotions and feelings were. In scripture, "bowels" means pity, compassion, and tenderness (Job 30:27, NKJV; 1 John 3:17, NKJV).

BRANCH — a stem or limb growing from the trunk of a tree. The arms of the golden lampstand made for the tabernacle are also called branches (Exod. 37:17–22). The most special use of this word in the Bible is when it is used as a symbolic title for the Messiah.

BREACH — exposed; a weak spot (2 Kings 22:5, NKJV).

BREAD — a food item made from flour or meal and mixed with a liquid. Sometimes yeast was added and then it was shaped into loaves and baked.

Bread had an important place in Israel's worship services and it was also a big part of trade and commerce (business).

On the night before Jesus was crucified, He met with his disciples. "While they were eating, Jesus took some bread. He thanked God for it and broke it. Then he gave it to his followers and said, 'Take this bread and eat it. This bread is my body'" (Matt. 26:26). By His sacrifice, Christ became the Bread of Life. This became known as the Lord's Supper or the Last Supper.

BREASTPLATE — a piece of armor (Eph. 6:14, NKJV); a religious garment (Exod. 28:15–30, NKJV).

BREECHES — a word for trousers [pants] (Exod. 28:42, KJV).

BRETHREN — refers to brothers in a family (Gen. 47:1, NKJV); also brothers in a spiritual family (Acts 20:32, NKJV).

BRIDE — a woman who has just gotten married or is about to be married. In biblical times, it was the custom that fathers picked wives for their sons (Gen. 38:6). Sometimes a son might ask his father for a certain bride, and his father would talk with the parents or guardians of the young woman and try to work it out (Gen. 34:4, 8). Once in a while, the father of the young woman might try to make a deal for a certain husband for his daughter (Exod. 2:21).

BRIDEGROOM — a man who has just gotten married or is about to be married. This word is also used as a title for the Messiah. John the Baptist called Jesus the "bridegroom" (John 3:29). Jesus referred to Himself as the "bridegroom" (Matt. 9:15). Jesus' bride is the church—those who are spiritually united with Him by faith.

BRIMSTONE — a bright yellow mineral usually found near active volcanoes. It burns very easily and it smells really bad when burning. The Hebrew and Greek words for "brimstone" mean divine fire (Gen. 19:24, NKJV; Ezek. 38:22, NKJV; Luke 17:29, NKJV). In other Bible versions, the word "sulphur" is used in place of brimstone.

BROOD — baby birds still in the nest (Luke 13:34, NKJV).

BUCKLER — a "shield" (1 Chron. 5:18); also a symbol for God's protection (Ps. 18:2).

BULL, BULLOCK — an animal used for sacrifice (Heb. 10:4; Exod. 29:11).

BULRUSH — large bunches of grass with hollow stems that grew beside the rivers in Egypt and Palestine. Moses' basket was woven from bulrushes (Exod. 2:3–6, NKJV).

BULWARKS — towers built along city walls. Soldiers stood in them to shoot arrows and throw large stones at their enemies (Ps. 48:13, NKJV; Isa. 26:1, NKJV).

BURDEN — a heavy load or weight. A burden can be an actual object (Exod. 23:5, NKJV) or a symbol or a feeling (Num. 11:11, 17, NKJV).

BURIED — placed in a grave (Num. 20:1). This word is also used as a symbol in a baptism (Rom. 6:4).

BURN — the action of fire. This word is used to mean actual burning, like in the story of the burning bush (Exod. 3:2) and the story of the fiery furnace (Dan. 3:20–25). The word is also used to describe anger (Exod. 32:10–11, NKJV), jealousy (Ps. 79:5), and strong emotions (Luke 24:32).

BURNING BUSH — the flaming shrub (tree) at Mount Horeb. This is where Moses first found out about the presence of God (Exod. 3:2–4). Moses saw the flames and he was very curious why the bush did not burn up. Some Bible teachers believe the burning bush was a symbol of Israel because Israel survived the "fiery trial" of being slaves in Egypt.

C

CAESAR [se´-zur] — a title given to several emperors of the Roman Empire. The first one was Augustus (Matt. 22:17).

CAESAREA [ses-a-re´-ah] *(pertaining to Caesar)* — an important seaport city. Herod the Great spent a lot of money to build the city between 25 and 13 B.C. He named it in honor of Caesar Augustus. This is the place where Paul spent two years in prison (Acts 23:33).

CAESAREA PHILIPPI [ses-a-re´-ah fil´-a-pi] *(Caesar's city of Philip)* — a city on the hills of Mount Hermon and a place where Jesus ministered (Matt. 16:13; Mark 8:27).

It was near Caesarea Philippi that Jesus asked His disciples who He was and God told Simon Peter to give this answer: "You are the Christ, the Son of the living God" (Matt. 16:16).

CAIAPHAS [cah´-ya-fus] — Caiaphas became a high priest about A.D. 18 when John the Baptist began preaching (Matt. 26:3, 57; Luke 3:2). He was a member of the Sadducees.

After Jesus raised Lazarus from the dead, the Jewish leaders were worried about Jesus becoming very popular. They called a meeting to decide what to do about Jesus. During the meeting Caiaphas said Jesus should be killed. Because he was a high priest, the people listened to him and did what he said (John 11:49–53). He also helped plan the arrest of

Ruins of the palaces of the Caesars, emperors of the Roman Empire, in the capital city of Rome.

Photo by Howard Vos

These man-made breakwaters built by the Romans turned Caesarea into a major Mediterranean port city.

Jesus (Matt. 26:3–4) and took part in the illegal trial of Jesus (Matt. 26:57–68).

CAIN *(metalworker)* — the oldest son of Adam and Eve and the brother of Abel (Gen. 4:1–25).

Cain was a farmer and brought some of his crops as a sacrifice to God. His brother Abel was a shepherd and brought a lamb as a sacrifice. Abel had a good attitude about what he gave to God and his sacrifice was accepted. Cain had a bad attitude about his gift to God, so God did not accept his sacrifice (Gen. 4:7). Cain was jealous and committed the first murder by killing his brother, Abel.

CALDRON — a ceramic or metal container used for boiling meat and for ceremonies (2 Chron. 35:13, NKJV; Mic. 3:3, NKJV).

CALEB [ca´-leb] *(dog)* — one of the twelve spies sent by Moses to learn about the Promised Land of Canaan (Num. 13:6, 30; 14:6, 24, 30, 38).

Joshua and Caleb had faith in God that He would help them get the land. They weren't afraid at all. They told Moses and Aaron and the Israelites to attack Canaan immediately (Num. 13:30).

The other ten spies were afraid to try to take the land. The Israelites listened to them instead of Joshua and Caleb. The Lord was very disappointed in the Israelites because of their lack of faith. Of all the adults alive at that time, only Caleb and Joshua were allowed to enter the Promised Land (Josh. 14:6–15).

CALENDAR — a system to keep track of time, usually based on a natural cycle like the seasons or the phases of the moon. A calendar usually covered a period of one year and included days of each month and the days of the week.

Calendars of biblical times, much like the calendars of today, were used to keep records and predict the time for the changing of the seasons. Calendars were also used to help people plan their work and to remember the religious festivals and when they were supposed to be celebrated.

CALL, CALLING — an important religious term used several different ways in the Bible.

Sometimes it referred to God's calling of people to salvation (Rom. 8:28–30; 1 Thess. 2:12). Other times it was used when talking

The Jewish Calendar

The Jews used two kinds of calendars:
Civil Calendar—official calendar of kings, childbirth, and contracts.
Sacred Calendar—from which festivals were computed.

NAMES OF MONTHS	CORRESPONDS WITH	NO. OF DAYS	MONTH OF CIVIL YEAR	MONTH OF SACRED YEAR
TISHRI	Sept.–Oct.	30 days	1st	7th
HESHVAN	Oct.–Nov.	29 or 30	2nd	8th
CHISLEV	Nov.–Dec.	29 or 30	3rd	9th
TEBETH	Dec.–Jan.	29	4th	10th
SHEBAT	Jan.–Feb.	30	5th	11th
ADAR	Feb.–Mar.	29 or 30	6th	12th
NISAN	Mar.–Apr.	30	7th	1st
IYAR	Apr.–May	29	8th	2nd
SIVAN	May–June	30	9th	3rd
TAMMUZ	June–July	29	10th	4th
AB	July–Aug.	30	11th	5th
*ELUL	Aug.–Sept.	29	12th	6th

The Jewish day was from sunset to sunset, in 8 equal parts:

FIRST WATCH . . . . .SUNSET TO 9 P.M.
SECOND WATCH . . . . .9 P.M. TO MIDNIGHT
THIRD WATCH . . . . .MIDNIGHT TO 3 A.M.
FOURTH WATCH . . . . .3 A.M. TO SUNRISE

FIRST HOUR . . . . .SUNRISE TO 9 A.M.
THIRD HOUR . . . . .9 A.M. TO NOON
SIXTH HOUR . . . . .NOON TO 3 P.M.
NINTH HOUR . . . . .3 P.M. TO SUNSET

*Hebrew months were alternately 30 and 29 days long. Their year, shorter than ours, had 354 days. Therefore, about every three years (7 times in 19 years) an extra 29-day month, VEADAR, was added between ADAR and NISAN.

about asking God for help, like prayer (Ps. 55:16–17). It is also the speaking of a person's name, for example, to call by name (Gen. 17:5, NKJV; Luke 1:13, NKJV).

CALVARY [cal´-va-ry] (from the Latin word *calvaria,* "the skull") — the name used in the KJV and NKJV for the place outside Jerusalem where Jesus was crucified (Luke 23:33).

CANA [ca´-nah] *(place of reeds)* — a small town in Galilee where Jesus performed his first miracle by turning water into wine (John 2:1), eight miles northeast of Nazareth.

CANAAN [ca´-na-an] *(land of purple)* — an area by the Mediterranean Sea where the Canaanites lived before the land was taken by the Israelites (Gen. 11:31; Josh. 5:12). Canaan is also the name of the fourth son of Ham. He was the grandson of Noah (Gen. 9:18–27; 10: 6, 15).

CANAANITES [ca´-na-an-ites] — an ancient tribe that lived in the land of Canaan before the Israelites took over.

CANON — a rule, standard, or a guide. Although this word is not used in the Bible, it does refer to the books of the Bible, which are inspired by God.

CANOPY — a high covering. The word is used twice in the Bible as a symbol, once when Elihu was declaring God's majesty by saying "the thunder from his canopy" (Job 36:29, NKJV) and another when David was talking about God the sovereign Creator, and said, "His canopy around him was dark waters" (Ps. 18:11, NKJV).

CAPERNAUM [ca-pur´-na-um] *(village of Nahum)* — a very important city located on the shore of the Sea of Galilee. Capernaum was the center of much of Jesus' ministry (Matt. 4:13–15).

Cana of Galilee, the village where Jesus performed His first miracle.

CAPTIVE — a person taken and held as a prisoner, especially by an enemy in war (2 Sam. 8:2, NKJV; 1 Kings 20:32, NKJV; 2 Kings 25:7, NKJV).

CAPTIVITY — being held as a prisoner or slave by an enemy, especially if it involves being taken to a foreign land. The term "captivity" is used to describe two periods when the nations of Israel (722 B.C.) and Judah (605 B.C. and later) were removed from their homelands.

CAREFUL — being worried, nervous, or afraid (Luke 10:41, NKJV). In today's language, the word means being cautious, caring, concerned, and paying attention to detail (Phil. 4:10; Titus 3:8).

CARMEL [car´-mel] *(garden/orchard of God)* — a town in the country of Judah (Josh. 15:55; 1 Sam. 25:2, 5, 7, 40). Carmel was the home of a very rich and very foolish man named Nabal.

Carmel is also a mountain range that is about thirteen miles long. A part of the mountain range sticks out into the Mediterranean Sea. That part is named Mount Carmel. It is nearly 470 feet high.

CARNAL — of the world, not spiritual. The apostle Paul compares spiritual people (those who listen to and obey the Holy Spirit) with carnal people (those who do whatever they want because it feels good or makes them happy) (1 Cor. 3:1–4, NKJV; Rom. 8:5–7, NKJV).

CENSER — a container used to carry burning hot coals. They were also used for burning incense (Num. 16:6, 17–18, 37–39, 46, NKJV). The censers in the tabernacle were made of

Photo by Werner Braun

Aerial view of the ruins of ancient Capernaum, a city on the shore of the Sea of Galilee.

bronze (Exod. 27:3, NKJV; Lev. 16:12, NKJV). The censers in the temple were made of "pure gold" (1 Kings 7:50; 2 Chron. 4:22).

CENSUS — to count and write down the people who live in a town. It was also a way to learn what property people owned so the government would know how much taxes to charge them (Luke 2:1–5, NKJV).

CENTURION — a leader in the Roman army who was in charge of one hundred soldiers (Matt. 8:5–10).

CEPHAS [se´-fas] *(rock)* — the Aramaic name Jesus gave to Simon, the son of Jonah (John 1:42).

CEREAL OFFERING — an offering given to God to show thanks for His blessings. Also called a grain offering (Lev. 2; Num. 15:1–9).

CHAFF — dry material-like husks (seed coverings) and other debris that is separated from the seeds of grain. In the Bible, chaff symbol-izes evil or wicked people (or things) that are about to be destroyed (Ps. 1:4; Matt. 3:12; Luke 3:17).

CHARITY — a word for love (Col. 3:14, KJV).

CHASTE — having pure thoughts and actions (1 Pet. 3:2, NKJV).

CHASTEN — correcting a person with the purpose of teaching, not just pointing out that they did something wrong (1 Cor. 11:32, NKJV).

CHASTISEMENT — the action of a harsh punishment. In the Bible the word "chastisement" usually refers to a punishment by God for the purpose of teaching (Job 4:3, NKJV), guiding (2 Tim. 2:25, NKJV), and discipline. Sometimes this can be a physical punishment (Prov. 22:15, NKJV; Heb. 12:5–11, NKJV; Rev. 3:19, NKJV).

CHEBAR [ke´-bar] *(great)* — a "river" of Chaldea. The prophet Ezekiel lived along the banks of this river (Ezek. 1:1, 3; 3:15, 23). It was

Photo by E. B. Trovillion

In prehistoric times, families lived in some of these caves in the vicinity of Mount Carmel.

here that he had many of his amazing visions (Ezek. 10:15, 20, 22; 43:3, NKJV; Kebar, ICB).

Chebar was probably not really a river. It was most likely the famous Grand Canal of Nebuchadnezzar that connected the Tigris and Euphrates rivers.

CHERUB [chair´-ub] — a place in Babylonia where some Jewish citizens lived during the Captivity. When they returned to Judah, they could not prove that they were really Israelites (Ezra 2:59; Neh. 7:61, NKJV; Kerub, ICB).

CHERUBIM [chair´-oo-bim] — angel-like creatures with wings that were usually associated with the worship and praising of God. Cherubim are first mentioned in the Bible when God sent Adam and Eve away from the Garden of Eden. He placed cherubim at the east of the garden, "and a flaming sword which turned every way, to guard the way to the tree of life" (Gen. 3:24, NKJV).

CHINNERETH, CHINNEROTH, CINNEROTH [kin´-ne-reth, kin´-ne-roth, sin´-e-roth] (lute, harp) — used to be the name of the Sea of Galilee (Num. 34:11, NKJV; Josh. 12:3, NKJV) and "Lake Tiberias" (John 6:1). The lake is shaped like the outline of a harp.

CHOOSE, CHOSEN — to appoint; to select; to call; one who is appointed, selected, or called out (Deut. 7:6–11).

CHOSEN PEOPLE — a name for the people of Israel. They were called this because God chose them for a special purpose. They were to be a holy people chosen to worship God and tell people all over the world about Him (Exod. 19:4–6; Deut. 7:6–8; Ps. 105:43).

CHRIST (anointed one) — a special name for Jesus. He was the one people had been waiting for to save them. For hundreds of years, the Jewish people had been telling about and looking for a Messiah. This Messiah would be someone who would save them and turn the world into a place of peace and prosperity. Jesus was identified as this Messiah when Peter said, "You are the Christ, the Son of the living God" (Matt. 16:16).

CHRISTIAN — a person who believes in Jesus and what He did and lives a Christlike life. You can find the word three times in the New Testament:

"In Antioch the followers were called Christians for the first time" (Acts 11:26).

Agrippa said to Paul, "Do you think you can persuade me to become a Christian in such a short time?" (Acts 26:28).

Peter exhorted, "But if you suffer because you are a Christian then do not be ashamed" (1 Pet. 4:16).

CHRONICLES, BOOKS OF FIRST AND SECOND — two books in the Old Testament. A lot of the material written in First and Second Chronicles is also written in the books of First and Second Samuel and First and Second Kings. The difference is that the writer of First and Second Chronicles wanted to give hope to the Israelites after they survived seventy years of captivity in Babylon. He wrote to remind them of the good times and give them hope for the future while they thought about what God had promised them.

CHURCH — a local group of believers (Matt. 16:18). Church is also a word that includes all believers from the past, the present, and the future who follow Jesus (1 Cor. 10:32).

CIRCUMCISION — the surgical removal of the foreskin of the male sex organ. Jewish boys were circumcised as a sign of keeping God's Covenant.

Moses and the prophets used the term "circumcised" as a symbol for purity of heart and readiness to hear and obey God (John 7:22; Acts 7:8).

CISTERN — a man-made place for storing liquids (especially water). It is usually an underground tank for catching and storing rainwater.

In the Bible, the word cistern is mostly used as a symbol (Prov. 5:15, NKJV; Jer. 2:13, NKJV).

CITIES OF REFUGE — cities where people who had accidentally killed someone could go to live without worrying about someone trying to punish them or get revenge (Num. 35:6–7, NKJV; Josh. 20:7–8, NKJV; Cities of Safety, ICB).

CITY — a place where people live. A city is bigger and has more people than a town or a village, or it is more important because it is a popular place for business or entertainment. In biblical times, a city had walls for defending itself, a town or village did not (Lev. 25:29–31; Ezek. 38:11).

CITY OF DAVID — a strong city belonging to the Jebusites that was later known as Jerusalem. King David and his men captured it (2 Sam. 5:7, 9). Jesus was born there (Luke 2:4, 11; John 7:42).

CLEAVE — hang on to tightly; stay married to your spouse (Gen. 2:24–25, NKJV); keep your relationship with God strong (Deut. 11:22, NKJV).

CLOVEN — divided; split; like an animal's hoof (Deut. 14:7, NKJV; divided, ICB).

COLLECTION — In the Old Testament, the word "collection" refers to a religious tax taken from the people of Israel by the Levites (2 Chron. 24:6, 9, NKJV). The people were not allowed to decide if they wanted to give, it was a mandatory tax. In the New Testament, "collection" refers to a voluntary offering from the churches to help needy Christians in Jerusalem (1 Cor. 16:1–4).

COLOSSE — a city in the Roman province of Asia (western Turkey), located in the Lycus River Valley about one hundred miles east of Ephesus. The apostle Paul wrote a letter to the church at Colosse (Col. 1:2).

COLOSSIANS, EPISTLE TO THE — one of four shorter epistles (letters) written by Paul while he was in prison. The other three were to the Philippians, the Ephesians, and Philemon. In this letter, Paul told the Colossians to really think about Jesus and his work and live a proper Christian life.

COMELINESS — beauty (Isa. 53:2, NKJV).

COMMEND — to praise (Luke 16:8, NKJV); to give with trust (Luke 23:46, NKJV).

COMMUNION — sharing with a feeling of closeness (1 Cor. 10:16, NKJV). (See Lord's Supper).

The mound of ancient Colosse, a city in Asia Minor where a church was established during the days of the apostle Paul.

COMPASSION — feel along with another (Lam. 3:22, NKJV).

CONCUBINE [con´-cue-bine] — in the Old Testament, a female slave that a man could have children with even though she was not his wife (Gen. 25:6, NKJV).

CONDEMN, CONDEMNATION — to say a person is guilty of doing wrong and that they should be punished (Matt. 12:37; Rom. 5:16, 18).

CONFESS, CONFESSION — to admit (1 John 1:9); to say; to tell (Phil. 2:11); a strong, proud statement of what you believe. The apostle Paul wrote: "If you use your mouth to say, 'Jesus is Lord,' and if you believe in your heart that God raised Jesus from death, then you will be saved. We believe with our hearts, and so we are made right with God. And we use our mouths to say that we believe, and so we are saved" (Rom. 10:9–10).

CONFOUND — confuse (Gen. 11:7, 9, NKJV).

CONGREGATION — a group or assembly of people who gather together for worship and religious teaching; a religious community, like the people of Israel or the Christian church (Acts 13:43, NKJV).

CONGREGATION, MOUNT OF — the place where God meets with His people, whether in heaven or on earth (Exod. 5:22, NKJV; 29:42–43, NKJV). Mount of Congregation is also used to describe a place where the Babylonians thought their gods lived (Isa. 14:13, NKJV).

CONSCIENCE — a person's inner thoughts about doing right (God's will) and feeling good about it (God's approval), or doing wrong (our own will) and feeling bad about it (condemnation) (Rom. 2:14–15, NKJV).

CONSECRATE — to set something or

someone aside (apart), especially for God's use (2 Chron. 29:31–33, NKJV).

CONSECRATION — the act of setting aside (apart), or dedicating something or someone for God's use. In the Old Testament, the temple and the things inside it were the most important objects consecrated to God (2 Chron. 7:5–9, NKJV; Ezra 6:16–17, NKJV). Aaron and his sons were consecrated to the priesthood (Exod. 29, NKJV; Lev. 8, NKJV), but other things could be consecrated also (Josh. 6:19, NKJV; Mic. 4:13, NKJV; Lev. 27:28, NKJV).

CONTENTMENT — freedom from anxiety or worry (1 Tim. 6:6, NKJV). Contentment is being happy with what you have and what is happening in your life.

CONTRITE — the kind of spirit (attitude) that is pleasing and acceptable to God (Ps. 34:18, NKJV). People who have a contrite spirit are truly sorry for their sins.

CONVERSATION — one person talking to another. The word is used only twice in the NKJV (Jer. 38:27; Luke 24:17). In the King James Version, the word is used to describe a person's conduct, behavior, or way of life. An example of this is when the writer of the Book of Hebrews wrote, "Let your conversation be without covetousness" (Heb. 13:5, KJV).

CONVERSION, CONVERT — the change in a person's attitude that brings them into a right relationship with God.

The best description of conversion is talked about by Saul of Tarsus (Paul) at his own conversion: "I send you to open their eyes that they may turn away from darkness to the light.

I send you that they may turn away from the power of Satan and turn to God. That their sins can be forgiven and they can have a place with those people who have been made holy by believing in me" (Acts 26:18).

CONVICT OF SIN, CONVICTION — the process of being condemned by your own conscience because you understand what God expects of you but you aren't doing those things.

The idea of conviction is found all through Scripture, but the word is hardly used (Ps. 32; 51; Acts 2:37; Rom. 7:7–25). The Holy Spirit is responsible for the act of conviction (John 16:7–11). Conviction usually happens because a person learns the Word of God (Acts 2:37) or God reveals what He wants through a person's conscience (Rom. 1:18–20; 2:15). God doesn't like for people to feel horrible, but he allows conviction so people will repent of their sins (Acts 2:37–38; Rom. 2:1–4) and turn to Him for salvation and eternal life.

CORBAN [cor´-ban] *(an offering brought near)* — a gift or offering in the temple that was dedicated to God in a special way (Mark 7:11, NKJV).

CORINTH [cor´-inth] — ancient Greece's most important city (Acts 18:1; 19:1; 1 Cor. 1:2; 2 Cor. 1:2; 2 Tim. 4:20). Because of its location, Corinth was the connecting link between Rome and the East. The apostle Paul established a strong, growing church at Corinth.

CORINTHIANS, EPISTLES TO THE — two letters the apostle Paul wrote to the church in Corinth. The first letter was written in Ephesus (1 Cor. 16:8) during Paul's third missionary journey, around A.D. 56. The second letter was written about twelve to fifteen months later from Macedonia (2 Cor. 2:12–17).

First Corinthians was written to help the church solve the problems they were having and to answer their questions. Second Corinthians was written to tell the Christians at Corinth that Paul understood the struggles they were having and he wanted to encourage them to stay faithful and not give up. Both letters show how much Paul cared about the people. He felt bad with them when they hurt and he celebrated with them when they were happy.

Photo by Gustav Jeeninga

The ruins of Corinth, one of the wealthiest and most immoral of ancient cities (1 Cor. 5:1; 6:9–11).

CORRUPTIBLE, CORRUPTION — perishable (Rom. 1:23, NKJV), decay of the body (Acts 2:27, 31, NKJV), and the decline of human life through the power of sin (2 Pet. 1:4, NKJV). But because of the resurrection of Christ, our bodies, sown in corruption (subject to the decay and dissolution of organic matter), will be raised in incorruption (1 Cor. 15:42, 50–54, NKJV).

COUNCIL — a group of people who meet to discuss important matters and make decisions (Acts 25:12, NKJV). Council can also be the place where the group meets.

COUNSEL — when used as a verb it means to give advice (John 18:14, NKJV); when used as a noun it means advice (Dan. 4:27, NKJV).

COUNSELOR — a person who gives counsel or advice (Prov. 11:14, NKJV), like the king's adviser (2 Sam. 15:12, NKJV; 1 Chron. 27:33, NKJV), or a person who works for the government (Isa. 1:26). The Holy Spirit is also called "the Counselor" in the NRSV and NIV (John 14:16, 26, NKJV; 15:26, NKJV; 16:7, NKJV).

COUNTENANCE — look or appearance (1 Sam. 16:7, NKJV); honor (Exod. 23:3, NKJV).

COURAGE — the strength and ability to stand against your fears or get through a difficult situation. Courage comes when a person trusts God and does whatever God asks them to do whenever He asks them to do it (2 Chron. 19:11).

COVENANT — an agreement between two people or two groups that involves promises. The idea of a covenant between God and His people is one of the most important truths in the Bible. Because of this, the word "covenant" is often used to talk about the two main sections of the Bible: Old Covenant (Old Testament) and New Covenant (New Testament).

COVERING THE HEAD — women used to wear a head covering in early Christian church services because the apostle Paul said that a woman participating in the services should have her head covered as a symbol of authority (1 Cor. 11:5–16).

COVETOUSNESS — a strong desire to possess (have or own) something (or someone) that belongs to another person. The Ten Commandments say this attitude is wrong (Exod. 20:17, NKJV; Deut. 5:21, NKJV). This is a greedy, self-centered, and disrespectful attitude that ignores God's law. The Bible says we should be careful to avoid this sin (Josh. 7:21, NKJV; Rom. 7:7, NKJV; 2 Pet. 2:10, NKJV).

CREATE, CREATION — the action God used in making the universe come into existence.

CREATURE — any created being, including humans, created as a result of God's power and authority. The Bible says that God is the sovereign Creator of all things. Through His might and power He brought the universe into existence (Gen. 1:3–24, NKJV; Ps. 33:6, NKJV; Heb. 11:3, NKJV). This means that all beings, even angels, are His creatures (John 1:3, NKJV; 1 Cor. 8:6, NKJV).

CRIMSON — a deep red color. The word "crimson" is also used as a symbol for sin (Isa. 1:18, NKJV).

CROSS — an upright wooden stake or post used in the execution (killing) of condemned people (John 19:17). After Jesus died on the cross, it became a symbol for the Christian faith.

CROWN OF THORNS — a rude, fake symbol of authority made by the Roman soldiers and placed on Jesus' head shortly before His crucifixion (Matt. 27:29; Mark 15:17; John 19:2, 5). Crowns were symbols of honor and

Photo by Howard Vos

God the Creator, from a painting by Michelangelo in the Sistine Chapel in Rome.

Photo by Howard Vos

Gold cups discovered by archaeologists in tombs at the ancient city of Mycene on the island of Crete.

authority in the Greek and Roman worlds but Jesus' crown of thorns was meant to make people laugh at Him and tease Him. With hate in their hearts, people yelled, "Hail, King of the Jews!" (Matt. 27:29; Mark 15:18; John 19:3). But Jesus' love was so strong that He patiently suffered through their teasing to accomplish God's will.

CRUCIFIXION — a method of torture and killing (execution) used by the Romans on Christ and others. At a crucifixion, the victim was usually nailed or tied to a wooden stake and left to die.

CUBIT — a unit of measurement; the distance from the elbow to the fingertip of an adult—about eighteen inches (Gen. 6:15, NKJV).

CUMMIN — a plant used for seasoning (Isa. 28:25, 27).

CUP — a small container used for drinking water (Matt. 10:42), wine (Jer. 35:5), and other liquids.

D

DAGON [day´-gun] — a pagan god of the Philistines (Judg. 16:23–30).

DAMASCUS [da-mas´-cus] — one of the oldest cities in the world and the capital of Syria (Isa. 7:8). Saul was on the road to Damascus when he saw Jesus. He became a Christian and God changed his name to Paul.

DAN *(a judge)* — the fifth son of Jacob (Gen. 30:1–6), and a city named after him.

DANIEL *(God is my judge)* — the name of four men in the Bible:

1. A son of David and Abigail (1 Chron. 3:1). He is also called Kileab (2 Sam. 3:3).

2. A priest of the family of Ithamar who returned with Ezra from the Captivity (Ezra 8:2). He sealed the covenant in the days of Nehemiah (Neh. 10:6).

3. A wise (Ezek. 28:3) and righteous man, mentioned together with Noah and Job (Ezek. 14:14, 20).

4. A prophet during the Captivity of God's covenant people in Babylon and Persia (Dan. 1:6–12:9; Matt. 24:15). Daniel also wrote the book in the Old Testament that bears his name.

DANIEL, BOOK OF — a major book of prophecy in the Old Testament. The book is named for Daniel because he wrote it. Part of

Photo by Howard Vos

An altar for pagan worship at the city of Dan. Portions of the altar were constructed by King Ahab of Israel.

the book tells of things that happened to Daniel and his friends. The other part of the book tells about things that would happen in the future (prophecy).

DARIUS [da-ri´-us] — the name of several rulers of ancient Persia like Darius I the Great, who ruled from about 522 to 485 B.C., Darius II Ochus, the son of Artaxerxes I, who ruled over Persia from about 424 to 405 B.C. (Neh. 12:22), and Darius III Codomannus, the king of Persia from 336 to 330 B.C. This Darius is probably the "fourth" king of Persia mentioned by the prophet Daniel (Dan. 11:12).

DARKNESS — the absence of light. Darkness existed before God created light (Gen. 1:2). Darkness was included as part of many different things like evil, bad luck, struggles (Job 17:12), death (Job 10:21–22; 38:17), and sin (Job 24:13–17).

Darkness also describes the condition of people who haven't found Jesus (John 1:4–5; 12:35) and the people who turn away from Jesus on purpose (John 3:19–20).

DAUGHTER — a female child. Sometimes the word "daughter" is used in the Bible to talk about other female relatives like a stepsister, niece, or a granddaughter (Gen. 20:12; 24:48).

DAVID *(beloved)* — the second king of Israel, an ancestor of Jesus Christ, and the writer of many psalms. The story of David's life is found in 1 Samuel 16–31; 2 Samuel 1–24; 1 Kings 1–2; and 1 Chronicles 10–29.

DAY OF THE LORD, THE — a special day at the end of time when God's will and purpose for humanity will be fulfilled (Phil. 1:6, 10, NKJV).

DEACON — a servant or minister (not a pastor) (1 Tim. 3:8–13).

Tombs of Darius I and Artaxerxes I at the royal city of Persepolis in ancient Persia.

DEAD SEA — a large salty lake in southern Israel. In the Old Testament it is called the Salt Sea; the Sea of the Arabah; and the Eastern Sea (Gen. 14:3; Josh. 3:16).

DEAD SEA SCROLLS — the name for a group of scrolls (around eight hundred) and fragments of scrolls that were found in eleven caves near Khirbet ("ruin of") Qumran on the northwest shore of the Dead Sea in 1947. The Dead Sea Scrolls have provided a lot of important information to Bible scholars.

DEATH — a word that means the end of life. But since humans are spiritual beings, death is only the end of our physical life (body), not the end of our existence (1 John 3:14; Rom. 6:4–8; Rev. 20:6).

DEBAUCHERY — the bad behavior of a person who is drunk (Gal. 5:19, NKJV; 1 Pet. 4:13, NIV).

DEBORAH [deb´-o-rah] *(bee)* — the name of two women in the Old Testament:
1. A nurse to Isaac's wife, Rebekah (Gen. 24:59; 35:8).

David's Triumphs

David was a man after God's own heart (1 Sam. 13:14), that is, his will was completely committed to the will of his Lord. As a dedicated servant of God, he was used by God to perform mighty acts for the sake of His chosen people Israel.	King of Judah (2:4) King of Israel (5:3) Conquers Jerusalem (5:7) Returns ark (6:12) Davidic covenant (7:16) Defeats Philistines (8:1) Defeats Moab (8:2) Defeats Ammon (10:16) Defeats Syria (10:19)

David's Troubles

Causes	Effects
Adultery (11:4)	Bathsheba bears a son (11:5)
Murder of Uriah (11:17)	Accused, repents, but the child dies (12:10, 13, 19)
Amnon's incest (13:14)	Amnon murdered (13:28, 29)
Absalom usurps throne (16:15, 16)	Absalom murdered (18:14, 15)
The census (24:2)	Plague (24:15)
Consistently illustrated in the life of David's household is the principle that a disobedient life is a troubled life.	

Photo by Howard Vos

Oasis at En Gedi where David hid from King Saul during his years as a fugitive (1 Sam. 23:29; 24:1).

2. The fifth judge of Israel and a prophetess. She was the only female judge (Judg. 4–5).

DECAPOLIS [de-cap´-o-lis] *(ten cities)* — a group of ten cities or "towns" in northern Palestine. Most of the people who lived there were Greek. Jesus healed and taught people from there (Matt. 4:25; Mark 5:20; Mark 7:31).

DECREE — an official order, command, or an announcement issued by a king or other person of authority. The decrees of kings were often delivered to faraway towns or cities by messengers and announced in a public place (Ezra 1:1; Amos 4:5). In the Bible we can learn about God's decrees, which are laws or rules the whole world is supposed to follow (Ps. 148:6, NKJV).

DEDICATE, DEDICATION — the act of setting apart, or making holy (Eph. 5:26). Dedication is the religious ceremony where a person or a thing is set aside or consecrated (made holy) for serving God. The temple (2 Chron. 2:4, NKJV), a field (Lev. 27:16, NKJV), a house (Lev. 27:14, NKJV), articles of precious metal (2 Sam. 8:10, NKJV), and even items won in battle (1 Chron. 26:27, NKJV) are all examples of things that were dedicated.

In one of the most beautiful passages in the Bible, Hannah dedicated her young son Samuel by giving him to God (1 Sam. 1:19–28). Hannah's prayer of thanksgiving to God (1 Sam. 2:1–10) is a good example of praise and dedication for everyone who wants to honor God with their lives.

DEDICATION, FEAST OF — a feast that is also known as Hanukkah and the Feast of Lights. It is only mentioned once in the Bible

(John 10:22). It was the celebration of the cleansing of the temple after Antiochus Epiphanes vandalized it. The Feast of Dedication is observed (held) on the twenty-fifth day of the ninth month on the Jewish calendar.

DEEP, THE — a massive space, huge area, or the abyss. In the Bible, the word is first used in Genesis 1:2: "The earth was without form, and void; and darkness was on the face of the deep" (NKJV). It is also used to refer to the oceans and to the large amount of water that came during the Flood (Gen. 7:11, NKJV; 8:2, NKJV). The deep also refers to the Abyss, or the abode (place) of the dead (Rom. 10:7, NKJV) and evil spirits (Luke 8:31, NKJV; Rev. 9:1–2, 11, NKJV; 20:1, NKJV).

"The deep" is also a symbol for something great or mighty (Ps. 36:6; 92:5; 1 Cor. 2:10).

DEFILE — to make unclean or impure. The Old Testament mentions five types of defilement: (1) ceremonial (Lev. 15:19); (2) ethical (Ezek. 37:23, NKJV); (3) physical (Song of Sol. 5:3, NKJV); (4) religious (Jer. 3:1); and (5) sexual (Lev. 15:24). God had these laws to help His chosen people stay pure. But the people spent too much time fighting over tiny little details of each law instead of focusing on how they were supposed to live. Jesus fixed the problem by making them understand what they were doing and reminding them how they were supposed to be living (Mark 7:15, 18, 20, 23, NKJV).

DEITY — any god including the one true God.

DELILAH [de-li´-lah] — a Philistine woman. Because Samson loved her, she was able to trick him into thinking that she loved him. He wasn't supposed to tell anyone the secret of his great strength, but he thought he could trust Delilah so he told her that the secret was his long hair. Long hair was a symbol of his Nazirite vow (promise) to God. She sold that information to the Philistines for 1,100 pieces of silver (Judg. 16:5). While Samson was asleep at her house, the Philistines snuck in and cut his hair. Because of this Samson lost his strength and was captured. They put him in prison and caused him to go blind.

DEMAS [de´-mas] — a friend and coworker of the apostle Paul. Later Demas left Paul because he loved the "world" too much (2 Tim. 4:10; Col. 4:14; Philem. 24).

DEMETRIUS [dah-me´-tre-us] — the name of a silversmith in Ephesus (Acts 19:24, 38) who made and sold silver statues of false gods. He became nervous that people would hear the gospel and stop buying his idols so he started a riot against the apostle Paul (Acts 19:28, 34; Acts 19:35–40; Acts 20:1).

There was another man named Demetrius who was a Christian. He received praise from John because he had "a good testimony from all" (3 John 12).

DEMONIAC — a person who is possessed by demons (Mark 5:15–16).

DEMONS — another name for fallen angels who joined Satan in the fight against God (Luke 10:17).

DENARIUS [de-nar´-e-us] — a silver coin (Matt. 20:1–16).

DENY — to say something is untrue or to

disown something. A person can deny God with their words or deeds (actions). Denial in word is saying that you don't know or have a relationship with God or Christ (Josh. 24:27, NKJV; Matt. 10:33, NKJV; 2 Pet. 2:1, NKJV). Denial in deed is to keep something from someone (Prov. 30:7, NKJV; 1 Tim. 5:8, NKJV), even yourself (Matt. 16:24, NKJV).

DERBE [der´-by] — a city in the southeastern part of Lycaonia. During their first missionary journey, Paul and Barnabas went there when the people of Lystra ran them off (Acts 14:6–20). Paul also visited Derbe on his second missionary journey (Acts 16:1).

DESOLATE — deserted; unoccupied (Jer. 33:12, NKJV).

DEUTERONOMY, BOOK OF — an Old Testament book written by Moses just before he died. The title of the book comes from the Greek word *Deuteronomion,* which means "second law." In this book, Moses talked about and repeated many of the laws that God gave the people at Mount Sinai about forty years earlier. He also reminded the people to stay faithful to their God and His commands as they prepared to enter the Promised Land.

DEVICE — thought (Prov. 19:21).

DEVIL *(accuser, slanderer)* — the main title for the fallen angelic being who is the worst enemy of God and mankind (Eph. 6:10–17). Satan is his usual name, and devil is what he is—an accuser or deceiver. The term comes from a Greek word that means "a false witness" or "malicious accuser."

DIADEM [di´-a-dem] — a band or wrapping around the turban of a king or his queen. It is proof of their royal authority. Rulers of the ancient Near East did not wear rigid gold crowns but cloth turbans wound around the head. These turbans were decorated with cloth diadems covered with jewels. The New Testament shows the difference between a diadem and a crown. A crown was a garland or a wreath awarded for faithful service, like a crown of righteousness, while a diadem was always a symbol of royal authority.

DIDYMUS [did´-ih-mus] *(twin)* — the Greek

The unexcavated mound of Derbe, a city visited by the apostle Paul (Acts 14:20; 16:1).

name of Thomas, one of the twelve disciples of Christ (John 11:16; 20:24; 21:2).

DISCERN — being able to tell the difference between good and bad (Job 6:30, NKJV; Heb. 5:14, NKJV).

DISCIPLE — a student, learner, or pupil. In the Bible the word usually refers to a follower of Jesus. The word is rarely used in the Old Testament. Isaiah used the term "disciples" or "followers" to refer to people who are taught or instructed (Isa. 8:16).

DISCIPLESHIP — the life and training of a disciple.

DISCIPLINE — to train by instruction and control (1 Cor. 9:27, NKJV). The biblical idea (concept) of discipline has a positive side (instruction, knowledge, and training) and a negative side (correction, punishment, and reproof).

DISOBEDIENCE — the unwillingness to follow the guidance of authority, especially refusing to follow God's will. The first act of disobedience happened when Adam and Eve ate the forbidden fruit (Gen. 3).

DISPENSATION — a period of time during which mankind must answer to God for how it has behaved. The word "dispensation" is found twice in the NKJV (Eph. 1:10; Eph. 3:2). The KJV uses the word four times (1 Cor. 9:17; Eph. 1:10; 3:2; Col. 1:25).

DISPERSE — to scatter; to spread (Prov. 15:7, NKJV; Ezek. 12:15, NKJV).

DISPERSION — the sending of Jewish people to other countries. This happened to the Hebrew people many times. The term comes from a Greek word meaning "to scatter." Sometimes the dispersions were voluntary, other times they were forced.

DIVERSE — various; many different ones (Mark 1:34, NKJV).

DIVINATION — fortunetelling (Ezek. 21:21, NKJV; Acts 16:16, NKJV).

DIVINE — of God or relating to God (Heb. 9:1, NKJV).

DIVORCE — the legal dissolution (ending) of a marriage (Deut. 24:1–4).

DOCTRINE — a set of beliefs about God, mankind, Jesus Christ, the church, and other related concepts considered important and accepted by all members of a community of faith (Prov. 4:2, NKJV).

DOMINION — rule; power (Gen. 1:26, NKJV).

DOOM — calamity (a terrible thing); destruction (Deut. 32:35).

DOOR — the covering over an entrance into a tent (Gen. 18:1), a house (Judg. 19:22), or a public building (Ezek. 47:1). The doors of Bible times were made of a wide variety of material, including animal hides, wood, and metal.

DOORKEEPER — a guard, but not a member of the military (Ps. 84:10).

DOORPOSTS — the two sides of a doorway,

similar to a doorframe. The Hebrew people were ordered by the Lord to spread the blood of a sacrificial lamb on the doorposts of their houses during the Passover. This was a sign of their loyalty to the Lord. It was also a sign for the destroying angel to pass over their houses when the firstborn of Egypt were killed during the tenth plague (Exod. 12:7). Later, the Hebrew people were told to write sacred words on the doorposts of their houses as a reminder of what God did for them (Deut. 6:9; 11:20).

DORCAS [dor´-cas] *(gazelle)* — a Christian woman from Joppa known for being nice to and helping the poor (Acts 9:36–43). Tabitha was her Aramaic name (it also means "gazelle"). She was raised from the dead by the apostle Peter.

DOUBLE-TONGUED — without integrity (1 Tim. 3:8, NKJV). One way of saying double-tongued in modern language is "two-faced." A two-faced person says one thing to one person, and another thing to another person usually to try and cause trouble.

DOVE — a small bird used for sacrifice (John 2:14).

DOWRY — a gift the groom gave to the father of his bride. This was not considered a payment or a purchase price for a wife, but payment to the father for the loss of her help as a daughter. The dowry could be money (Exod. 22:16–17), service (Gen. 29:15–30), or the performance of a specific job (1 Sam. 18:25–27; Judg. 1:12). Laban tricked Jacob into serving fourteen years of labor as a dowry for Rachel (Gen. 29:15–30).

DOXOLOGY — a declaration of praise to God; a brief hymn (song) expressing His power and glory.

DRACHMA [drock´-ma] — a silver coin similar to a Roman denarius.

DREAD — fear (1 Chron. 22:13).

DREAM — a time where images, thoughts, and ideas pass through the mind of a sleeping person. In ancient times, dreams (especially those of kings and priests) were thought to be messages from God (Num. 12:6; Gen. 31:10–13).

DRUNK, DRUNKENNESS — a drugged or crazy condition that results from drinking alcoholic beverages (1 Cor. 5:11; 6:10; Eph. 5:18). Drunkenness is listed several times in the New Testament as a sin to avoid (Luke 21:34; Rom. 13:13; Gal. 5:21).

DULCIMER — a musical instrument. Some Bible teachers think it may have been similar to a Greek instrument known as the symphonia, which consisted of two pipes thrust through a leather sack (Dan. 3:5, 10, 15).

DULL — not sharp; slow to learn (Heb. 5:11, NKJV).

DUMB — silent or mute (Mark 7:37).

DUNG — waste produced by humans and animals as a part of the process of digesting food (Job 20:7). Sometimes this word is used to describe an item that is useless, rejected, or despised (Jer. 16:4).

DUNG HILL — a phrase for a pile or pit of human and animal wastes. It was used to fertilize plants in Bible times (Isa. 25:10; refuse heap, NKJV; manure, ICB).

DURST — dared (Esther 7:5; Luke 20:40).

DUST — loose earth. God made Adam out of the dust of the earth (Gen. 2:7). Because he led people to sin, the serpent was cursed to eat dust as he crawled on his belly (Gen. 3:14). Dust was poured on the head as a sign of mourning. Dust is also used as a symbol for a great number of people (too many to count) (Gen. 13:16), for death (Gen. 3:19; Job 10:9; Eccles. 12:7), and for the grave (Dan. 12:2).

E

EARNEST — a down payment or guarantee given by a buyer to a seller as part of a contract. This contract was a promise that the full amount would be paid at a later time. Paul wrote, God has "put his Spirit in our hearts to be a guarantee for all he has promised" (2 Cor. 1:22; earnest, KJV) or as a guarantee of our inheritance (2 Cor. 5:5; Eph. 1:14; earnest, KJV).

EARTH, EARTHLY — the planet where mankind lives. God is in control of the entire earth. The Israelites were promised that if they obeyed God's will and kept His laws, the earth would produce fruitful harvests, but if they were disobedient, the crops would fail and famine would come (Deut. 28).

EAST, MEN OF THE — the people who lived east of Palestine (Job 1:3).

EAST WIND — a destructive desert wind (Gen. 41:27).

EBED-MELECH [e´-bed-me´-lek] *(servant of the king)* — an Ethiopian eunuch who served Zedekiah, king of Judah. Ebed-Melech saved the prophet Jeremiah from a dungeon (Jer. 38:7–13). Later, Jeremiah told him that he would be saved when the Babylonians captured Jerusalem (Jer. 39:15–18).

EBENEZER [eb-en-e´-zer] *(stone of help)* — the place where Israel was defeated by the Philistines and the Ark of the Covenant was captured (1 Sam. 5:1).

ECCLESIASTES, BOOK OF — an Old Testament book that was probably written by Solomon. Its name comes from the Greek word *ekklesiastes,* which means "teacher."

The Book of Ecclesiastes teaches that just being rich and famous does not bring true happiness. True happiness comes from serving God and following His will for our lives. Another important lesson from Ecclesiastes is that life is to be enjoyed (3:12–13).

EDEN [e´-dun] *(delight)* — the first place Adam and Eve lived (Gen. 2–3).

Photo by Gustav Jeeninga

Petra, situated in ancient Edom, is the site of numerous buildings carved from red sandstone cliffs by the Nabateans about 300 B.C.

EDICT — an official order (Esther 1:20, NKJV; Heb. 11:23, NKJV).

EDIFY, EDIFICATION — to build up; to strengthen; to encourage (Eph. 4:12, 29, NKJV).

EDOM [e´-dum] *(red)* — another name for Esau. Esau traded his birthright to his brother Jacob for a meal of red stew (Gen. 25:29–34). Edom is also the name of the land where Esau's family lived (Gen. 32:3; 36:8).

EDOMITES [e´-dum-ites] — the descendants (family) of Edom or Esau. They were enemies of the Israelites.

EGYPT [e´-jipt] — a large country in the northeast corner of Africa. The Israelites spent 430 years in this land (Exod. 12:40) between the time of Joseph and Moses. Jesus lived in Egypt when he was a baby (Matt. 2:13–15).

ELAM [e´-lam] *(highland)* — the name of eight or nine men in the Bible, but most of the time it is talking about the son of Shem and grandson of Noah (Gen. 10:22). Elam is also a geographical region east of the Tigris River.

ELDER — a word used all through the Bible, but it means different ideas at different times in biblical history. It can mean age, experience, and authority, as well as a specific leadership role (Acts 20:17–38).

ELEAZAR [el-e-a´-zar] *(God is helper)* — the name of seven men in the Bible, but most of the time it is talking about Aaron's third son by his wife Elisheba (Exod. 6:23). Eleazar was the father of Phinehas (Exod. 6:25). Eleazar was consecrated as a priest and made chief of the Levites after his older brothers, Nadab and Abihu, were killed for offering a bad sacrifice (unholy fire) (Lev. 10:1–7).

Photo by Howard Vos

The Sphinx and the Great Pyramid, timeless symbols of the land of Egypt and its people.

Photo by Howard Vos

The step pyramid of the Pharaoh Zoser at Saqqarah near Cairo—the oldest known Egyptian pyramid (2700 B.C.)—with accompanying temple.

ELECTION — the process of God inviting people to be part of His kingdom and to receive great benefits of His love and blessings (2 Pet. 1:10, NKJV). The Bible uses the word "election" in three different ways: (1) God's choice of Israel and the church for special service and privileges, (2) the choice of a specific individual to some office or to perform a special service, and (3) the invitation to be a child of God and receive the gift of eternal life (salvation).

ELI [e´-li] *(the Lord is high)* — a judge and high priest. When the prophet Samuel was a child, he lived with Eli (1 Sam. 1–4; 14:3).

ELI, ELI, LAMA SABACHTHANI [e´-li, e´-li, la´-ma, sa-bock´-tan-ni´] — the heart-broken cry of Jesus from the cross (Matt. 27:46). The first two words (Eli, Eli) are spoken in Hebrew and they mean "my God, my God." The final words (lama sabachthani) are spoken in Aramaic and mean "Why have you left me alone?" These are the words Jesus said at the moment he took the sins of the world upon

Himself and had to experience the righteous judgment of God against sin for all human beings. We can see that even in His loneliest, saddest moment He still had faith in God because He cried out to His Father calling Him "*My* God."

ELIEZER [el-e-e´-zer] *(my God is helper)* — Eliezer of Damascus was the name of Abraham's head servant (Gen. 15:2). If Abraham had not had a son, Eliezer would have been Abraham's heir.

ELIJAH [e-li´-jah] *(the Lord is my God)* — the son of Jeroham, a Benjamite (1 Chron. 8:27); another man named Elijah was the son of Harim (Ezra 10:21). It believed that he is the same Elijah who divorced his foreign wife after the Captivity in Babylon (Ezra 10:26). The most important man named Elijah was a prophet who lived in the ninth century B.C. during the time of Ahab and Ahaziah in the northern kingdom of Israel. Elijah was a very good man and the Israelites had great respect for him.

ELISHA [e-li´-shah] *(my God saves)* — an early Hebrew prophet who took Elijah's place (1 Kings 19:16). The period of his ministry dates from about 850 to 800 B.C. Elisha's work consisted of presenting the Word of God through prophecy, advising kings, anointing kings, helping the needy, and performing several miracles.

ELIZABETH [e-liz´-a-beth] *(God is my oath)* — the wife of the priest Zechariah. Zechariah and Elizabeth had been unable to have children (Luke 1:6–7). God performed a miracle and they had a son who came to be known as John the Baptist.

EMMANUEL [em-man´-uel] — another way of saying Immanuel (Isa. 7:14; Matt. 1:23).

EMMAUS [em´-ma-us] *(warm wells)* — a small town (village) in Judea where Jesus showed Himself to two disciples after His resurrection. Jesus went with them to Emmaus, and they invited Him to stay there with them (Luke 24:28).

ENCHANTMENT — the practice of magic or sorcery. In the Bible, enchantment is used as a word that can mean several things, including fortunetelling, calling up demons, and controlling evil spirits. Most ancient civilizations believed in enchantment, but the Mosaic Law said these practices were bad (abominations) and forbidden (Deut. 18:10–12).

EN-GEDI [en-ghe´-di] *(spring of a kid)* — an oasis on the western shore of the Dead Sea about thirty-five miles southeast of Jerusalem. It contained many hideouts where David

Photo by Levant Photo Service

Statue of the prophet Elijah at the Muhraqah on Mount Carmel, commemorating his victory over the pagan worshipers of Baal.

sometimes hid when he was fleeing from King Saul (1 Sam. 23:29–24:1).

ENMITY — a deep-seated animosity or hatred. The apostle Paul said that the human mind in its natural state is in "enmity against God" (Rom. 8:7, NKJV). This enmity can only be changed by the redeeming power of Christ.

ENOCH [e´-nok] *(initiated or dedicated)* — the firstborn son of Cain (Gen. 4:17–18). Enoch was also the name of a city built by Cain in the land of Nod and named after his son (Gen. 4:17). The son of Jared was also named Enoch and he was the father of Methuselah (Gen. 5:18–24).

ENSAMPLE — model, example (Phil. 3:17).

ENVY — a feeling of resentment and jealousy toward others because of their possessions or good qualities. Christians are warned to be careful not to commit the sin of envy (Rom. 13:13; 1 Pet. 2:1).

EPHAH [e´-fah] — a unit for measuring volume (Judg. 6:19, NKJV). Ephah is also the name of two men, one woman, and a tribe in the Bible.

EPHESIANS [e-fe´-zheuns] — people who were born in or who lived in Ephesus (Acts 19:35).

EPHESIANS, EPISTLE TO THE — one of four shorter epistles written by the apostle Paul while he was in prison; the other three are Philippians, Colossians, and Philemon.

In this letter to the Ephesians, Paul wants them to understand how important God's plan is and how important it is for there to be peace and unity in the church. He also explains how family members should behave and how Christians need to stand strong against Satan.

EPHESUS [ef´-e-sus] — a large and important city on the west coast of Asia Minor. The apostle Paul started a church there.

EPHOD OF HIGH PRIEST [e´-fod] — a vest worn by the high priest when he was at the altar (Exod. 28:4–14, NKJV; 39:2–7, NKJV). The ephod was made of fine linen interwoven with some threads of pure gold and other

Photo by Ben Chapman

The great theater of the city of Ephesus, showing the marble boulevard leading to the nearby harbor, now silted in because of erosion.

threads that were blue, purple, and scarlet in color. It was worn over a blue robe (Exod. 28:31–35).

On the shoulders of the ephod, there were two onyx stones set in gold. The names of the twelve tribes of Israel were engraved on these stones. The front of the vest, also called the breastplate, was fastened to the shoulder straps by two golden chains (Exod. 28:14) and by a blue cord (Exod. 28:28). Associate priests were allowed to wear ephods at a later point in time (1 Sam. 22:18).

EPHRAIM [e´-fra-im] *(doubly fruitful)* — the second son of Joseph. His mother was Asenath.

When Ephraim was born, Joseph chose the name Ephraim because it meant "fruitful" (Gen. 41:52). Joseph was a foreigner (a Hebrew) in Egypt but God blessed him and he earned a high position in the Egyptian government. Joseph had two sons, Ephraim and Manasseh. Eventually Ephraim's thousands of descendants (family) settled in the land of Canaan. They were one of the largest tribes in Israel (Gen. 48:17; Num. 1:10).

EPICUREANS [ep-i-cu-re´-ans] — Greek philosophers who attended a school founded by Epicurus about 306 B.C. The Epicureans cared about practical things, not spiritual things. Their main interest in life was pleasure. They believed they could find happiness by seeking physical and mental pleasure and avoiding the things that caused pain (Acts 17:16–33).

EPISTLE — a letter of correspondence between two or more people or groups. Several books of the New Testament were originally written as

The spring at En-Gedi, where David hid from King Saul (1 Sam. 24:1).

epistles (2 Pet. 3:16). An epistle is almost the same as a letter, except an epistle is usually more formal and a letter is more personal.

ER [ur] — the name of three men in the Bible:
1. A son of Judah (Gen. 38:3, 6–7).
2. A son of Shelah, the youngest son of Judah (1 Chron. 4:21)
3. An ancestor of Jesus who lived between the time of David and Zerubbabel (Luke 3:28).

ESAU [e´-saw] — a son of Isaac and Rebekah and the twin brother of Jacob. Esau was also known as Edom (Gen. 25:24–28; Deut. 2:4–8).

Esau was a hunter and outdoorsman. He was his father's favorite and his brother Jacob was his mother's favorite (Gen. 25:27–28).

Esau was more honest and dependable than Jacob, but he committed a great sin by

55

Photo by Gustav Jeeninga

Top: An epistle, or letter, in the Greek language from the third century A.D., written to a person named Aphrodite.

Bottom: Reverse side of the letter to Aphrodite, showing how two pieces of papyrus were pressed together in crisscross fashion to produce a piece of writing material.

ignoring the importance of his birthright. A birthright allowed the oldest son to inherit most of the father's property and the right to lead the family after the father's death. To the ancient Hebrews, a birthright actually had a high spiritual value. Esau did not have the faith to accept his privileges and responsibilities. It was an insult to sell this important gift for a small meal (Heb. 12:16–17).

ESCHATOLOGY [es-ca-tol´-ogy] — the study of what will happen at the end of time, especially the Second Coming of Christ. The word comes from two Greek words, *eschatos* (last) and *logos* (study). A simple definition would be "the study of last things."

ESTABLISH — to make; to strengthen; to confirm (Prov. 8:28, NKJV; Heb. 13:9, NKJV).

ESTHER [es´-tur] *(star)* — the Jewish queen of the Persian king Ahasuerus (Xerxes). Esther saved her people, the Jews, from a plot to kill them. After her mother and father died, Esther's cousin Mordecai raised her. Her Jewish name was Hadassah, which means "myrtle" (Esther 2:7).

ESTHER, BOOK OF — a historical book of the Old Testament named for its main character, Queen Esther of Persia. It was her courage and quick thinking that saved the Jewish people from disaster. The Book of Esther is a reminder of how God always keeps His promises.

Some Bible scholars believe Esther has no place in the Bible because it never mentions the word "God."

The Book of Esther is valuable because it teaches important spiritual lessons about fasting (4:16) and God's protection of His people (4:14). The book also teaches a valuable lesson about God's power and timing.

ESTRANGE, ESTRANGED — to make unknown, to become unloved (Jer. 19:4).

ETERNAL LIFE — a person's new life in Jesus Christ. This is God's gift to all believers. The idea of eternal life is implied by the prophets in their pictures of the glorious future promised to God's people (John 3:16).

ETHIOPIA [e-the-o´-pe-ah] *(burnt face)* — the Greek name for the ancient nation south of Egypt (Acts 8:26–40). Its Hebrew name was Cush. Modern Ethiopia (Abyssinia), in the horn of East Africa, is hundreds of miles away from ancient Ethiopia.

ETHIOPIAN — a person who was born in or lived in Ethiopia (Jer. 13:23, NKJV).

EUNUCH [yu´-nuk] — a male servant of a royal household in Bible times.

EUPHRATES [yu-fra´-teze] — the longest river of Western Asia and one of two major rivers in Mesopotamia. The river begins in the mountains of Armenia in modern-day Turkey. It then heads west toward the Mediterranean Sea, turns to the south, swings in a wide bow through Syria, and then flows some one thousand miles southeast to join the Tigris River before it empties into the Persian Gulf.

EUTYCHUS [yu´-tik-us] *(fortunate)* — a young man of Troas who was sitting in a tall building listening to the apostle Paul preach. He went to sleep and fell from the building and died from the fall. Paul performed a miracle and brought Eutychus back to life (Acts 20:9–10).

EVANGELIST, EVANGELIZE — a person authorized to share the gospel of Christ with others; to tell others about Jesus. The exact meaning of the word evangelist is "one who proclaims good tidings" (Eph. 4:11, NKJV; 2 Tim. 4:5, NKJV).

EVE [eev] *(life-giving)* — the first woman (Gen. 3:20; 4:1), created from one of Adam's ribs to be "a helper" to him (Gen. 2:18–22).

EVERLASTING — lasting forever, eternal. The Bible speaks of the everlasting God (Isa. 40:28, NKJV), Father (Isa. 9:6, NKJV), King (Jer. 10:10, NKJV), and Redeemer (Isa. 63:16, NKJV). The Lord is a God of everlasting kindness (Isa. 54:8, NKJV), love (Jer. 31:3, NKJV), and mercy (Ps. 100:5, NKJV; 103:17, NKJV) who has established an everlasting covenant with His people (Heb. 13:20, NKJV). His kingdom is everlasting (2 Pet. 1:11, NKJV), as is His salvation (Ps. 45:17, NKJV).

EVIL — a force that opposes God and His work (Rom. 7:8–19).

EVIL ONE — Satan, the devil (John 17:15; 1 John 3:12).

EWE — a female sheep (Lev. 14:10, NKJV).

EXALT — to lift up (Exod. 15:2, NKJV).

EXCEEDING — abundant; more than is needed (Eph. 1:19, NKJV).

EXECRATION — an oath or curse (Jer. 42:18; 44:12).

EXHORT, EXHORTATION — a message of warning or encouragement used to motivate a person or group of people to do something. The apostle Paul often exhorted his fellow Christians to live out their calling as ministers of the Lord Jesus (Rom. 12:8, NKJV; 2 Cor. 8:17, NKJV).

EXILE — to place a person or group of people

in captivity and remove them from their homeland.

EXODUS, THE — the journey of the Israelites out of captivity, led by Moses.

EXODUS, BOOK OF — an important Old Testament book about the nation of Israel. It takes its name from the event known as the Exodus, the dramatic deliverance of the Hebrew people from slavery in Egypt.

The Bible's entire message of redemption begins with the covenant relationship between God and His people described in this book. The Book of Exodus is a dramatic testimony to the power of God. The signs and plagues sent by God to break Pharaoh's stubbornness are clear demonstrations of His power. The Book of Exodus also shows the weakness of Egypt's false gods. The puny idols of Egypt are powerless before the mighty God of Israel.

EXORCIST — one who drives away demons (Acts 19:13, NKJV).

EXPEDIENT, EXPEDIENCY — doing what is necessary to reach a specific goal (John 11:50, NKJV; 18:14, NKJV).

EXTOL — to exalt or praise; to glorify (Ps. 68:4, NKJV).

EYESERVICE — the outward show of service, in order to impress others. The apostle Paul spoke harshly against this kind of action (Eph. 6:6, NKJV; Col. 3:22, NKJV).

EZEKIEL [ih-zeek´-e-uhl] *(God will strengthen)* — a prophet who was taken captive and sent to Babylon in 597 B.C. He shows us just how ugly and serious our sin is.

EZEKIEL, BOOK OF — a prophetic book of the Old Testament. The Book of Ezekiel is

Photo by Howard Vos

The rugged Sinai Desert, through which the Israelites passed during the Exodus from Egypt.

named for its author, the prophet Ezekiel, who received his prophetic messages from God in a series of visions. He addressed these prophecies to the Jewish exiles in Babylonia, where he lived among them.

EZRA [ez´-rah] *([God is] a help)* — the name of three men in the Bible:

1. A descendant of Judah (1 Chron. 4:17)

2. A scribe and priest who led the captives in Jerusalem to make a new commitment to God's Law.

3. A priest who returned from the Captivity with Zerubbabel (Neh. 12:1, 13).

EZRA, BOOK OF — a historical book of the Old Testament that tells about the resettlement of the Jewish people in their homeland after their long exile in Babylonia. The book is named for its author and central figure, Ezra the priest, who led the exiles in a new commitment to God's Law after their return.

F

FACE — the part of the human body that contains a person's unique identifying characteristics. In the Bible, "face" is also used as a symbol for the presence of God. In the Garden of Eden, Adam and Eve "hid themselves from the presence [literally, face] of the Lord God" (Gen. 3:8, NKJV).

FAINT — weak (Isa. 40:30, NKJV).

FAITH — a belief in or confident attitude toward God. This includes a commitment to following His will.

FAITHFUL — true; unwavering; continuing or staying (Deut. 7:9).

FAITHFULNESS — dependability, loyalty, and stability, especially in reference to God and His relationship to human believers. The faithfulness of God and His Word is a constant theme in the Bible. It is particularly prominent in Psalms 89 and 119. God is "the faithful God" (Deut. 7:9) and chooses Israel (Isa. 49:7).

FALL, THE — the disobedience and sin of Adam and Eve that caused them to lose their innocence. This event plunged them and all of mankind into a state of sin and corruption (Gen. 3).

FALLOW — a deer (Deut. 14:5, NKJV); unplowed ground (Jer. 4:3, NKJV).

FALSE, FALSEHOOD — a lie (Deut. 5:20, NKJV).

FAMILY — a group of people related by marriage or blood and generally living together in the same household (Exod. 12:21).

FAMINE — not having enough food or water for everyone. This word occurs often in the Bible. Sometimes it is talking about an actual famine and sometimes it is talking about a spiritual famine.

FARE — peace; prosperity (1 Sam. 17:18, NKJV).

FAST, FASTING — going without food or drink voluntarily, usually for religious reasons. Fasting could also be done for other reasons. Sometimes it was done as a sign of distress, grief, or repentance (Acts 12:2, 3; 14:23).

FATHER — the male parent of a household (Gen. 2:24). The father had the responsibility of providing for the family and giving religious instruction to the children.

FATHOM — a unit of measure for water, approximately six feet (Acts 27:28, NKJV).

FATLING — a grain-fed lamb, calf, or kid (baby goat) that was raised for meat (1 Sam. 15:9, NKJV). Because of the cost of feed, these animals were very valuable in Bible times. They were a luxury the poor could not afford.

FAULT — error; mistake; sin (Dan. 6:4, NKJV; Gal. 6:1, NKJV).

FAVOR — grace (Esther 2:15, NKJV).

FEAR — a feeling of reverence, awe, and respect (Acts 2:43, NKJV). Also an unpleasant emotion (feeling) caused by a sense of danger. Fear can be directed toward God or mankind, and depending on the situation, it can healthy or harmful.

FEASTS AND FESTIVALS — holy gatherings, or the regular gathering of the people of Israel for worship.

The feasts and festivals of the nation were scheduled at specific times of the year and they could be both civil and religious in nature. Some feasts and festivals marked the beginning or the end of the agricultural year, while others were in memory of historic events. This was always a time of thanksgiving and joyous feasting.

FEET WASHING — *(See Foot Washing.)*

FELIX [fe´-lix] *(happy)* — a Roman governor of Judea. The apostle Paul had to appear before him (Acts 24:27).

Jewish Feasts

Feast of	Month on Jewish Calendar	Day	Corresponding Month	References
Passover	Nisan	14	Mar.–Apr.	Exod. 12:1–14; Matt. 26:17–20
*Unleavened Bread	Nisan	15–21	Mar.–Apr.	Exod. 12:15–20
Firstfruits	Nisan or Sivan	16 6	Mar.–Apr. May–June	Lev. 23:9–14; Num. 28:26
*Pentecost (Harvest or Weeks)	Sivan	6 (50 days after barley harvest)	May–June	Deut. 16:9–12; Acts 2:1
Trumpets, *Rosh Hashanah*	Tishri	1, 2	Sept.–Oct.	Num. 29:1–6
Day of Atonement, *Yom Kippur*	Tishri	10	Sept.–Oct.	Lev. 23:26–32; Heb. 9:7
*Tabernacles (Booths or Ingathering)	Tishri	15–22	Sept.–Oct.	Neh. 8:13–18; John 7:2
Dedication (Lights), *Hanukkah*	Chislev	25 (8 days)	Nov.–Dec.	John 10:22
Purim (Lots)	Adar	14, 15	Feb.–Mar.	Esther 9:18–32

*The three major feasts for which all males of Israel were required to travel to the temple in Jerusalem (Exod. 23:14–19).

FELLOWSHIP — sharing things in common with others (1 John 1:3–7). Fellowship can be either positive or negative.

FESTUS, PORCIUS [fes´-tus por´-shih-us] — the Roman procurator, or governor, of Judea after Felix (Acts 24:27).

FETTERS — shackles or chains attached to the ankles of prisoners to make it difficult for them to walk (Ps. 105:18, NKJV). Fetters were usually made of iron or bronze.

FIDELITY — faithfulness; loyalty. The word occurs only once in the Bible (Titus 2:10, NKJV). The apostle Paul wrote to Titus instructing him to exhort slaves to show "all good fidelity" to their own masters.

FIG, FIG TREE — a fruit-producing plant that could be either a tall tree or a low-spreading shrub. The size of the tree depended on its location and soil. The blooms of the fig tree always appear before the leaves in spring. There were usually two crops of figs a year.

Figs were eaten fresh (2 Kings 18:31) and pressed into cakes (1 Sam. 25:18). Sycamore figs were similar to the fig but were smaller and not as good (Amos 7:14). Poor people could not afford the better variety so they usually ate those.

FILLETS — fasteners (Exod. 27:10).

FILTH, FILTHINESS — foul or dirty; also a symbol of ceremonial uncleanness or spiritual corruption. "All our righteousnesses," declared the prophet Isaiah, "are like filthy pieces of cloth" (Isa. 64:6). But God will forgive and cleanse the sinner who repents and believes in Christ (1 John 1:7–9).

FIRE — the flames of something that is burning. In the Bible, fire is often used as a symbol of God's presence and power (Gen. 15:17–18).

FIRM — strong and stable (Heb. 3:6, NKJV).

FIRMAMENT — the enormous area of sky and space where the stars and planets are set. God made the firmament on the second day of creation to divide the waters that covered the earth from those that were above it (Gen. 1:7, NKJV). The firmament actually includes more than just the space between the seas of earth and the rain clouds of the sky. It is hard to understand just how far this space reaches. On the fourth day of creation God placed the stars, the sun, and the moon in the "firmament of the heavens" (Gen. 1:15–18, NKJV).

FIRSTBORN — the first offspring of human beings or animals (Exod. 4:22; Heb. 1:6).

FIRSTFRUITS — the firstborn of the flocks and the first vegetables and grains to be gathered at harvest time. The Hebrew people strongly believed the "firstfruits" belonged to God. They were dedicated or presented to God on the day of the firstfruits, a part of the celebration of Pentecost (Num. 28:26).

FIRSTLING — the firstborn of animals or the first of the harvest from a crop. Abel brought the firstlings of his flock as an offering to God (Gen. 4:4). The law of the firstborn is recorded in Exodus 13:11–16.

FISH GATE — a gate in Jerusalem, place for a fish market (2 Chron. 33:14).

FLAGON [FLAG gon] — a word for raisin cake (KJV).

FLATTER — to compliment (say something nice) for selfish reasons (Prov. 28:23, NKJV).

FLEE — to leave quickly with the intention of getting away from someone or something (Gen. 16:8, NKJV; Matt. 2:13, NKJV).

FLESH, FLESHLY — the physical bodies of humans or animals. When God removed a rib from Adam to create Eve, he closed up the place with flesh (Gen. 2:21). The apostle Paul spoke of the flesh of men, beasts, fish, and birds (1 Cor. 15:39).

FLINT — a rock used for making tools and weapons (Deut. 8:15, NKJV).

Photo by Howard Vos

Inscribed stone tablet from Babylon that describes a great flood. Unlike the Babylonian stories, the biblical account of the Flood emphasizes the sin of people and the power and moral judgment of God.

FLOCK — a herd of animals that included both sheep and goats. Both kinds of animals grazed and traveled together (Gen. 30:31–32). These animals were difficult to tell apart except at close range. This explains Jesus' teaching about separating sheep from goats at the last judgment (Matt. 25:32). In Old Testament times, the size of a person's flocks and herds was a way to measure their wealth (1 Sam. 25:2; Job 1:3).

FLOOD, THE — the deluge (huge flood) that God sent to destroy the sinful people during the time of Noah (Gen. 6–8).

FOLD — a place for animals (Num. 32:16, NKJV); also means flock (John 10:16, NKJV).

FOOD — nourishing substances eaten by people and animals.

FOOL, FOOLISHNESS — a stupid person or a senseless act. In the Bible, the most foolish person of all is one who denies God: "A wicked fool says to himself, 'There is no God'" (Ps. 14:1; 53:1).

The use of the word "fool" in Matthew 5:22 is a special case. Jesus warned against using the word "fool" as a form of abuse. This word showed the hatred in a person's heart toward others.

FOOT WASHING — an expression of hospitality shown to guests in Bible times. People traveling dusty roads in Palestine needed to wash their feet for comfort and cleanliness. Usually the lowliest servant in the household performed the foot washing (Luke 7:44). Sometimes guests were offered water and vessels to wash their own feet (Gen. 18:4; Judg. 19:21).

At the Last Supper, Jesus washed His disciples' feet. He explained that this act was an example of the humble ministry that they should always be ready to perform for each other (John 13:5–17).

FORBEAR, FORBEARANCE — tolerate (Eph. 4:2, NKJV), tolerance or mercy. Although human sin deserves punishment, God in His forbearance, or mercy (longsuffering patience), gives a chance for repentance (Rom. 2:4, NKJV).

FORD — a shallow place that provides easy passage across a body of water (Josh. 2:7, NKJV; Judg. 3:28, NKJV).

FOREFATHERS — ancestors, family that lived before (Jer. 11:10).

FOREIGNER — a person whose citizenship and loyalty belong to a different country (Deut. 15:3).

FOREKNOW, FOREKNOWLEDGE — the unique knowledge of God that makes Him able to know everything before it happens.

FORESKIN — the skin that covers the end of the male sex organ. The removal of the foreskin took place during the circumcision. It was a sign of the Abrahamic covenant (Gen. 17:10–25). Circumcision happened eight days after birth (Lev. 12:3).

FORGIVE, FORGIVENESS — the act of excusing or pardoning others even though they made a mistake. That is what God does when He forgives the sins of human beings.

FORM — to make or create; bring forth (Gen. 2:7).

FORNICATION — having a sexual relationship without being married. Seven times in the New Testament, Paul writes a list of sins. The word "fornication" is found in five of those lists (Rom. 13:13; 1 Cor. 5:11; Gal. 5:19, NKJV; Eph. 5:3, NKJV; Col. 3:5, NKJV).

FORSAKE — to abandon (Matt. 19:27).

FORTRESS — a safe place (Isa. 25:12, NKJV; Ps. 18:2, NKJV).

FOUL — offensive; unclean (Mark 9:25).

FOUNDATION — the strong, stable base on which a building is constructed. Jesus taught that believers should build their faith on the strong foundation of practicing His teachings (Matt. 7:24–27, NKJV). The apostle Paul also referred to Christ as a foundation for believers (1 Cor. 3:11).

FOWL — a bird, birds (Gen. 1:21).

FRAME — when used as a verb it means to establish or make (Jer. 18:11); when used as a noun it is a form or what something is made of (Ps. 103:14, NKJV).

FRANKINCENSE — a fragrant substance made from tree resin (Matt. 2:11).

FREE, FREEDOM — the absence of slavery; the ability to go wherever and do whatever a person wants (John 8:36; Rom. 6:18).

FREEWILL OFFERING — a voluntary offering (Lev. 22:18, NKJV).

FRONTLET — a small container that held scripture (Deut. 6:8, NKJV).

FROWARD — corrupt; bad (Prov. 2:15).

FRUIT — food (Gen. 1:11). The word "fruit" is also a reference to children (Exod. 21:22), and spiritually speaking, a reference to good qualities (characteristics) (Gal. 5:22, NKJV).

FRUSTRATE — set aside (in Bible times) (Gal. 2:21, NKJV).

FUGITIVE — a runaway or escapee (Gen. 4:14, NKJV).

FULFILL — complete (Matt. 3:15, NKJV).

FULLNESS OF TIME — an exact or specific time (Gal. 4:4, NKJV).

FUNERAL — a burial ceremony. The Bible doesn't give many details about the actual rituals involved in burying the dead in ancient Palestine. Corpses (dead bodies) were generally buried (Gen. 23:4, 6, 8), but only Joseph was embalmed and put in a coffin (Gen. 50:26).

Mourners at funerals included family members (Gen. 37:34) and friends (1 Sam. 15:35). Sometimes people called professional mourners were paid to attend the funeral (Eccles. 12:5).

Mourning customs included weeping (Gen. 23:2), wearing sackcloth (Isa. 15:3), cutting hair (Jer. 7:29), fasting (2 Sam. 1:11), and putting ashes on (Ezek. 27:30). A line of mourners usually carried the body to the burial site (2 Sam. 3:31–34).

FURNACE — an oven (Dan. 3:6).

FURY — a violent and intense anger; rage. The Bible speaks often of the fury of the LORD (Isa. 51:13, 22, NKJV). This phrase refers to the judgment of a holy God against the sinful rebellion of human beings.

FUTURE — a time that hasn't happened yet (Ps. 37:37–38, NKJV). The Christian believer is confident of the future because he belongs to Jesus Christ.

G

GABRIEL [ga´-bre-el] *(God is great)* — an archangel who acts as the messenger of God; he appeared to Daniel (Dan. 8:16), Zechariah (Luke 1:19), and the Virgin Mary (Luke 1:26–38).

GAD *(good fortune)* — the seventh son of Jacob's twelve sons. Gad was the firstborn son of Zilpah (Leah's maid). Moses praised Gad for his bravery and faithfulness to duty (Deut. 33:20–21). Except for Ezbon, Gad's seven sons all founded tribal families (Num. 26:15–18).

There was also a prophet named Gad. He was called David's "seer" (1 Chron. 21:9). He told David to buy the threshing floor of Araunah the Jebusite, and it became the site of the temple. He also helped arrange the tabernacle music (2 Chron. 29:25) and wrote about David's time as king (1 Chron. 29:29).

GADARA [gad´-ar-a] *(walls)* — a city of Transjordan about six miles southeast of the Sea of Galilee. Gadara was mainly a Greek city and one of the cities of the Decapolis. It was also the capital city of Perea. The ruins of Gadara, known in modern times as Um Qeis, include two theaters, a church, bathhouses, and a street lined with columns. These ruins

Photo by Howard Vos

Remains of a church at ancient Gergesa which memorialized Jesus' healing of the demoniac (Matt. 8:28–34). This region east of the Sea of Galilee was also known as Gadara and Gerasa.

are proof that Gadara was once a large and beautiful city.

GADARENES [gad-a-renes'] — the people who were born in or lived in Gadara. The Gadarenes are mentioned in the story of Jesus healing a demon–possessed man (Mark 5:1–20, NKJV).

GALATIA [ga-la-she'-a] — a region in central Asia Minor (modern Turkey). The northern part of the region was settled in the third century B.C. by Celtic tribes that had been driven out of Gaul (France). The region received its name, Galatia, from those tribes.

GALATIANS [ga-la-she'-ans] — the people who were born in or lived in Galatia (Gal. 3:1).

GALATIANS, EPISTLE TO THE — a short, exciting letter from the apostle Paul to the Christians of Galatia. The Book of Galatians is full of valuable information about Paul's life between his conversion and his missionary journeys (1:11–2:14). Galatians also teaches the doctrine of justification by faith alone (Christians are accepted by God when they believe that Jesus died on the cross for their sins and that He rose again).

GALILEE [gal'-i-lee] *(circle or circuit)* — a Roman province of Palestine during the time of Jesus.

GALILEE, SEA OF — a freshwater lake, fed by the Jordan River. This body of water was closely associated with Jesus' ministry.

GALL — a bitter thing (Matt. 27:34).

GAMALIEL [gam-a'-le-el] *(God is my recompense)* — a leader of the tribe of Manasseh

Photo by Willem A. VanGemeren

The Sea, or Lake, of Galilee, at the point where the Jordan River flows into the northern end of the lake.

chosen to help take the census during Israel's wandering in the wilderness (Num. 1:10).

Another man named Gamaliel was a famous member of the Jewish Sanhedrin and a teacher of the Law who had taught the apostle Paul (Acts 22:3). He told the Sanhedrin not to worry about the apostles of the Christian church. Gamaliel felt that if Jesus was a false prophet (there had been several), the little group would fall apart. But if the works of Jesus truly were "from God," he pointed out to the others, "you will not be able to stop them" (Acts 5:39).

GARMENT — a piece of clothing (Matt. 9:16, NKJV).

GARRISON — a fort or a company of soldiers stationed in a fort. During Saul's reign as king of Israel, the Philistines had garrisons deep inside Israel—at Geba (1 Sam. 13:3, NKJV) and Bethlehem (2 Sam. 23:14, NKJV; 1 Chron. 11:16, NKJV). In later years, David drove out the Philistines and placed his own garrisons in Damascus (2 Sam. 8:6, NKJV) and Edom (2 Sam. 8:14, NKJV; 1 Chron. 18:13, NKJV).

In the New Testament, the word "garrison" always means a group of Roman soldiers who were stationed in Palestine (Matt. 27:27, NKJV) or in one of the surrounding nations visited by the apostle Paul (2 Cor. 11:32, NKJV). Paul was once rescued from an angry mob by a garrison of soldiers (Acts 21:31, NKJV).

GATE — an entrance (Acts 3:10).

GAZA [ga´-za] *(stronghold)* — one of the five main cities of the Philistines. Gaza was located on the great caravan route between Mesopotamia and Egypt. This made Gaza an ideal rest stop and business center for merchants and travelers.

GEHENNA [ge-hen´-na] — a word used in reference to hell (Deut. 32:22).

GENEALOGY — a list of a person's ancestors. The genealogy of Jesus is found in Matthew 1:1–17 and Luke 3:23–28.

GENERATION — a group of people who lived at a specific time in history (Deut. 32:5, NKJV).

The word "generation" also means a single line of individuals who share a common ancestor (Gen. 17:7, NKJV; Exod. 1:6, NKJV; Matt. 1:17, NKJV). This use of the word usually occurs when the Bible gives a family or tribal history (1 Chron. 5:6–7, NKJV).

GENESIS, BOOK OF — the first book of the Bible. Genesis is the first of the five books of Moses, known as the Pentateuch.

Genesis is the book of beginnings. The word "Genesis" means "the origin, source, creation, or coming into being of something." The Hebrew name for the book is *bereshith,* the first word in the Hebrew text, which is translated as "in the beginning" (Gen. 1:1). Genesis describes such important beginnings as the Creation, the fall of man, and the early years of the nation of Israel.

GENNESARET [ghen-nes´-a-ret] — the "Lake of Gennesaret" (Luke 5:1, NKJV) is Lake Galilee (Matt. 4:18) and is sometimes called "the lake" (Luke 5:2).

The district of Gennesaret was called the land of Gennesaret (Mark 6:53). It was a plain with rich soil. Figs, olives, palms, and a variety of other trees were grown there.

The town of Gennesaret was a city of Naphtali (Josh. 19:35), also known as Kinnereth.

GENTILES — a word used by Jewish people to refer to foreigners, or any other people who were not Jewish.

GERGESENES [ghur´-ghes-enes´] — another name for Gadarenes (Matt. 8:28, NKJV).

GETHSEMANE [geth-sem´-a-ne] *(olive press)* — the garden where Jesus often went alone or with His disciples for prayer, rest, or fellowship. This is also the site where He was betrayed by Judas on the night before His crucifixion (Matt. 26:36–50; Mark 14:32).

GIANTS — human beings of abnormal size

The Garden of Gethsemane, where Jesus agonized in prayer on the night before His crucifixion (Matt. 26:36–46). The roots of these giant olive trees may date from the time of Christ or before.

and strength. Races of giants are first mentioned in the Old Testament in Genesis 6:4, where large godlike beings were produced by the union of "the sons of God" and "the daughters of men." God did not approve of these abnormal unions (Gen. 6:5–6).

GIDEON [ghid´-e-on] — a military hero and spiritual leader who saved Israel from the Midianites (Judg. 6:13–14).

GIFT, GIVING — the act of granting favor or presenting an item to another person without expecting anything in return. The purpose of a gift may be to honor (Dan. 2:48), celebrate (Rev. 11:10), or simply to provide help (Esther 9:22).

God is the giver of every good and perfect gift (Matt. 7:11; James 1:5, 17), including eternal life (Rom. 6:23), salvation (Eph. 2:8), the necessities of life (Matt. 6:11), ability to work (Eccles. 3:13; 5:19; Deut. 8:18), the Holy Spirit (Acts 2:38; 5:32), spiritual abilities (1 Cor. 12:4), and His best gift (2 Cor. 9:15), His Son (John 3:16).

GIFTS, SPIRITUAL — special abilities given by God (1 Cor. 7:7).

GILEAD [ghil´-e-ad] — the son of Machir and grandson of Manasseh (Josh. 17:1). He was the founder of a tribal family called the Gileadites.

Gilead is also a mountain region east of the Jordan River and the name of a mountain on the edge of the Jezreel valley (Judg. 7:3) where Gideon and his men were camped when Gideon decided to take a smaller army to fight the Midianites.

Two other men named Gilead were the father of Jephthah, a judge of Israel (Judg. 11:1–12:7), and the head of the family of Gad (1 Chron. 5:14).

GILGAL [gil´-gal] *(circle)* — the village where the prophet Elijah ascended into heaven (2 Kings 2:1).

Gilgal was also the name of the first campsite of the people of Israel after they crossed the Jordan River and entered the Promised Land (Josh. 4:19–20). They took stones from the Jordan and set them up at Gilgal as a memorial to God's deliverance. The first Passover in Canaan was held at Gilgal (Josh. 5:9–10).

There was also a small town between Dor and Tirzah (Josh. 12:23) that was known as Gilgal.

Does the Bible Really Say That?

Saying or Phrase	Meaning Today	Original Context or Meaning
A Garden of Eden	A paradise of unspoiled beauty and unlimited resources.	The place where God originally put Adam and Eve, before their sin (Gen. 2:8, 15).
Forbidden fruit	A pleasure or delight that we shouldn't enjoy, but which is also more attractive because it is off-limits.	The fruit of the tree of the knowledge of good and evil, which Adam and Eve were told not to eat (Gen. 2:17; 3:3).
Adam's apple	The hard lump of cartilage that is often prominent in a man's throat.	The tradition that a piece of the forbidden fruit (popularly thought of as an apple) became stuck in Adam's throat (Gen. 3:6).
Fig leaf	In art, a small covering for the genitalia; figuratively, any means of protecting oneself from embarrassment.	The coverings that Adam and Eve made after they sinned and became aware of their nakedness (Gen. 3:7).
Am I my brother's keeper?	A rhetorical question asked to evade responsibility in regard to someone else.	The question with which Cain replied when the Lord asked him where Abel was, whom Cain had murdered (Gen. 4:9).
Forty days and forty nights	A long passage of time.	The duration of the downpour that caused the flood of Noah's time (Gen. 7:12).
Babel, or a Tower of Babel	A symbol of confusion and chaos.	The place where God confused the languages of the nations in order to disperse them throughout the earth (Gen. 11:1–9).
The Promised Land	An image of ultimate freedom, happiness, and self-determination.	The phrase used to describe the land that God promised to give Abraham's descendants, the land of Canaan, said to be flowing with milk and honey (Gen. 12:7; 15:18–21).
A mess of pottage	An allusion to being cheated or shortchanged.	The bargain by which Jacob gained the family birthright from his elder brother Esau in exchange for a bowl of red stew called "pottage" in some translations (Gen. 25:27–34).

GIRD — to put on and fasten (Acts 12:8, NKJV).

GIRDLE — a belt (2 Kings 1:8; Mark 1:6); also called loincloth.

GLEAN, GLEANING — the process of gathering grain or other produce left in the fields after the harvest (Judg. 8:2, NKJV; Ruth 2, NKJV; Isa. 17:6, NKJV). The Old Testament Law required that property owners leave the gleanings of their produce in the fields so they might be gathered by "the poor and the stranger" (Lev. 19:9–10, NKJV; 23:22, NKJV).

GLORIFICATION — the process of making holy and pure.

GLORIFY — praise (Ps. 86:9, NKJV).

GLORY — beauty; power; honor; a quality of God's character that shows His greatness and authority (Acts 7:2; James 2:1).

GLUTTON — a person who eats way too much. Gluttony is more than overeating though; it is an attitude of disrespect for what is acceptable. It is also associated with drunkenness (Prov. 23:21, NKJV; Deut. 21:20, NKJV).

GNASH, GNASHING OF TEETH — to grate or grind one's teeth together as an expression of hatred and scorn (Job. 16:9, NKJV).

GNAT — a tiny insect (Matt. 23:24, NKJV).

GNOSTICISM [nos´-ti-siz-im] — a system of false teachings that existed during the early centuries of Christianity. Its name came from *gnosis,* the Greek word for knowledge. The Gnostics believed that knowledge was the way to salvation instead of Jesus.

GOD — the creator of the universe who has provided mankind with a revelation of Himself through the natural world and through His Son, Jesus Christ.

Old Testament Names for God	
1. Elohim, "God," i.e., His power and might	Gen. 1:1; Ps. 19:1
2. El-Elyon, "The most high God"	Gen. 14:17-20; Isa. 14:13,14
3. El-Olam, "The everlasting God"	Isa. 40:28-31
4. El-Roi, "The strong one who sees"	Gen. 16:13
5. El-Shaddai, "God Almighty"	Gen. 17:1; Ps. 91:1
6. Adonai, "Lord," i.e., the Lordship of God	Mal. 1:6
7. Jehovah (Yahweh), "The LORD," i.e., God's eternal nature	Gen. 2:4
8. Jehovah-Jireh, "The LORD will provide"	Gen. 22:13,14
9. Jehovah-Maccaddeshem, "The LORD your sanctifier"	Exod. 31:13
10. Jehovah-Nissi, "The LORD our banner"	Exod. 17:15
11. Jehovah-Rapha, "The LORD our healer"	Exod. 15:26
12. Jehovah-Rohi, "The LORD my shepherd"	Ps. 23:1
13. Jehovah-Sabbaoth, "The LORD of Hosts"	Isa. 6:1-3
14. Jehovah-Shalom, "The LORD is peace"	Judg. 6:24
15. Jehovah-Shammah, "The LORD who is present"	Ezek. 48:35
16. Jehovah-Tsidkenu, "The LORD our righteousness"	Jer. 23:6

God is often described by his attributes. An attribute is a characteristic of a person or being. We aren't able to understand God completely, but we can learn about Him by studying His attributes as they are shown to us in the Bible.

GOD, NAMES OF — the titles given to God throughout the Bible. In the ancient world, knowing a person's name was a special privilege that meant you had access to that person. God gave His people access to Him by sharing several of His names with them. Knowing these names allowed them to have a better understanding of His love and righteousness.

GODS, PAGAN — the false gods and idols worshiped by people during Bible times—especially the false gods of Egypt, Mesopotamia (Assyria and Babylon), Canaan, Greece, and Rome.

GOD'S WILL — God's plan and desire for us (Matt. 6:10).

GOLGOTHA [gol´-gath-a] *(place of a skull)* — a hill just outside the walls of Jerusalem where Jesus was crucified (Mark 15:22).

GOLIATH [go-li´-ath] — a Philistine giant. David killed him with a stone from his sling (1 Sam. 17:4–51). Goliath lived in the Philistine city of Gath. He was probably a descendant of a tribe of giants known as the Anakites, or descendants of Anak (Num. 13:33).

GOMORRAH [go-mor´-rah] *(submersion)* — one of the five "cities of the plain" located in the Valley of Siddim (Salt Sea or Dead Sea). The other cities were Sodom, Admah, Zeboiim,

and Zoar (Gen. 14:2–3). Because the cities of Sodom and Gomorrah became so evil and full of sin, they were destroyed by fire (Gen. 19:24, 28). The destruction of Sodom and Gomorrah is a clear example of God's judgment against the worst sinners (Isa. 13:19; Jer. 49:18; Amos 4:11; Matt. 10:15; 2 Pet. 2:6; Jude 7).

GOOD — a word with two distinct meanings in the Bible. As an adjective, "good" means "pleasing" (Prov. 15:23), "kind," and "gracious" (1 Sam. 25:15). As a noun, "good" basically means God Himself (Mark 10:18). The Bible also speaks of God's works, gifts, and commands as good.

GOPHERWOOD — the type of wood used for building Noah's ark. Gopher wood is probably a lot like cypress wood (Gen. 6:14, NKJV).

Photo by Howard Vos

A bust of Zeus in the Ephesus Museum. Zeus was the chief pagan god of the ancient Greeks.

Pagan Gods of Egypt

Name	Responsibility	Form or Sacred Animal
Aker	Earth-god • Helper of the dead	Two lion heads
Amon	Wind-god • God of Thebes • Helper of the pious	Human (ram and goose sacred)
Anubis	Glorifier of the dead	Jackal-headed, black-skinned
Apis	Ensures fertility	Bull
Aton	Sun-god	
Atum	Primordial creature-god	Serpent-human
Bes	Protection at birth • Dispenser of masculinity	Group of demons
Edjo	Goddess of Delta/Lower Egypt	Uraeus serpent
Geb	Earth-god • Consort of Nut • Begetter of Osiris	Human
Hathor	Sky-goddess • Goddess of love, dance, alcohol	Cow
Heket	Primordial goddess	Frog
Horus	Sky-god	Falcon
Isis	Goddess of life, healing • Daughter of Geb Consort/sister of Osiris • Mother of Horus	Human
Khepri	Primordial god • Rising sun	Scarabaeus
Khnum	Giver of the Nile • Creator of mankind	Human with ram's head
Khons	Moon-god	Human
Maat	Justice • Daughter of Ra	Human
Meskhenet	Goddess protector of newborns and of destiny	
Min	God of masculinity and reproduction	
Mut	"Eye of the sun" • consort of Amon	Vulture or human
Nekhbet	Goddess of Upper Egypt	
Nut	Sky-goddess • Consort of Geb Mother of Osiris and Seth • Mother of heavenly bodies	
Osiris	Dead pharoahs • Ruler of dead, life, vegetation	
Ptah	Creator-god • Lord of artisans	
Ra	God of sun, earth and sky • Father of Maat • National god	Human with falcon head
Sekhmet	Goddess of war and sickness	Human with lion head
Selket	Guardian of life • Protector of dead	Scorpion
Seshat	Goddess of writing and books	
Seth	God of chaos, desert and storm, crops • Brother of Osiris	
Shu	God of air • bearer of heaven	
Sobek	Creator-god	Crocodile
Sothis	God of Nile floodwaters	
Thermuthis	Goddess of fertility and harvest • fate	Serpent
Thoth	God of wisdom, moon, chronology • Messenger of gods	Ibis or baboon
Thoueris	Goddess of fertility and women in labor	Hippopotamus

GOSHEN [go´-shen] — the name of two areas and a city in the Old Testament but usually a reference to the northeastern territory of the Nile Delta in Egypt. Jacob and his family were given permission to live in this fertile area during Joseph's rule as prime minister of Egypt (Gen. 46:28).

During the time of the Exodus, Goshen was protected from the plagues of flies (Exod. 8:22) and hail (Exod. 9:26) that covered the rest of Egypt. The area was small but it had two main cities: Rameses and Pithom.

GOSPEL — the joyous good news of salvation in Jesus Christ. The Greek word translated as "gospel" means "good news." In Isaiah 40:9, the prophet shared the "good tidings" that God would rescue His people from captivity. Jesus said, "The Spirit of the Lord is in me. This is because God chose me to tell the Good News to the poor" (Luke 4:18).

GOSPELS — the first four books of the New Testament. These books are all about the saving work of God in His Son Jesus Christ. The gospels are not true biographies of Jesus, because apart from certain events surrounding His birth (Matt. 1–2; Luke 1–2) and one from His youth (Luke 2:41–52), they record only the last two or three years of Jesus' life.

The authors of the gospels wrote to share knowledge about Jesus as a person and to call us to commit to Him as Lord.

GOVERNMENT — an earthly authority; those who rule over others in order to keep society stable and orderly (2 Pet. 2:10).

Why Four Gospels?

Gospel	Matthew	Mark	Luke	John
Audience	Jews	Romans	Hellenists	Greek World
Portrait of Jesus	Jesus is the **Messiah/King** who fulfills Old Testament prophecy and expectations	Jesus is the authoritative Son of God	Jesus is the perfect **Son of Man** who came to save and minister to all people through the power of the Holy Spirit and prayer	Jesus is the fully **divine Son of God** in whom we should believe to receive eternal life (the "I AM" of God)
Key Verses	Matthew 1:1; 16:16; 20:28	Mark 1:1; 8:27; 10:45; 15:34	Luke 19:10	John 20:31
Key Words	Fulfilled	Immediately	Son of Man	Believe; Eternal Life

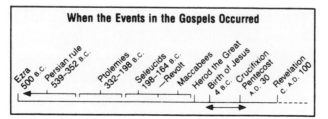

When the Events in the Gospels Occurred

Ezra 500 B.C. / Persian rule 539–352 B.C. / Ptolemies 332–198 B.C. / Seleucids 198–164 B.C.—Revolt / Maccabees / Herod the Great / Birth of Jesus 4 B.C. / Crucifixion A.D. 30 / Pentecost / Revelation c. A.D. 100

GOVERNOR — a regional agent or officer for the Roman emperor during New Testament times (Luke 2:2).

GRACE — favor or kindness shown without caring if a person deserves it. Grace is one of the key attributes of God. Grace is almost always associated with mercy, love, compassion, and patience (Rom. 5:1, 2, 8).

GRANT — to give; to allow (Ps. 85:7, NKJV; Rev. 3:21, NKJV).

GRAVE — a place where the dead are buried. Typically, the Hebrew people buried their dead in graves much like we do today, except that they were not as deep. Burial grounds were located outside the city limits (Luke 7:12; John 11:30). Plain stones or a stone slab were used to cover the grave to keep it safe from animals and to mark the burial place (2 Sam. 18:17). In some instances cut stones were used. Occasionally expensive pillars were used as memorials (2 Kings 23:17). Jacob built a pillar over Rachel's grave (Gen. 35:20). Now there is a building that marks her grave on top of the traditional site.

GREECE — a region or country in southeastern Europe between Italy and Asia Minor. The Old Testament name for Greece was Javan (Gen. 10:2, 4; Isa. 66:19).

In the early years of its history, Greece was a self-governing country. Because the people came from such different backgrounds, they disagreed about many things. This kept them from becoming a unified nation.

Greece is important to Christianity because of its language. In New Testament times, Greek was the language spoken by the common people of the ancient world. Most of the New Testament was written originally in Greek.

GREEK — the language spoken in Greece.

GREEKS — people who were born in Greece or who had Greek parents. In the New Testament, "Greeks" is sometimes used as a reference for those who were not Jews.

GRIEF — an emotion of sorrow; the experience of emotional distress or pain. Today the word "grief" is usually used to express what a person feels in periods of intense sadness, as in the time of death. The Bible uses the word more freely and, more often than not, in reference to things other than death. Grief is a response to the trouble an enemy causes (Ps. 6:7, NKJV; 31:10, NKJV) or to the foolishness of a child (Prov. 10:1, NKJV).

GROPE — to clumsily feel; to search (Job 12:25, NKJV).

GROW — mature, can be used in reference to the physical and spiritual (Gen. 21:20; Luke 2:40).

GUARANTEE — a promise or assurance; something given or held as security. The apostle Paul declared that the Holy Spirit, who lives in our hearts, is the guarantee that we shall receive our full inheritance from God (2 Cor. 5:5).

GUILT, GUILTY — the act of accepting responsibility for wrong actions; knowing you have done something wrong and feeling sorry about it (Lev. 4:3; Ezra 9:13, 15). Although the word "guilt" is not specifically used, some classic examples of guilt in the Bible are: Adam and Eve (Gen. 3:7–8), Cain (Gen. 4:8–9), and David (2 Sam. 11; Ps. 51).

H

HABAKKUK [hab´-ak-uk] — a courageous Old Testament prophet and the author of the Book of Habakkuk. The Scriptures don't tell us anything about his family or his birthplace. Habakkuk was both a poet and a prophet. His deep faith led him to write a beautiful poem of praise about the mysterious ways of God (Hab. 3).

HABAKKUK, BOOK OF — a short prophetic book of the Old Testament that deals with the age-old problems of evil and human suffering. The book is named for its author, the prophet Habakkuk.

Habakkuk contains three short chapters. In the first two, Habakkuk protests, complains, and questions God. But the final chapter is a beautiful psalm of praise. Habakkuk apparently used this complaining and questioning technique to make his point concerning the approaching judgment of God. The lesson in this is that God allows Himself to be questioned by one of His followers of His long-suffering mercy and grace.

HABITATION — a dwelling place. Solomon referred to the temple as God's "house of habitation" (2 Chron. 6:2, KJV). The church is also called "a habitation of God through the Spirit" (Eph. 2:22, KJV).

HADES [ha´-dees] — the place of the dead (Rev. 1:18).

HAGAR [ha´-gar] — the Egyptian slave-woman of Sarah. Hagar had a son named Ishmael with Abraham (Gen. 16:1–16). After waiting ten years for God to fulfill His promise to give them a son, Sarah quit trusting God and presented Hagar to Abraham so he could have a child with her. This was the custom during that time period. Because Abraham agreed to Sarah's plan, it showed their lack of faith in God.

HAGGAI [hag´-ga-i] *(festive)* — an Old Testament prophet and author of the Book of Haggai. As God's spokesman, he encouraged the captives who had returned to Jerusalem to complete the reconstruction of the temple. This work started shortly after the first captives returned from Babylon in 538 B.C. The building activity soon stopped though, because the people felt discouraged and overwhelmed. Beginning in 520 B.C., Haggai and his fellow prophet, Zechariah, convinced the people to start building again. The temple was completed five years later, about 515 B.C. (Ezra 5:1).

HAGGAI, BOOK OF — a short prophetic book of the Old Testament written to encourage the people of Israel who had returned to their native land after the captivity in Babylon. The two short chapters of Haggai contain four important messages. He called on the people to rebuild the temple, to remain faithful to God's promises, to be holy and enjoy God's great provisions, and to keep their hope set on the coming of the Messiah and the establishment of His kingdom.

HAIL — a greeting that involves a wish for the good health and peace of the person addressed. Judas didn't mean it when he walked up to Jesus in the Garden of Gethsemane and said, "Greetings [Hail, KJV], Teacher!" (Matt. 26:49).

HALF-TRIBE — a term used in the Old Testament to refer to the two separate settlements of the tribe of Manasseh—one east of the Jordan River and the other in central Palestine west of the Jordan. During the days of Moses, half of the people of the tribe of Manasseh requested permission to settle the territory east of the Jordan after the land was conquered. Moses agreed to this request, on the condition that the entire tribe helped in the conquest of Canaan (Num. 32:33–42; Deut. 3:12–13; Josh. 1:12–18).

HALLELUJAH — a form of Alleluia.

HALLOWED — holy; set apart (Matt. 6:9, NKJV).

HAMAN [ha´-man] — the evil prime minister of Ahasuerus (Xerxes I), king of Persia (485–464 B.C.). When Mordecai refused to bow to Haman, Haman decided to kill Mordecai and his family, as well as all of the Jews in the Persian Empire. But Esther intervened (stepped in) and saved her people. Haman died on the gallows (a place for hanging) he had built for Mordecai (Esther 3:1–9:25). This reminds us that God is always in control, even when wickedness and evil seem to be winning.

HANANIAH [han-a-ni´-ah] *(the Lord is gracious)* — the name of fifteen men in the Old Testament but most notably the Hebrew name given to Shadrach (Dan. 1:6–7).

HANDMAID — a female slave or servant (Luke 1:38, KJV).

HANNAH [han´-nah] *(gracious)* — one of the wives of Elkanah (1 Sam. 1:1–2:21). Because Hannah was unable to bear children, she was harassed and teased by Elkanah's other wife, Peninnah. Peninnah had given birth to several children. Hannah promised that if she were to give birth to a son, she would devote him to the Lord's service. The Lord answered her prayers, and she gave birth to a son who became the prophet Samuel.

Since Hannah kept her promise, God rewarded Hannah with three more sons and two daughters. Hannah's beautiful thanksgiving prayer (2:1–10) is similar to the song that Mary sang when she learned she would be the mother of Jesus (Luke 1:46–55).

HANUKKAH [han´-na-ka] — a Jewish feast or holiday also known as the Feast of Dedication or the Feast of Lights (John 10:22).

HARAN [ha´-ran] — the third son of Terah and the younger brother of Abraham. Haran was the father of Lot, Milcah, and Iscah (Gen. 11:26–31).

The son of Caleb was also named Haran. His mother was Ephah, Caleb's concubine. Haran was the father of Gazez (1 Chron. 2:46).

A Levite from the family of Gershon (the son of Shimei) was given the name Haran. He lived during David's time as king (1 Chron. 23:9).

Abraham and his father lived in a city named Haran (Gen. 11:31–32; 12:4–5). The family of Abraham's brother Nahor, and Jacob and his wife Rachel, also lived in this city for a time (Gen. 28:10; 29:4–5). The city was on the Balikh, a small branch of the Euphrates River.

HARD BY — close to (Lev. 3:9, KJV).

HARDHEARTED, HARDHEARTEDNESS — stubbornness in opposition to God's will (1 Sam. 6:6, NKJV). The most famous example of this kind of disobedience was the Pharaoh of Egypt, who refused to release the Hebrew people in spite of repeated displays of God's power (Exod. 4:21; 7:3; 14:4, 17, NKJV).

HARLOT — a prostitute. The word "harlot" is often used as a symbol in the Old Testament to describe the wicked behavior of the nation of Israel in worshiping false gods (Isa. 1:21, NKJV; Jer. 2:20, NKJV; Ezek. 16, NKJV).

HASTE — an extreme hurry (Exod. 12:11, NKJV).

HAUGHTY — arrogant, proud (Ezek. 16:50, NKJV).

HEAP — to place upon (Prov. 25:22, NKJV).

HEARKEN — to pay attention (Acts 27:21, KJV).

HEART — the inner part of a person that thinks, feels, and makes decisions (Acts 2:46).

HEARTH — a dug-out depression in a house or tent where fires were built for heating or cooking. The smoke from the fire was let out through a hole in the wall, usually translated as "chimney" (Hosea 13:3).

HEATHEN — one of several words used for the non-Jewish peoples of the world. The distinction between the Israelites and the other nations was important because God's relationship with Israel was special. He chose Israel, res-

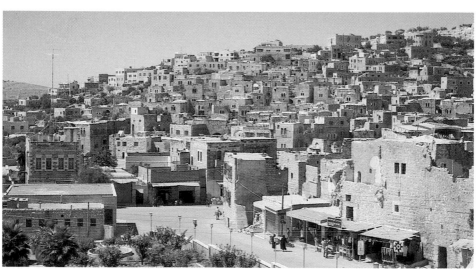

Photo by Howard Vos

Modern Hebron, successor to the ancient city of the same name where Abraham bought a burial cave for Sarah and his descendants (Gen. 23).

cued the people from Egypt, entered into a covenant with them, and gave them His laws.

God planned to bring light and salvation to all nations through Israel (Gen. 12:3; Isa. 2:1–3), but that required them to keep separate from the sinful ways of the surrounding nations (Lev. 18:24).

HEAVEN — the dwelling place of God (John 3:13; 6:38–40; Acts 7:56; 2 Cor. 5:1–10; 1 Peter 1:4).

HEBREW [he´-broo] — a descendant of Abraham (Gen. 14:13); the language the Old Testament is written in.

HEBREWS, EPISTLE TO THE — the nineteenth book in the New Testament. Hebrews is a letter written by an unknown Christian. The author teaches and encourages his readers to stay close to Jesus. The author uses a lot of Old Testament quotations to show how Jesus was the fulfillment of Old Testament prophesies and that He is the supreme Mediator between God and humankind.

HEBRON [he´-brun] (*alliance*) — a city located nineteen miles southwest of Jerusalem on the road to Beersheba. Originally Hebron was called Kiriath Arba (Gen. 23:2).

Hebron was also the name of the third son of Kohath (Exod. 6:18). He was an uncle of Moses, Aaron, and Miriam. His descendants were called Hebronites (Num. 3:27).

A descendant of Caleb (1 Chron. 2:42–43) also had the name Hebron and so did a town

Peasants appear before an Egyptian nobleman in this painting from a royal tomb. In their early history, the Hebrew people were enslaved by the Egyptians.

in Asher (Josh. 19:28, KJV). It is possible that the town of Hebron was also called Abdon (Josh. 21:30).

HEIFER — a young cow (Gen. 15:9, NKJV).

HEIR — a person who inherits (Gal. 4:1). (See Inheritance).

HELL — the place of eternal punishment for the wicked; the abode (place) of the dead (Matt. 5:22, 29–30).

HELLENISM — a Greek way of living that spread the Greek language and culture to the Mediterranean world after the conquests of Alexander the Great.

In the Bible, the words "Hellenists" (NKJV) and "Grecians" (KJV) in Acts 6:1 and 9:29 mean Greek-speaking Jews.

HELMET — a protective head covering worn in battle (1 Sam. 17:5); also a symbol for salvation (Eph. 6:17).

HEMORRHAGE — heavy bleeding (Mark 5:25).

HENCEFORTH, HENCEFORWARD — from now on (John 15:15, NKJV).

HERALD — an officer sent by a king or other high official to tell a message or announce good news (Dan. 3:4, NKJV).

HERB — grass; plant (Luke 11:42, NKJV).

HERITAGE — something inherited from an ancestor (Exod. 6:8, NKJV; 1 Pet. 5:3, NKJV). It can be a spiritual lesson or an actual object.

HERMENEUTICS [hur-me-newt´-ics] — the ideas and methods used to interpret Scripture. Bible scholars believe a biblical text must be interpreted according to the language it was written in, its place in history, who the author was, why the author wrote it, and the reason it was originally written.

HEROD [her´-od] — the name of several Roman rulers in Palestine during Jesus' ministry and the times shortly before His birth and after His resurrection.

Antipater was a descendant of Esau. Julius Caesar gave him the title of procurator of Judea in 47 B.C. He placed two of his sons into ruling positions. One of them was Herod, known as "Herod the Great." He was appointed governor of Judea.

HERODIANS [he-ro´-de-ans] — wealthy, powerful Jews who were agreeable with Greek customs and Roman law in New Testament times. The Herodians were not the same as the Sadducees. They agreed with the Sadducees about the Romans and they disagreed with the Pharisees because they were against the Romans. The Herodians did agree with the Pharisees about Jesus, though.

HERODIAS [he-ro´-de-as] — the queen who asked for John the Baptist's head on a platter as a present (Matt. 14:1–12). She was the granddaughter of Herod the Great.

HESHBON [hesh´-bon] — a city located in Transjordan about fifty miles east of Jerusalem and approximately fourteen miles southwest of modern Amman, Jordan. Heshbon was captured by the Israelites (Josh. 12:1–2), then rebuilt and populated by the tribes of Reuben

(Josh. 13:17) and Gad (1 Chron. 6:81). Later, Mesha, the king of Moab, captured it. The prophets spoke harshly about this city (Isa. 15:4; 16:8–9).

HEW — to cut with hard hits from a heavy cutting instrument like when chopping firewood (2 Chron. 2:10, KJV) or quarrying and cutting stone for building purposes (Amos 5:11, NKJV).

HEZEKIAH [hez-e-ki´-ah] *(the Lord is my strength)* — the thirteenth king of Judah. He was the son of Ahaz and Abijah, the daughter of Zechariah. Hezekiah became known as one of Judah's godly kings. Hezekiah's father (Ahaz) had allowed the kingdom to practice idolatry, but when Hezekiah became king, he was strong and courageous and made the kingdom change their ways (2 Kings 18:4). The fact that an ungodly man like Ahaz could have a godly son is a sure sign of God's grace. This man was probably the great-great-grandfather of the prophet Zephaniah (Zeph. 1:1; Hizkiah, KJV).

Neariah had a son named Hezekiah who was a descendant of David (1 Chron. 3:23). Another man named Hezekiah was the head of a family who returned from the Captivity in Babylon (Neh. 7:21).

HIGH PLACES — elevated or hilltop sites used just for the worship of pagan gods. People used to build their shrines on hilltops. In Mesopotamia, where the land is flat, they built artificial mountains in the shape of step pyramids called ziggurats. The tower of Babel (Gen. 11:1–9) was probably a ziggurat.

HIGH PRIEST — the highest religious position for the Hebrews (Matt. 26:3, 57). Aaron was the first high priest.

Excavated remains of a structure in Jerusalem built by Herod the Great. This Herod was known as a builder of many magnificent buildings, including a temple for use by Jewish worshipers.

The Valley of Hinnom west and south of Jerusalem. In Jeremiah's time this valley was associated with worship of the pagan god Molech in rites that required child sacrifices (Jer. 19:1–9).

HILKIAH [hil-ki´-ah] *(the Lord is my portion)* — the name of several men in the Old Testament. The high priest during the reign of King Josiah (2 Kings 22:4–14) and the priest who helped Ezra read the Book of the Law to the people (Neh. 8:4; 11:11) are the two best known.

HIN — a unit of measure for measuring liquid (Exod. 30:24, NKJV).

HINNOM [hin´-nom] — an unknown person whose name appears in the phrase "the Valley of Hinnom" (Josh. 15:8; Neh. 11:30). This person might have been the original Jebusite owner of this valley outside Jerusalem.

HIRAM [hi´-ram] *(my brother is exalted)* — a king of Tyre and a friend of both David and Solomon (2 Sam. 5:11; 1 Kings 10:11, 22; 2 Chron. 8:2, 18).

Another man named Hiram was a skilled laborer who worked on Solomon's temple (1 Kings 7:13, 40, 45).

HIRE — to employ. The word "hire" can also mean bribe (Ezek. 16:33, NKJV).

HISS, HISSING — a sound made by pushing air between the tongue and the teeth to show contempt, insult, and scorn (Job 27:23, NKJV). People often clapped their hands, wagged their head, and grinded their teeth while hissing (Lam. 2:15–16, NKJV).

HITHER — here (Gen. 15:16, KJV).

HITHERTO — until now (John 16:24, NKJV).

HITTITES [hit´-tites] — the people who lived in Asia Minor between about 1900 and

1200 B.C. The name Hittite comes from Hatti, another name for Anatolia. The Old Testament contains many references to the Hittites (Gen. 15:20; Num. 13:29; 1 Kings 10:29; Ezra 9:1; Ezek. 16:3, 45).

HOLY — pure, godly, humble, and willing to serve. Holiness is one of the most important characteristics of God.

HOLY GHOST — another name for the Holy Spirit (Matt. 1:18).

HOLY OF HOLIES — a phrase for Holy Place (KJV).

HOLY PLACE — a term used for the most sacred inner room in the Holy Tent and the temple. Only the high priest was allowed to go in there. This room was separated from the rest of the worship area by a sacred veil (curtain) that was a symbol for the presence of God. Once a year the high priest would enter the Holy Place and sprinkle the Ark of the Covenant with sacrificial blood and ask God to forgive the sins of the people.

HOLY SPIRIT — the third person of the Trinity (the other two are God and Jesus). The Holy Spirit provides the power of God and Jesus to Christians.

HOMER — a standard unit for dry measure (Ezek. 45:11–14). This unit contained about 6 1/4 bushels. It was a large measure weighing the equivalent of the normal load a donkey could carry (the Hebrew word for "donkey" is *hamor*). In Leviticus 27:16 (NKJV), a homer of barley is worth fifty shekels of silver. (See Weights and Measures of the Bible.)

HOMOSEXUALITY — the act of feeling sexual desire toward a person of the same sex. The Bible says homosexual behavior is wrong (Lev. 20:13). It was one of the reasons why God placed such a harsh judgment against Sodom and Gomorrah (Gen. 19:4–5, 12–13). The apostle Paul said people who practice homosexual behavior would not inherit the kingdom of God (1 Cor. 6:9). He also said that the behavior is wrong for both men and women (Rom. 1:26–27).

HONOR — admiration and respect. To honor God is to give Him the highest admiration and respect. Only God is worthy of our highest honor (1 Chron. 16:25; Rev. 4:9–11). Jesus taught that if a person is going to honor God the Father, he must also honor the Son (John 5:23).

Honor should also be given to our spiritual leaders in the church (1 Tim. 5:17; Heb. 13:7, KJV).

HOPE — confidently expecting something to happen. In the Bible, the word "hope" stands for both the act of hoping (Rom. 4:18; 1 Cor. 9:10) and the thing hoped for (Col. 1:5; 1 Pet. 1:3). Hope isn't wishing for something that may or may not happen. Hope is being sure about something unseen and still in the future (Rom. 8:24–25; Heb. 11:1, 7). As Christians, our hope is in God (Ps. 39:7).

HOR, MOUNT [hoer] — the mountain where Aaron died and was buried (Num. 20:22–29; Deut. 32:50).

A mountain in northern Palestine was also named Mount Hor (Num. 34:7–8).

HOREB, MOUNT [ho´-reb] *(waste)* — the

83

"mountain of God" (Exod. 18:5) in the Sinai Peninsula where Moses heard God speaking through the burning bush (Exod. 3:1). It is also where the law was given to the nation of Israel. "Horeb" is another name for Mount Sinai used many times in the Book of Deuteronomy.

HOSANNA [ho´-san-na] *(save us now)* — a word the crowd shouted at Jesus' triumphal entry into Jerusalem (Matt. 21:9, 15, NKJV; Mark 11:9–10, NKJV; John 12:13, NKJV). The word originally was a prayer requesting God's help, but by this time in Jewish history it had become a cry of joy or a shout of welcome.

HOSEA [ho-zay´-ah] *(deliverance)* — an Old Testament prophet who wrote the Book of Hosea. Hosea was the son of Beeri (Hos. 1:1). He ministered in the northern kingdom of Israel. The style of his writing shows that he was probably wealthy and well educated. His writing style also shows that he was a very compassionate and trustworthy man. He paid attention to the political events happening in the world and he understood what they meant. As a prophet, he was deeply committed to God and His will.

HOSEA, BOOK OF — a prophetic book of the Old Testament that shows God's unending love for His people, even though they kept sinning and turning away from Him. The prophet Hosea demonstrated God's unending love by staying true to his wife even though she was unfaithful to him.

Through his actions and his prophetic message, Hosea gives a good example of God's unending love for His people.

HOSPITALITY — the act of taking care of guests even if they are strangers. In the New Testament, the Greek word translated "hospitality" means "love of strangers" (Rom. 12:13, NKJV).

As Christians we should always take care of each other. In the Old Testament, Abraham

Photo by Levant Photo Service

The barren mountain traditionally identified as Mount Hor, the place where Aaron was buried along the border of ancient Edom (Num. 20:22–29).

invited strangers into his house, washed their feet, prepared fresh meat for them, had Sarah bake bread for them, and escorted them when they left (Gen. 18:1–15). Later Abraham found out those strangers were really God's angels.

HOST — a person who takes care of guests and shows hospitality to strangers. Being a good host was considered a sign of faithfulness to God (Job 31:32; Isa. 58:7).

HOUSE — a building where a person or family lives. A house could be the hut of a peasant, the palace of a king, or even the temple of God. There were many different kinds and sizes of houses in biblical times. The style and size of the house usually depended on how much money a family had. Those with a lot of money usually had two-story homes with many rooms. Local customs and available building materials determined how the house was designed and built.

HUMILITY — a good attitude that comes from understanding that everything we have is a gift from God. The Greek philosophers thought humility was a sign of weakness. Biblical humility is not a sign of weakness or low self-esteem (Matt. 6:16–18; Rom. 12:3). It is the ability to think of others and put them first, especially God and Christ (John 3:30; Phil. 2:3). Humble people focus more on God and others than on themselves.

HYPOCRITE — a person who acts like they are good when they really aren't; a person who points out other people's mistakes and asks them to change even though they make the same mistakes and aren't willing to change (Matt. 6:2, 5, 16).

HYSSOP — a small, bushy plant used as a brush. Hyssop is the same plant we call marjoram (Exod. 12:22; John 19:29).

I

I AM — a name of God.

ICONIUM [i-co´-ne-um] — the capital of Lycaonia in central Asia Minor. Paul and Barnabus visited there when they were forced to leave Antioch of Pisidia (Acts 13:51). Paul's ministry at Iconium was very successful and many people were saved (Acts 14:1). Eventually they had to flee for their lives because of persecution (Acts 14:19, 21). Iconium is known today as Konya, or Konia.

IDLE — useless; inactive; lazy. The Bible says that an idle person will be poor and hungry (Prov. 19:15).

IDOL, IMAGE — a man-made symbol or an object of worship; a false god. There are a few places in the Bible where the word "image" appears, but not as a reference to a man-made object of worship (Gen. 1:26; Lev. 19:4).

IDOLATRY — the worship of something created instead of the worship of the Creator Himself (God). Idolatry is mentioned many times in the Bible. It was probably the greatest temptation for people in Bible times. This sin was so serious that it was placed near the beginning of the Ten Commandments (Exod. 20:4–6).

IMAGE — a likeness (Gen. 1:26).

IMAGE OF GOD — the characteristics God gave humans at creation. This is one thing that makes people stand out from the rest of God's creatures.

IMMANUEL [im-man´-u-el] *(with us is God)* — a symbolic name from the prophecy of Isaiah that was later given to Jesus the Messiah (Isa. 7:14; Matt. 1:23).

The "I AM" Statements

Twenty-three times in all we find Jesus' "I AM" (*ego eimi*, Gk.) in the Greek text of John's Gospel (4:26; 6:20, 35, 41, 48, 51; 8:12, 18, 24, 28, 58; 10:7, 9, 11, 14; 11:25; 13:19; 14:6; 15:1, 5; 18:5, 6, 8). In several of these, Jesus joins His "I AM" with seven metaphors which show how He loves and desires to save the world.

"I AM the bread that gives life" (6:35, 41, 48, 51)
"I AM the light of the world" (8:12).
"I AM the door for the sheep" (10:7, 9).
"I AM the good shepherd" (10:11, 14).
"I AM the resurrection and the life" (11:25).
"I AM the way. And I am the truth and the life" (14:6).
"I AM the true vine" (15:1).

IMMORALITY — behavior that goes against established moral principles. The word is used to describe Israel's worship of pagan gods (Ezek. 23:8, 17, NKJV), an adulterous woman (Prov. 2:16, NKJV), and sexual impurity (1 Cor. 5:1, NKJV).

IMMORTALITY — the ability to live forever. In the Bible, the word "immortality" is usually talking about the spirit, but it is also used as a reference to the resurrected body.

IMPART — to give (Rom. 1:11, NKJV).

IMPORTUNITY — a word that means

This incense burner, decorated with sacred serpents, was discovered in the excavation of the Canaanite temple at Beth Shan.

having persistence when asking for something; boldness. In Jesus' parable of the persistent friend (Luke 11:5–8, KJV), a man was rewarded for his importunity because he kept knocking on the door. Jesus taught that we should have this kind of persistence with our prayers.

IMPUTE, IMPUTATION — the act of charging something to a person's account.

INCARNATION — a word that refers to the act of Jesus becoming a human being. This word is not used in the Bible, but it is based on clear references in the New Testament (Rom. 8:3; Eph. 2:15; Col. 1:22).

INCENSE — a sweet-smelling substance that was burned as an offering to God on the altar in the tabernacle and the temple. The purpose of this incense offering was to honor God. Incense was a symbol for the prayers of the Hebrew people, which were like a pleasant aroma offered to God.

INCREASE — when used as a noun it means fruit (Lev. 26:4, KJV); when used as a verb it means to grow (Prov. 1:5, NKJV; Acts 6:7, KJV).

INDIGNATION — anger (Ps. 69:24, NKJV; Rev. 14:10, NKJV).

INFINITY — forever, no beginning and no end; a word that shows that God has always been and will always be (Col. 1:15; Heb. 1:3).

INFIRMITY — sickness; weakness (John 5:5, NKJV).

INHABITANT — a person who dwells

87

(lives) in a certain place (Gen. 19:25, NKJV; Rev. 17:2, NKJV).

INHERITANCE — something (like property or money) that is given to someone else in a family, usually after someone dies (Gen. 15:7, NKJV; Luke 10:25, NKJV; Deut. 21:16, KJV). In the Bible it was after the father died.

To the Hebrews, the land of Canaan was regarded as an inheritance from the Lord because God had promised the land to Abraham and his descendants (Num. 33:53). Both Moses and Joshua were told by the Lord to divide the land of Canaan among the tribes "as an inheritance" (Num. 26:52–53, NKJV; Josh. 13:6, NKJV).

INIQUITY — unrighteousness; lawlessness (sin). The Bible uses this word to describe all kinds of sin (2 Pet. 2:16, NKJV; Rev. 18:5, NKJV; 1 Cor. 13:6, NKJV; Gen. 15:16, NKJV).

INJUSTICE — a wrong; an injury (Job 16:17, KJV).

INNOCENCE — blamelessness; freedom from sin and guilt (Gen. 20:5; Ps. 26:6). Since the fall of man, when Adam and Eve brought disobedience into the world (Gen. 3:1–24), no one except Jesus has been totally sinless and blameless (Rom. 3:9–18; 2 Cor. 5:21).

INNOCENT — without guilt (Matt. 27:4). People can be called "innocent" only because they have been forgiven of sin and been declared new creations through faith in Christ.

INSPIRATION — a technical term for the Holy Spirit's supernatural guidance of those who received special revelation from God as they wrote the books of the Bible. The result of this inspiration is that the Bible contains the truths that God wanted His people to know and share with the world (2 Tim. 3:16, NKJV).

INSTRUCT — to train; to teach (2 Tim. 2:25, KJV).

INSURRECTION — an act of rebellion against the government (Ezra 4:19, KJV; Ps. 64:2, KJV; Acts 21:38). Barabbas, the criminal who was released by Pilate before Jesus' crucifixion, was guilty of this crime against the Roman government (Mark 15:7, KJV).

INTEGRITY — honesty; sincerity. In the Old Testament, Noah (Gen. 6:9), Abraham (Gen. 17:1), Jacob (Gen. 25:27), David (1 Kings 9:4, NKJV), and Job (Job 2:3, 9; 4:6; 27:5; 31:6, NKJV) were called people of integrity. Although Jesus

Photo by Howard Vos

Michelangelo's painting of the prophet Isaiah in the Sistine Chapel in Rome.

The famous Isaiah Scroll is one of the best-preserved manuscripts discovered among the Dead Sea Scrolls. It contains the entire text of the Book of Isaiah.

did not use the word "integrity," he told people to have a pure heart and a pure motive (Matt. 5:8; Matt. 6:1–6).

INTERCESSION — the act of asking God or praying on behalf of another person or group (Isa. 53:12, NKJV; Heb. 7:25, NKJV).

INTEREST — an additional payment or a fee, especially in reference to loans.

ISAAC [i´-zak] *([God] laughs)* — the only son of Abraham by his wife Sarah and the father of Jacob and Esau. God promised to make Abraham's descendants a great nation that would become God's chosen people. Abraham and Sarah laughed when they heard they would have a son at their ages (Gen. 17:17–19;

18:9–15). Isaac was born when Abraham was one hundred years old and Sarah was ninety (Gen. 17:17; 21:5).

God asked Abraham to sacrifice his only son. When God saw that Abraham would obey him no matter what, He stopped Abraham and saved Isaac's life (Gen. 22:1–19).

ISAIAH [i´-za-ah] *(the Lord has saved)* — a famous Old Testament prophet who predicted the coming of the Messiah. He also wrote the Book of Isaiah. Isaiah was probably born in Jerusalem to a family that was related to the royal house of Judah. He recorded the events during the reign of King Uzziah of Judah (2 Chron. 26:22). When Uzziah died (740 B.C.), Isaiah had a vision of God in the temple (Isa. 6). That vision was his calling to become a prophet.

ISAIAH, BOOK OF — a major prophetic book of the Old Testament. Because of the way this book talks about God and His purpose of salvation, it is sometimes called "the fifth gospel." The book is named for its author, the great prophet Isaiah, whose name means "the Lord has saved."

ISCARIOT [is-car´-e-ot] *(man of Kerioth)* — the last name of Judas. He was the disciple who betrayed Jesus (John 6:71; 12:4; 13:2, 26).

ISHMAEL [ish´-ma-el] *(God hears)* — the name of six men in the Old Testament but usually refers to Abraham's son by his wife's Egyptian maidservant, Hagar.

Sarah wasn't very nice to Hagar, so she ran away. Then Hagar met the angel of God. The angel told her to go back to Sarah and have a good attitude. The angel promised Hagar that her son, who would be named Ishmael, would also have many descendants. Hagar went back to Abraham and Sarah and gave birth to her son (Gen. 16:4–15). She named him Ishmael just like the angel said.

ISRAEL [iz´-ra-el] *(he strives with God)* — the name given to Jacob after his great struggle with God at Peniel (Gen. 32:28; 35:10). Later, the name was given to the descendants of Jacob. The twelve tribes were called "Israelites," "children of Israel," and "house of Israel," identifying them as the descendants of Israel through his sons and grandsons.

ISRAELITE [iz´-ra-el-ite] — a descendant of Israel, or Jacob (Lev. 23:42–43). Israelites were considered to be children of the covenant, faithful servants of the Lord, and heirs to the promises made to Abraham (Rom. 11:1).

J

JACOB [ja´-cub] *(he supplants)* — a twin son of Isaac and Rebekah who later became known as Israel (Gen. 32:28). His brother was Esau.

He was named Jacob because when he was born, "he was holding on to Esau's heel" (25:26). Jacob took his brother's birthright (25:29–34), his father's blessing (27:1–29), and his father-in-law's flocks and herds (30:25–43; 31:1).

JAIRUS [ja-i´-rus] — a leader at a synagogue whose daughter was raised from the dead by Jesus (Mark 5:21–23, 35–43).

JAMES — the name of five men in the New Testament. The two best known are:

1. James, the son of Zebedee, one of Jesus' twelve apostles. In lists of the twelve apostles, James and his brother John are always mentioned with two other brothers, Peter and Andrew. These four men fished together on the Sea of Galilee. The first thing Jesus did when he began his public ministry was to ask them to follow him (join him in ministry) (Matt. 4:18–22; Mark 1:16–20).

2. James, the son of Alphaeus. This James was also one of the twelve apostles. In each list of the apostles, he is the ninth one mentioned (Matt. 10:3; Mark 3:18; Luke 6:15; Acts 1:13).

JAMES, EPISTLE OF — a New Testament book filled with practical, straightforward teaching. Every chapter is full of examples and reminders written to make Christians want to be more like Jesus.

JAPHETH [ja´-feth] — one of Noah's three sons (Gen. 5:32; 6:10; 1 Chron. 1:4). Japheth and his wife were two of the eight people who entered the ark and were saved from the destructive waters of the Flood (Gen. 7:7; 1 Pet. 3:20).

JEBUSITES [jeb´-u-site] — the people who first lived in the city of Jebus (Judg. 19:10–11; 1 Chron. 11:4–6). Jebus is an ancient name for Jerusalem.

JEHOIACHIN [je-hoy´-a-kin] *(the Lord establishes)* — the son of Jehoiakim (2 Chron. 36:8–9; Ezek. 1:2). Jehoiachin was a bad king just like his father. He wasn't able to do much though, because he was only king for three months. Nebuchadnezzar's armies took over Jerusalem, and when the city surrendered, Jehoiachin was exiled to Babylonia (2 Kings 24:6–15).

JEHOIADA [je-hoy´-a-dah] *(the Lord knows)* — the name of six men in the Old Testament, but the best known was a priest who helped hide the young king, Joash, from the wrath of Queen Athaliah (2 Kings 11:1–12:16; 2 Chron. 22:10–12).

JEHOIAKIM [je-hoy´-a-kim] *(the Lord raises up)* — an evil king of Judah. The prophet Jeremiah predicted the things that would happen to him.

JEHORAM [je-ho´-ram] *(the Lord is exalted)* — was the name of the fifth king of Judah, the ninth king of Judah, and a priest sent by King Jehoshaphat to instruct the people in the law (2 Chron. 17:8). Both of the kings were also called Joram.

JEHOSHAPHAT [je-hosh´-a-fat] *(the Lord is judge)* — a son of Asa who became king of Judah after his father (1 Kings 15:24). Jehoshaphat was thirty-five years old when he became king, and he reigned twenty-five years in Jerusalem (2 Chron. 20:31), from about 873 B.C. to about 848 B.C. There were also four other men in the Old Testament named Jehoshaphat.

JEHU [je-hu] *(the Lord is He)* — the eleventh king of Israel (2 Chron. 22:7–9). Elisha the prophet anointed Jehu as king. There were also four other men named Jehu in the Old Testament.

JEREMIAH [jer-e-mi´-ah] *(the Lord hurls)* — the name of nine men in the Old Testament. The best known was the prophet Jeremiah who wrote the Book of Jeremiah. He prophesied during the rulerships of the last five kings of Judah.

JEREMIAH, BOOK OF — a major prophetic book of the Old Testament. The book is named for its author and main character, the great prophet Jeremiah. He faithfully delivered God's message of judgment even though everyone was against him and didn't want to hear what he had to say.

Jeremiah's greatest lesson was his idea of the new covenant (31:31–34). A new covenant between God and His people was necessary because the people had broken the old covenant. No matter how many times God allowed the

Photo by Howard Vos

King Jehu of Israel bows before Shalmaneser III of Assyria, in this obelisk, or stone monument, discovered in ancient Assyria.

The mound of ancient Jericho, believed by many archaeologists to be the oldest settlement in Palestine and possibly the oldest city in the ancient world.

IEREMIA

A woven tapestry that portrays the prophet Jeremiah, from the Church of San Vitale In Ravenna, Italy.

old covenant to be renewed, the people still continued to break the promises they had made to God. Jeremiah saw and understood that a new type of covenant was needed between God and His people. This covenant would be one of grace and forgiveness instead of a covenant of rules engraved in stone.

JERICHO [jer´-ik-o] — one of the oldest cities in the world. Because the Israelites obeyed God, He gave them a victory at Jericho under the leadership of Joshua by causing the walls of the city to fall down.

JEROBOAM [jer-o-bo´-am] *(let the kinsman plead)* — the name of two kings of the northern kingdom of Israel:

1. Jeroboam I, the first king of Israel (1 Kings 11:26–14:20). He was the son of Nebat and Zeruah. He reigned over Israel for twenty-two years (1 Kings 14:20).

2. Jeroboam II, the fourteenth king of Israel, who reigned for forty-one years (793–753 B.C.). He was the son of Joash (or Jehoash), the grandson of Jehoahaz, and the great-grandson of Jehu (2 Kings 13:1, 13; 1 Chron. 5:17). The Bible says that Jeroboam "did what the Lord says was wrong" (2 Kings 14:24).

JERUB-BAAL [je-rub´-ba-al] *(let Baal plead)* — a name given to Gideon by his father after he destroyed the altar of Baal at Ophrah (Judg. 6:32).

JERUSALEM [je-ru´-sa-lem] *(city of peace)* — a sacred city and the capital of Palestine during Bible times. Jerusalem is still a great city even today.

JERUSALEM, NEW — the holy city described by John in Revelation 21–22. This city is not built by human hands; it is a heavenly city built and provided by God Himself (Rev. 21:2).

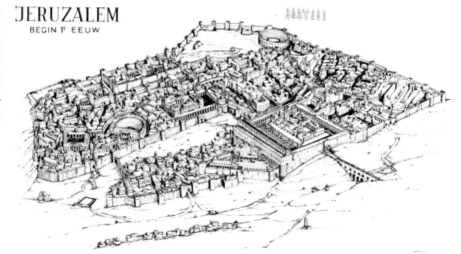

Photo by Amsterdam Bible Museum

An artist's sketch of what Jerusalem might have looked like in New Testament times. The beautiful temple built by Herod appears within the square wall structure in the foreground.

Photo by Howard Vos

Traditional site of the baptism of Jesus in the Jordan River at the beginning of His public ministry (Matt. 3:13–17).

JESUS CHRIST — the Son of God born to the Virgin Mary. Jesus was born to fulfill God's eternal plan of salvation. He lived a perfect life so He could be the perfect sacrifice. The Old Testament is full of prophecies about His coming. The New Testament is the story of His birth, life, ministry, death, and resurrection.

JESSE [jes´-se] *(meaning unknown)* — the father of King David (1 Sam. 16:18–19) and an ancestor of Jesus. Jesse was the father of eight sons—Eliab, Abinadab, Shimea (Shammah), Nethanel, Raddai, Ozem, Elihu, and David— and two daughters, Zeruiah and Abigail (1 Chron. 2:13–16).

JETHRO [je´-thro] *(his excellency)* — the father-in-law of Moses (Exod. 3:1). He was also called Reuel (Exod. 2:18), Hobab (Judg. 4:11; Num. 10:29).

JEWS — a name first used to describe the people living in Judah (when the Israelites were divided into the two kingdoms of Israel and Judah). After the Babylonian Captivity, all the descendants of Abraham were called "Jews."

In the New Testament the word is used to describe all Israelites. People who were not Jewish were called Gentiles.

Photo by Ben Chapman

The modern city of Jerusalem, showing the Dome of the Rock and the hill on which Solomon's temple was built. The hill in the distance is the site of the Mount of Olives.

A menorah, or seven-branched lampstand, symbolizes Judaism and the Jewish state of Israel.

JEZEBEL [jez´-e-bel] (*there is no prince*) — the name of two women in the Bible:

1. The wife of Ahab, king of Israel, and the mother of Ahaziah, Jehoram, and Athaliah (1 Kings 16:31). Jezebel was a mean woman. She bullied her husband into worshiping false idols and since he was king, the rest of the nation also worshiped false idols.

2. A prophetess of Thyatira who convinced Christians "to take part in sexual sins and to eat food that is offered to idols" (Rev. 2:20). John probably called this woman "Jezebel" because her bad behavior reminded him of Ahab's horrible wife.

JEZREEL [jez´-re-el] (*God scatters*) — a common name in the Old Testament. There was a man from the tribe of Judah named Jezreel (1 Chron. 4:3), the prophet Hosea called his oldest son Jezreel (Hos. 1:4), and there were two cities and a valley called Jezreel.

JOAB [jo´-ab] (*the Lord is father*) — one of the three sons of Zeruiah (David's half-sister) (2 Sam. 2:13; 8:16; 14:1; 17:25; 23:18, 37; 1 Kings 1:7; 2:5, 22; 1 Chron. 11:6, 39; 18:15; 26:28; 27:24). He was the "general" or commander-in-chief of David's army (1 Chron. 11:6; 27:34).

JOASH, JEHOASH [jo´-ash, je-ho´-ash] (*the Lord supports*) — the eighth king of Judah. He was a son of King Ahaziah (2 Kings 11:2) by Zibiah (2 Kings 12:1). Joash was seven years old when he became king, and he

The Sea, or Lake, of Galilee, scene of many of Jesus' miracles and teachings (Matt. 14:13–33).

An excavated area in ancient Jerusalem known as The Pavement, identified by some scholars as the place where Pilate rendered judgment against Jesus (John 19:13).

Titles of Christ		
Name or Title	**Significance**	**Biblical Reference**
Adam, Last Adam	First of the new race of the redeemed	1 Cor. 15:45
Alpha and Omega	The beginning and ending of all things	Rev. 21:6
Bread of Life	The one essential food	John 6:35
Chief Cornerstone	A sure foundation for life	Eph. 2:20
Chief Shepherd	Protector, sustainer, and guide	1 Pet. 5:4
Firstborn from the Dead	Leads us into resurrection and eternal life	Col. 1:18
Good Shepherd	Provider and caretaker	John 10:11
Great Shepherd of the Sheep	Trustworthy guide and protector	Heb. 13:20
High Priest	A perfect sacrifice for our sins	Heb. 3:1
Holy One of God	Sinless in His nature	Mark 1:24
Immanuel (God With Us)	Stands with us in all life's circumstances	Matt. 1:23
King of Kings, Lord of Lords	The Almighty, before whom every knee will bow	Rev. 19:16
Lamb of God	Gave His life as a sacrifice on our behalf	John 1:29
Light of the World	Brings hope in the midst of darkness	John 9:5
Lord of Glory	The power and presence of the living God	1 Cor. 2:8
Mediator between God and Men	Brings us into God's presence redeemed and forgiven	1 Tim. 2:5
Only Begotten of the Father	The unique, one-of-a-kind Son of God	John 1:14
Prophet	Faithful proclaimer of the truths of God	Acts 3:22
Savior	Delivers from sin and death	Luke 1:47
Seed of Abraham	Mediator of God's covenant	Gal. 3:16
Son of Man	Identifies with us in our humanity	Matt. 18:11
The Word	Present with God at the creation	John 1:1

Photo by Howard Vos

reigned forty years in Jerusalem (2 Chron. 24:1), from about 835 B.C. until 796 B.C.

Another man named Joash was the thirteenth king of Israel. He was the son of King Jehoahaz and the grandson of King Jehu. He was also called Jehoash (2 Kings 13:10, 25; 14:8–17) and he reigned in Samaria for sixteen years (2 Kings 13:9–10).

There are six other men named Joash in the Old Testament.

JOB [jobe] — the third son of Issachar, and founder of a tribal family called the Jashubites. This man was also called Jashub (Num. 26:24; Gen. 46:13; 1 Chron. 7:1).

There is another man named Job and he is the main character in the Book of Job. This man was very faithful to God during some very difficult times. He lost everything—his money, his health, and his family—and he still praised God. He didn't understand why those things happened to him, but he trusted God anyway. God blessed him by giving him much more than he ever had before.

JOB, BOOK OF — an Old Testament book that deals with the question: Why do bad things happen to good people? The Book of Job is the same type of book as Proverbs, Ecclesiastes, and the Song of Solomon. These books are called Books of Wisdom, because there is so much we can learn from them.

The Book of Job teaches us to trust God in every situation. Sometimes when we are hurting, we aren't going to understand the reason why. The Book of Job also teaches us that God is good, just, and fair in everything He does. God always helps us through our problems and makes things right when we are faithful to Him and trust Him.

This ancient papyrus fragment, written in the Greek language, contains verses 1–14 of the first chapter of John's Gospel. It dates from about A.D. 200.

A mosaic of the prophet Joel, who prophesied about the outpouring of God's Spirit in the latter days (Joel 2:28).

Photo by Howard Vos

Traditional tomb of the apostle John in the Church of St. John at Ephesus.

JOEL [jo´-el *(the Lord is God)* — an Old Testament prophet and the author of the Book of Joel. He was a citizen of Jerusalem and he spoke a lot about the priests and their duties (Joel 1:9, 13–14, 16).

JOEL, BOOK OF — a short prophetic book of the Old Testament.

The Book of Joel shows that a message from God can come in the form of a natural disaster. Joel describes the terrible invasion of locusts and teaches us that the Lord can use a natural disaster to remind people that they need Him and they need to be obedient to Him.

JOHN THE APOSTLE — the son of Zebedee and the brother of James. Before Jesus called him to be one of His twelve disciples, John was a fisherman (Matt. 4:18–22; Mark 1:16–20). His mother was probably Salome (Matt. 27:56; Mark 15:40), who may have been a sister of Mary (John 19:25), the mother of Jesus.

JOHN THE BAPTIST — the son of

Remains of Machaerus, fortress of King Herod, where John the Baptist was beheaded, according to the Jewish historian Josephus.

99

Zechariah and Elizabeth. Elizabeth and Mary, the mothers of John and Jesus, were probably related (Luke 1:36). When John was older, he preached about the coming of the Messiah (Jesus). He warned the people to be careful how they lived and to change their evil ways. Jesus came to John to be baptized in the Jordan River. Herod killed John the Baptist by cutting off his head.

JOHN, EPISTLES OF — three letters written by the author of the Gospel of John.

Like the Gospel of John, the Epistles of John are about love, truth, sin, the world, life, light, and the Holy Spirit. John teaches that we must obey God and ask for forgiveness from our sins. He also warns people to stay away from false prophets.

JOHN, GOSPEL OF — the fourth Gospel of the New Testament. The first three Gospels (Matthew, Mark, and Luke) mainly talk about the miracles Jesus did and His teachings. The Gospel of John is different. It provides important information about Jesus' life. John doesn't use difficult words, but his words are very symbolic.

JONAH [jo´-nah] *(a dove)* — the prophet who was swallowed by a big fish because he refused to obey when God told him to go to Nineveh and tell the people to repent.

JONAH, BOOK OF — a short Old Testament book that shows God's love for all people. The book is named for its main character, the prophet Jonah. An important lesson in the Book of Jonah is that God can use people who do not want to be used by Him.

But the greatest lesson is that God wants to

Photo by Howard Vos

Traditional tomb of Joseph at Shechem (Exod. 13:19).

show mercy and grace to everyone in the world. He loves everyone. The Hebrew people were supposed to preach this message of God's love to the whole world (Gen. 12:1–3), but they forgot their purpose and decided that God only loved them and that His blessings were only for them. The Book of Jonah shows how wrong they were and that God's love is for everyone.

JONATHAN [jon´-a-than] *(the Lord has given)* — the name of fourteen men in the Old Testament, but the best known was the oldest son of King Saul and a close friend of David (1 Sam. 14:1).

JOPPA [jop´-pah] *(beautiful)* — an ancient city on the Mediterranean Sea about thirty-five miles northwest of Jerusalem.

JORAM [jo´-ram] *(the Lord is exalted)* — the name of four men in the Old Testament, but the best known was the tenth king of Israel who was killed by Jehu (2 Kings 8:16–29; 9:14–29). He was the son of Ahab and Jezebel.

He became king after his brother, Ahaziah. He was also called Jehoram (2 Kings 1:17). He was king for twelve years and even though he wasn't a good king, he did stop people from worshiping Baal, a false god (2 Kings 3:3).

JORDAN [jor´-dan] *(descending, flowing)* — the name of the longest and most important river in Palestine (Josh. 1:2; Mark 1:9).

JOSEPH [jo´-zef] *(may he add)* — the name of several men in the Bible. The two best known are:

1. The eleventh son of Jacob (Gen. 30:24), who was sold into slavery and later had an important job with Egyptian government. The story of Joseph's life is found in Genesis 37–50.

2. The husband of Mary, who was the mother of Jesus (Matt. 1:16–24; 2:13; Luke 1:27; 2:4).

JOSHUA [josh´-u-ah] *(the Lord is salvation)* — the man who led the Israelites into the Promised Land. He had been Moses's helper and Moses chose him to take his (Moses) place.

Joshua was born in Egypt. He went through the great events of the Passover and the Exodus with Moses and all the Hebrew people who escaped from slavery in Egypt with God's help. In the wilderness of Sinai, Moses took Joshua with him when he went into the mountains to talk with God (Exod. 24:13). Moses also gave Joshua a special place at the tabernacle. Joshua had to stay there while Moses was gone to talk with God (Exod. 33:11).

JOSHUA, BOOK OF — an Old Testament book that tells about the conquest and division of the land of Canaan by the Hebrew people. The book is named for its main character, Joshua, who was the leader of Israel after Moses.

Joshua warned the people against worshiping false gods and encouraged them to remain faithful to God. He was setting a good example for his own people as well as future generations, when he said: "As for me and my family, we will serve the Lord" (Josh. 24:15).

JOSIAH [jo-si´-ah] — the sixteenth king of Judah. He was the son of Amon and the grandson of Manasseh (2 Kings 21:23–23:30). Josiah ruled for over thirty years. It was a time of peace, prosperity, and reform (good changes). King Josiah truly wanted to please God, and the kingdom of Judah was very happy while he was king. It was hard to believe that a wicked king like Amon could have such a godly son. This shows how amazing God's grace really is.

Another man named Josiah was a captive who returned to Jerusalem from Babylon during the time of Zechariah (Zech. 6:10).

JOSIAS [jo-si´-as] — another name for Josiah.

JOT — the English meaning of the Greek word *iota* (Matt. 5:18, NKJV). Jot is the smallest letter of the Greek alphabet. The word is used to describe something that seems to be small and unimportant (trivial).

JOY — a positive attitude or pleasant emotion; delight (Ps. 94:1). Many kinds of joy are mentioned in the Bible, even the wicked experience joy in their triumphs over the righteous. Words used to describe different levels of joy are gladness, contentment, and cheerfulness.

JUBILEE [ju-ba-lee] — a Jewish event that happened every fifty years (Lev. 25:8–55).

The Jubilee year began with a blast from a

ram's horn on the Day of Atonement. This was a time of joy and freedom. It was the beginning of a year for doing good and showing mercy.

JUDAH [ju´-dah] *(praise)* — the fourth son of Jacob and Leah. His descendants were called the tribe of Judah (Gen. 29:35; Num. 26:19–21; Matt. 1:2). David and his family were from this tribe.

There were six other men named Judah in the Old Testament, and Judah was also the name of a place.

JUDAS [ju´-das] *(praise)* — the name of six men in the New Testament:

1. One of the four brothers of Jesus (Matt. 13:55; Mark 6:3; Juda, KJV).

2. One of the twelve apostles of Jesus—also called Thaddeus—but not Judas Iscariot (John 14:22).

3. Judas of Galilee, who led a revolt against Rome (Acts 5:37).

4. After the apostle Paul was converted, he stayed in Damascus with a man named Judas (Acts 9:11).

5. A disciple who belonged to the church in Jerusalem. He was chosen along with Silas to go with Paul and Barnabas to Antioch.

JUDE [jood] *(praise)* — the author of the Epistle of Jude. Jude is an English form of the name Judas.

The Period of the Judges

Events and Judges	Years
Israel serves Cushan-Rishathaim (3:7, 8)	8
Peace following Othniel's deliverance (3:7–11)	40
Israel serves Moab (3:12)	18
Peace follows Ehud's deliverance (3:12–30)	80
Shamgar delivers Israel from Philistines (3:31)	1
Israel serves Canaan (4:1–3)	20
Peace following deliverance by Deborah and Barak (4:1–5:31)	40
Israel serves Midian (6:1–6)	7
Peace following Gideon's deliverance (6:1–8:35)	40
Abimelech, king of Israel (9:1–57)	3
Tola's career (10:1, 2)	23
Jair's career (10:3–5)	22
Israel serves Ammon and Philistia (10:6–10)	18
Jephthah's career (10:6–12:7)	6
Ibzan's career (12:8–10)	7
Elon's career (12:11, 12)	10
Abdon's career (12:13–15)	8
Israel serves Philistia (13:1)	40
Samson's career (12:1–16:31)	20

JUDE, EPISTLE OF — the last of the letters of the New Testament, and the next to the last book of the Bible. Jude is a short, powerful epistle (letter) written by a man who refused to let negative influences destroy the church. Jude writes to defend his faith (v. 3) and he reminds people to watch out for false prophets (v. 12). He tells believers to study the teaching of the apostles (v. 17) and to stay strong in God's love (v. 21).

JUDEA [ju-de´-ah] — the Greco-Roman name for the land of Judah. Judea is first mentioned in Ezra 5:8 (NKJV) as part of the Persian Empire. The word "Judea" comes from the adjective "Jewish," a word that was used to describe the Babylonian captives who returned to the Promised Land. Most of them were from the tribe of Judah.

JUDGE — when used as a noun it is a public official who helps interpret the laws (Ezra 7:25; Matt. 5:25); when used as a verb it means to discern (know) or criticize (Gen. 15:14; Matt. 7:1).

JUDGES, BOOK OF — a historical book of the Old Testament that covers a period of over three hundred years. The book is named after military leaders (called "judges") that God used to save His people from their enemies. Twelve of these leaders are mentioned in the book.

The Book of Judges points out the need for an eternal deliverer or a savior. The deliverance of the human judges never lasted for very long and was never complete. Some of the judges had problems and weren't focused on what was best for the people. The Book of Judges leads us to Jesus Christ who is the judge (Ps. 110:6), King, and Savior of His people.

JUDGMENT — knowing the difference between good and evil. God judges people and their actions according to the standards of His law. Judgment can also be used as a word for the punishment given out to the people who bring about God's wrath and condemnation (John 5:24).

JUST — right, fair (Gen. 6:9, NKJV; Rom. 1:17, NKJV).

JUSTICE — the practice of what is right and just. Justice (or "judgment," KJV) specifies what is right, not only based on laws, but also by what makes for right relationships, harmony, and peace.

JUSTIFICATION — the process by which sinful human beings are made acceptable to a holy God.

JUSTIFIED — to be made right (Gal. 2:16, NKJV).

K

KADESH, KADESH BARNEA [ka´-desh bar-ne´-ah] *(consecrated)* — an area of wilderness between Egypt and the land of Canaan. The Hebrew people camped there after the Exodus.

KERYGMA [ke-rig´-ma] — the preaching of the gospel in the New Testament church (1 Cor. 1:21).

KIDRON [kid´-ron] *(gloomy)* — a valley on the eastern slope of Jerusalem.

KIN, KINSMAN, KINDRED — relatives. Family was important to the Hebrew people. The family had the responsibility of protecting and saving its members from others' wrongdoing (Gen. 34:1–31). In the Old Testament, the word "kinsman" is sometimes used as a word that means redeemer.

KINDLE — cause to burn (Acts 28:2, NKJV).

KINDNESS, LOVINGKINDNESS — God's love and favor toward His people. In the Old Testament, the word refers to God's long-suffering love. God will keep His promises to His people even though they constantly sin and turn away from Him (Deut. 7:12; Hosea 2:14–23, NKJV).

In the New Testament, the word refers to God's grace. Because God has been gracious toward believers, they should treat others with kindness or grace (Luke 6:35). Being kind to someone who has sinned isn't a sign of approval. We are kind to help the sinner find their way back to God (Rom. 2:4).

KINE — cows, cattle (Amos 4:1, KJV). (See Ox, Oxen.)

KING, KINGDOM — a ruler of a nation or territory, especially one who inherits his position and rules for life; a state or nation with a form of government in which a king or queen serves as supreme ruler (Matt. 6:10).

The Kidron Valley, just outside the eastern wall of Jerusalem. Jesus and His disciples crossed this valley and its brook on their way to the Garden of Gethsemane (John 18:1).

An exhausted traveler rests in the shade of a broom bush in the wilderness of Kadesh (Num. 20:16).

KINGDOM OF GOD, KINGDOM OF HEAVEN — God's rule of grace in the world, a future period foretold by the prophets of the Old Testament and that begins Jesus' public ministry. The kingdom of God is like the Garden of Eden. It is a time with no evil or wickedness and the people who live in the kingdom know only happiness, peace, and joy. This was the main expectation of the Old Testament prophets about the future (Matt. 6:10).

KINGS, BOOKS OF — two Old Testament books that tell the history of God's chosen people from 970 to 586 B.C. The books are organized around the various kings who ruled during that time. These books cover about four hundred years of Judah and Israel's history and are written in chronological order.

KISH — the name of four men in the Old Testament:

1. The father of King Saul (1 Chron. 12:1).
2. A Levite who lived in David's time (1 Chron. 23:21–22; 24:29).
3. A Levite who helped cleanse the temple (2 Chron. 29:12).
4. A Benjamite ancestor of Mordecai (Esther 2:5).

KISHON [ki´-shon] — a river in Palestine. Because the Kishon falls slightly as it crosses the level plain, it often swells up and floods much of the valley during the rainy season.

KISS — a symbolic act done by placing the lips on certain parts of another person's body, especially their cheeks, forehead, lips, or feet (Prov. 24:26). A kiss usually shows a close relationship to another person.

The most common type of kiss was a kiss between relatives (family kiss) (Gen. 29:11–13). A kiss could mean hello, or welcome (Exod. 4:27), or it could also mean good-bye (Ruth 1:9, 14; Acts 20:37). In the New Testament, the family kiss was also used between believers (Christian family) (1 Cor. 16:20; 1 Pet. 5:14).

A kiss can also be a sign of betrayal. When

Photo by Howard Vos

The gold mask buried with Pharaoh Tutankhamun of Egypt about 1350 B.C., illustrating the wealth of his kingdom.

Judas betrayed Christ, he did so with a kiss (Luke 22:47–48).

KNEEL — to get down on the knees; to bow (Ps. 95:6; Acts 9:40).

KNEELING — falling to one's knees as a sign of reverence, obedience, or respect. In the dedication of the temple in Jerusalem, Solomon knelt before God (1 Kings 8:54). Daniel knelt in prayer three times a day (Dan. 6:10).

KNOW — to understand intimately. The Bible also uses this word to mean the sexual relationship between a husband and wife (Gen. 4:1, NKJV; Luke 1:34, NKJV).

KNOWLEDGE — the truth or facts of life that a person learns from daily life or by thinking. The greatest truth that a person can learn through experience is truth about God (Ps. 46:10; John 8:31–32).

KORAH — the name of four men in the Old Testament. The two best known were Korah the Levite, who led a revolt against Moses and Aaron (Num. 16:1–49), and Korah the son of Izhar, a first cousin of Moses and Aaron (Exod. 6:21).

Photo by Denis Baly

These tourists are overshadowed by a gigantic urn at Petra, a city built by the Nebateans in southern Palestine. They inhabited the land of the ancient Edomites, a people mentioned often in the Books of 1 and 2 Kings.

L

LABAN [la´-ban] *(white)* — father-in-law of Jacob. He lived in the city of Nahor in Padan Aram where Abraham sent his servant to find a wife for Isaac. Laban was Rebekah's brother. When he found out the servant was there and saw the golden jewelry given to Rebekah, he invited him into their home (Gen. 24:29–60). Laban took control of the marriage arrangements. He was stubborn and greedy. This was discovered in his later dealings with Rebekah's son, Jacob.

LABOR — work (1 Cor. 3:8, NKJV).

LAD — a child (John 6:9, NKJV).

LAMB — a young sheep used as a sacrificial offering (Exod. 29:38).

LAMB OF GOD — a phrase used by John the Baptist to describe Jesus (John 1:29, 36). John publicly identified Jesus as "the Lamb of God" who "takes away the sin of the world!"

LAME, LAMENESS — a disability in one or more limbs, especially in a foot or leg. This makes it hard for a person to walk. Lameness is one of the physical imperfections that kept a priest from entering the Holy Place or offering sacrifices (Lev. 21:17–21, NKJV). Jesus healed many lame people (Matt. 11:5, NKJV; Luke 7:22, NKJV). Peter and John also healed a man who had been lame from birth (Acts 3:1–11, NKJV).

LAMECH [la´-mek] — a descendant of Cain (Gen. 4:18–24). Lamech is the first man mentioned in the Bible as having two wives (Gen. 4:19). By Adah he had two sons, Jabal and Jubal; and by Zillah he had a son, Tubal-Cain, and a daughter, Naamah.

Another man named Lamech was the first son of Methuselah, and the father of Noah (Gen. 5:25–26, 28–31). He lived to be 777 years old (Gen. 5:31). He is mentioned in the genealogy of Jesus (Luke 3:36).

LAMENTATIONS, BOOK OF — a short Old Testament book, written in poetic form. It expresses (tells) the deep sadness felt about the destruction of the city of Jerusalem and the temple. Its English title comes from a Greek verb meaning "to cry aloud."

LANGUISH — to become weak; to fade away; to lose strength (Hosea 4:3, NKJV).

LAODICEA [la´-od-i-se´-ah] — a city in the Lycus Valley where one of the seven churches of Asia Minor was located (Rev. 3:14).

LASCIVIOUSNESS — another word for licentiousness (KJV).

LAST SUPPER — *(See Lord's Supper.)*

LATIN — the Roman language (John 19:20).

LAVER — a basin (bowl) that the priests washed their hands and feet in before offering sacrifices (Exod. 30:18–21, NKJV).

LAW — a system of rules and regulations to keep the people under control. In the Old Testament, God gave the people a unique law code by direct revelation. He told them what to do in their worship, how to behave in their relationship to Him, and how to behave in their relationships with each other.

LAWFUL — authorized, allowed or permitted (Matt. 12:2, NKJV).

LAWLESS — unauthorized; allowed; permitted (1 Tim. 1:9, NKJV).

LAYING ON OF HANDS — the act of placing hands on a person to bless them, or for the purpose of dedication and consecration (Acts 6:6, NKJV).

LAZARUS [laz´-a-rus] *(God has helped)* — the brother of Martha and Mary who died and Jesus brought him back to life (John 11). Because everyone was talking about what Jesus had done, the chief priest got angry and made a plan to kill Lazarus (John 12:9–11). Another man named Lazarus was the beggar in Jesus' story about a rich man and a poor man (Luke 16:19–25).

LEAH [le´-ah] — the older daughter of Laban. Laban tricked Jacob into marrying her instead of her younger sister Rachel (Gen. 29:16–30). God blessed Leah and Jacob with six sons—Reuben, Simeon, Levi, Judah (Gen. 29:31–35), Issachar, and Zebulun (Gen. 30:17–20)—and a daughter, Dinah (Gen. 30:21). Leah's maid, Zilpah, had two sons named Gad and Asher (Gen. 30:9–13).

LEARN — to gain knowledge and understanding (Deut. 5:1; Matt. 11:29).

LEAVEN — a substance used to make dough rise (Exod. 12:15, 19–20, NKJV; yeast, ICB). In Bible times, leaven was usually a piece of fermented dough saved from a previous baking that was placed in the new dough to make it rise.

LEBANON [leb´-a-non] *(white)* — a nation of the Middle East that includes much of what was ancient Phoenicia in Bible times.

Photo by Gustav Jeeninga

Ruins of the city gate in the wall of ancient Laodicea. The church of Laodicea was rebuked by John because of its lukewarm spirit (Rev. 3:14–22).

This laver on a stand with wheels dates to about the twelfth century B.C. It was discovered in the excavation of a tomb on the island of Cyprus.

This territory has been an important trade center linking Europe and Asia for more than four thousand years.

LEES — the leftover residue from wine after it was fermented. In Bible times, the word was used in reference to the happiness and enjoyment of the righteous (Isa. 25:6, NKJV).

LEFT — the side of the body where the heart is located. The left side is a position of honor next to a king (Matt. 20:21–27).

LEGACY — an inheritance (Prov. 3:35, NKJV).

LEGION — the principal (main) unit of the Roman army. There were between three thousand and six thousand infantry troops and one hundred to two hundred cavalrymen in a legion. The New Testament uses the word "legion" to mean a large number. When Jesus healed a man possessed by demons, He asked the man his name. The man said, "My name is Legion; for we are many" (Mark 5:9). The man had many demons inside of him.

LENTIL — a pea-like seed used for food, especially in soups and stews (2 Sam. 17:28, NKJV).

LEPER, LEPROSY — a horrible skin disease that had no cure. In the Bible the word "leprosy" refers to a variety of symptoms (Matt. 8:3). Modern medicine has discovered some of those symptoms were actually other diseases and not leprosy.

LEST — in fear of (Matt. 7:6, NKJV).

LET — to allow (Matt. 8:22).

Photo by Howard Vos

Traditional tomb of Lazarus, who was raised from the dead by Jesus (John 11:1–44).

109

Photo by Gustav Jeeninga

Cedars of Lebanon on the mountainsides of Lebanon. Reckless cutting of these magnificent trees across the centuries has almost eliminated them from the landscape.

LETTERS — written messages between people who were separated by distance. Epistle was another word for letter (Acts 15:30). In Bible times, letters were written on sheets of parchment (animal skins), fragments of pottery, papyrus, and tablets made of clay.

LEVI [le´-vi] *(joined)* — the name of four men and one tribe in the Bible:

1. The third son of Jacob and Leah (Gen. 29:34).

2. A tribe descended from Levi (Exod. 6:19).

3. Another name for Matthew, one of the twelve apostles (Mark 2:14).

4. An ancestor of Jesus (Luke 3:24) who was a son of Melki.

5. Another ancestor of Jesus (Luke 3:29) who was a son of Simeon.

LEVIATHAN [le-vi´-a-than] — a large sea creature (Job 41) that was sometimes a symbol for a cruel enemy defeated by God (Job 3:8).

LEVITES [le´-vites] — the descendants of Levi who served as assistants (helpers) to the priests in the worship system of the nation of Israel. Aaron and his sons were Levites, and they had the responsibility of the priesthood. They offered burnt offerings and led the people in worship and confession. Any Levite who was not a blood relative of Aaron had to serve as priestly assistants. They took care of the tabernacle and the temple and performed other small jobs (Num. 8:6).

LEVITICUS, BOOK OF — an Old Testament book filled with worship instructions for God's chosen people. The Levites were the priestly family of the nation, and the title of the book seems to mean that its instructions were given specifically for them. But because of its directions on three important Spiritual truths: holiness, sacrifice, and atonement, the Book of Leviticus has an important message for modern believers too.

Without the information in Leviticus, we

Photo by Howard Vos

The mound of Gibeon, a city assigned to the Levites and priests at the time of Joshua's conquest of Canaan (Josh. 21:17). The modern village of el-Jib is on the right.

could not understand the fulfillment of these truths in the life and ministry of Jesus.

LEVY — a forced labor, fine, or taxation (Num. 31:28, NKJV).

LEWD, LEWDNESS — always having bad thoughts about sex; lust (Judg. 20:6, NKJV; Hosea 2:10, NKJV; 6:9, NKJV; Rom. 13:13, NKJV).

LIBERAL, LIBERALITY — generosity, the opposite of stinginess. The apostle Paul taught that Christians should be liberal and generous in their financial giving (Rom. 12:8, NKJV; 2 Cor. 8:2, NKJV).

LIBYA [lib´-e-ah] — a country in northern Africa (Ezek. 27:10, NKJV).

LICENTIOUSNESS — undisciplined (bad) behavior, especially concerning sex (Mark 7:22; 2 Cor. 12:21; lasciviousness, KJV). The Greek word translated as licentiousness means "outrageous conduct." It is a behavior that goes beyond accidental sin. It is a total disregard for what is right.

LIE — any statement or act designed to deceive (trick) another person. People usually lie to hurt someone (Rom. 3:13, KJV) or to protect one's self because of fear or pride (Matt. 26:69–75; Acts 5:1–11, KJV).

LIFE, BOOK OF — (See Book of Life.)

LIGHT — illumination; the opposite of darkness (Gen. 1:3–4). The Bible also speaks of light as the symbol of God's presence and righteous activity.

LIKENESS — in the image of (Gen. 1:26).

LOATHE, LOATHSOME — when used as a verb it means to hate or despise (Job 7:16, NKJV); when used as an adjective it means rejected (Prov. 13:5, NKJV).

LOCUST — a flying insect with a strong appetite. They usually travel together in large groups (swarms) and cause large amounts of damage (Joel 2:25).

LODGE, LODGING — to spend the night.

Most of the words translated "lodge" in the Bible are referring to the idea of a temporary resting place (Josh. 2:1, NKJV; Acts 10:18, NKJV).

LOFTY — high (Isa. 57:7, NKJV); proud (Isa. 2:12, NKJV).

LOINS — the lower abdomen, including the reproductive organs. When a man was ready to work, he put a belt around his waist and tucked his robe up into the belt so he could move his legs without his robe getting in the way. This is the meaning of "girded up his loins" (1 Kings 18:46, NKJV).

LOINCLOTH — a piece of clothing worn by men (Job 12:18, NIV).

LONGING — desire (Ps. 119:20, NKJV).

LORD — a name for God and Jesus.

LORD'S PRAYER — the prayer that Jesus taught His disciples (Matt. 6:5–15; Luke 11:1–4). In the Sermon on the Mount, Jesus taught that a person's attitude in prayer is very important. We aren't supposed to say the same prayer over and over again just trying to get God's attention. We need to tell God our needs and trust Him to take care of us.

LORD'S SUPPER — a ceremony where Christians eat bread and drink wine (or grape juice). It is a time to remember how Jesus died for our sins. The bread is a symbol of his body and the wine is a symbol of his blood.

The first Lord's Supper (Matt. 26:17–30; Mark 14:12–26; Luke 22:1–23; 1 Cor. 11:23–25) happened on the night before Jesus died at a meal commonly known as the Last Supper.

LOT [laht] — Abraham's nephew. Lot traveled with Abraham from Mesopotamia to Canaan and to Egypt and back (Gen. 11:27–31; 12:4–5; 13:1). Lot and Abraham both had large herds of cattle. The men who took care of their cattle (herdsmen) were always fighting over their pasturelands so Abraham decided it might be a good idea for them to separate.

Abraham let Lot choose which land he wanted. Lot chose the Jordan River valley instead of the rocky hill country. He ended up living in the sinful city of Sodom. The people in that city were so bad that God decided to destroy it and all the people who lived there. An angel of the Lord told Lot and his family to leave the city and never look back. Lot's wife looked back and was turned into a pillar of salt (Gen. 19:26).

LOTS, CASTING OF — a way of making decisions in Bible times, sort of like drawing straws or throwing dice. The casting of lots happened in early times when little of the Bible was available. At that point in time, God approved of this method for determining His will (Prov. 16:33).

LOVE — strong feelings of care and concern. There are hundreds of references to love in the Bible. God loves us so much that He sent His Son to die on the cross (John 3:16; 1 John 4:10).

LOVINGKINDNESS — merciful and steady; God's love (Ps. 17:7, NKJV). (See Kindness.)

LOW, LOWLY — humble (Isa. 2:12, NKJV; Luke 1:52, NKJV).

LUCIFER [lu´-sif-er] *(morning star)* — the word "Lucifer" is found only once in the Bible: "How you are fallen from heaven, O Lucifer, son of the morning! How you are cut down to the ground, you who weakened the nations!" (Isa. 14:12, NKJV). This passage describes the overthrow of the evil king of Babylon, but many Bible scholars say this passage is actually a description of Satan, who rebelled against the throne of God and was "brought down to Sheol, to the lowest depths of the pit" (Isa. 14:15, NKJV).

LUKE — a man who traveled with the apostle Paul (Philem. 24) and the author of the Gospel of Luke and the Acts of the Apostles. He was a doctor (Col. 4:14).

LUKE, GOSPEL OF — the third gospel in the New Testament written by Luke.

Luke cared a lot about people and their problems. The stories he shares in the Gospel of Luke really show how much compassion Jesus had for everyone. Luke was probably not Jewish. Matthew traces Jesus' family history back to Abraham, the father of the Hebrew people (1:2). Luke traces it back to Adam, the father of the human race (3:38). In the Gospel of Matthew, Jesus sends his disciples only "to the people of Israel," because they were like lost sheep (10:6). Luke says that Jesus sent his disciples to everyone.

LUST — a desire for what is forbidden. God allows certain desires (Deut. 12:15, 20–21, NKJV), but lust refers to the desire for things that are against the will of God. Christians are able to resist lust by the power of the Holy Spirit.

Photo by Howard Vos

The Chapel of Lydia by the riverside at Philippi. Lydia was converted to Christianity through the ministry of the apostle Paul (Acts 16:13–15).

The mound of ancient Lystra, a city in the province of Lycaonia where Paul was stoned by a mob (Acts 14:8–20).

LUZ [luhz] *(almond tree)* — a Canaanite city that was renamed Bethel by Jacob (Gen. 28:19). Another city named Luz was a city of the Hittites (Judg. 1:26).

LYDIA [lid´-e-ah] — a wealthy business-woman from the city of Thyatira who became a Christian after hearing the apostle Paul preach a sermon in the city of Philippi (Acts 16:12–15, 40).

Lydia is also the name of a large territory in western Asia Minor (modern Turkey). The Lydians are mentioned by the prophet Ezekiel as "men of war," who fought to defend Tyre (Ezek. 27:10) and who made an alliance with Egypt (Ezek. 30:5).

LYRE — a small harp.

LYSTRA [lis´-trah] — a city of Lycaonia where Paul preached after being asked to leave Iconium (Acts 14).

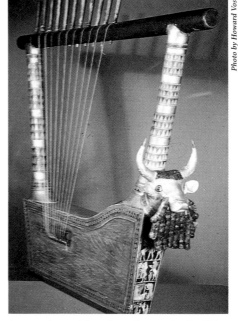

A reconstructed lyre from Mesopotamia. This was a popular musical instrument about 2500 B.C., several centuries before Abraham's time.

M

MACEDONIA [mas-e-do´-nee-ah] — a mountainous country north of Greece (Achaia). This area was visited two or three times by the apostle Paul (Acts 16).

MACEDONIANS [mas-e-do´-nee-ans] — the people who were born in or who lived in Macedonia (Acts 19:29; 2 Cor. 9:2).

MADNESS — a state of mental instability (1 Sam. 21:13; Eccles. 1:17, NKJV; John 10:20).

MAGDALA [mag´-da-lah] *(tower)* — a place on the Sea of Galilee about three miles northwest of Tiberias. Jesus and His disciples went to Magdala after the feeding of the four thousand (Matt. 15:39, NKJV; Magadan, ICB). Magdala was either the birthplace or the home of Mary Magdalene.

MAGDALENE [mag´-da-leen] *(from Magdala)* — a name given to a woman named Mary to distinguish her from the other women named Mary. She was a disciple of Jesus. Mary Magdalene is first spoken of in Luke 8:2, which mentions her as one of the people who were ministering to Jesus. Mary Magdalene has sometimes been described as a woman of bad character and loose morals just because Mark 16:9 states that Jesus had cast seven demons out of her. There is no proof of that, and there is no reason to think that she was the same person as the sinful woman whom Simon the Pharisee treated badly (Luke 7:36–50).

MAGISTRATE — a judge (Ezra 7:25).

MAGNIFY — to exalt; to praise; to glorify (Luke 1:46, KJV).

MAGOG [ma´-gog] *(land of Gog)* — the second son of Japheth and a grandson of Noah (Gen. 10:2).

MAHANAIM [ma-ha´na´-im] *(two armies)* — an ancient town in Gilead, east of the Jordan River near the River Jabbok. Mahanaim was located on the border between the tribes of Manasseh and Gad (Josh. 13:26, 30). It was later given to the Merarite Levites (Josh. 21:38).

MAIMED — missing a limb (arm or leg) or having a damaged limb (Mark 9:43, NKJV; Luke 14:13–14, NKJV).

MAKER — a creator (Hab. 2:18, NKJV), often used as a reference to God (Job 35:10, NKJV).

MALACHI [mal´-a-ki] *(my messenger)* — an Old Testament prophet and the author of the Book of Malachi. Very little is known about Malachi's life.

MALACHI, BOOK OF — a short prophetic book of the Old Testament written to scold the people of Israel for their unfaithful worship practices. This book tells about God's love but reminds the people how mighty and powerful God is and that He will punish those who do not obey Him.

MALCHUS [mal´-kus] *(ruler)* — a servant of the high priest who was present at the arrest of Jesus in the Garden of Gethsemane. Simon Peter struck Malchus with a sword and cut off his ear (John 18:10).

MALEFACTOR — a KJV translation of two Greek words meaning "evildoer" (John 18:30) and "evil worker" (Luke 23:32–33, 39). The two thieves crucified with Jesus were malefactors. (Luke 23:32–33, 39; criminals, NKJV).

MALICE, MALICIOUSNESS — the vicious desire of one person to hurt another (Titus 3:3, NKJV). Malice usually happens because a person falsely believes that another person is going to hurt them. A person can't feel malice and love at the same time. Christians are taught to eliminate (get rid of) malice in their lives (Eph. 4:31–32, NKJV).

MALTA [mal´-ta] — a small island in the Mediterranean Sea between Sicily and Africa, about ninety miles southwest of Syracuse. The apostle Paul was shipwrecked on Malta (Acts 28:1).

MAMMON [mam´-mon] *(riches)* — wealth that is used against God (Matt. 6:24; Luke 16:9, 11, 13, NKJV).

MAMRE [mam´-re] — an Amorite chief who formed an alliance with Abraham against Chedorlaomer (Gen. 14:13, 24).

Mamre was also a place in the district of Hebron, where Abraham lived. It was known for its "terebinth trees" (Gen. 13:18; 18:1), or "oaks" (NRSV). The cave of Machpelah was near Mamre. Abraham, Isaac, and Jacob and their wives, Sarah, Rebekah, and Leah were buried in that cave (Gen. 49:13).

MAN, MANKIND — God's highest creation, made in God's own image; human beings.

MANASSEH [ma-na´-seh] *(causing to forget)* — the name of five men in the Old Testament:

1. Joseph's firstborn son who was born in Egypt to Asenath (Gen. 41:51).

2. The grandfather of Jonathan (one of the priests of the graven image erected by the tribe of Dan).

3. The son of Hezekiah and Hephzibah and the fourteenth king of Judah. He reigned longer (fifty-five years) than any other Israelite king and was Judah's most wicked king. He became king at the age of twelve, although he probably co-reigned with his father for ten years. He could have followed the godly example of his father, but he chose to be evil like his grandfather, Ahaz.

4. A descendant of Pahath-Moab.

5. An Israelite from the family of Hashum.

MANASSEH, TRIBE OF [ma-na´-seh] — the descendants of Joseph's son, Manasseh.

Photo by Howard Vos

St. Paul's Bay at Malta. The beach on which Paul's ship ran aground (Acts 27:39–28:10) has eroded across the centuries, leaving this rocky shore.

MANDRAKE — a wild plant (Gen. 30:14–16).

MANGER — a feeding trough, or open box in a stable built to hold fodder (coarsely chopped hay and straw) for livestock (Luke 2:7, NKJV). In Bible times, mangers were made of clay mixed with straw, or from stones cemented with mud.

MANIFEST — to show, to make visible or apparent (John 2:11, NKJV).

MANIFOLD — abundant, many (Eph. 3:10, NKJV).

MANNA — the food that God provided for the Israelites in the wilderness during their Exodus (Exod. 16:15, 31, 33; Num. 11:6–9).

MANTLE — a covering like a robe (2 Kings 2:8).

MARK, GOSPEL OF — the second book of the New Testament. The Gospel of Mark focuses more on the actions of Jesus instead of the words of Jesus.

MARK, JOHN — a man who knew Peter and Paul. He is probably the author of the Gospel of Mark.

John Mark's mother, Mary, was a wealthy woman of Jerusalem. She owned a large house with servants. Christians gathered at her house when Peter was in prison to pray for his release (Acts 12:12).

John Mark went with Barnabas and Paul to Antioch (Acts 12:25) and later he traveled with them on their first missionary journey. He served as an assistant (Acts 13:5). He probably made travel, food, and lodging arrangements. He might have done some teaching, too.

MARRIAGE — the union of a man and a woman as husband and wife (Gen. 2:24–25). Marriage is the foundation for a home and family.

MARTHA [mar´-tha] (lady, mistress) — the sister of Mary and Lazarus (Luke 10:38–41; John 11:1–44; 12:1–3). Martha, Mary, and Lazarus were sincere followers of Jesus, but Mary and Martha showed their love for Him in different ways and they argued about which one of them was right. Martha was always busy doing the household chores (Luke 10:40). Her sister Mary thought it was more important to sit down and listen to Jesus (Luke 10:39). As Christians, we need to realize that they were both right. It is important to do our jobs, but we have to make time to worship and study so that we can grow as Christians.

MARY [ma´-ry] — the name of six women in the New Testament:

1. Mary, the mother of Jesus (Luke 1–2).

2. Mary Magdalene, a woman from Magdala who became a follower of Jesus after He cast seven demons out of her (Luke 8:1–2).

3. Mary of Bethany, sister of Martha and Lazarus (Luke 10:38–42).

4. Mary, the mother of the disciple James and Joses (Matt. 27:55–61).

5. Mary, the mother of John Mark (Acts 12:12).

6. Mary of Rome (Rom. 16:6).

MASTER — a person having authority, power, and control over the actions of other people (Gen. 24:12; Matt. 8:19, KJV).

MATTHEW [math´-ew] *(gift of the Lord)* — a tax collector who became one of the twelve apostles of Jesus (Matt. 9:9).

MATTHEW, GOSPEL OF — the first book of the New Testament.

Matthew is the story of Jesus and His teachings. The early church used the book for teaching new Christians. There are many passages in the book that show how the promises of God were kept (Jesus fulfilled the Old Testament prophecies).

MATTHIAS [mat´-thias] *(gift of the Lord)* — a disciple chosen to take the place of Judas Iscariot as an apostle (Acts 1:23, 26).

MEAT — the edible flesh of animals (not usually fish and poultry) (Num. 11:4; Deut. 12:15, 20).

Meat was often sacrificed on pagan altars and dedicated to pagan gods in Paul's day. Later this meat was offered for sale in the public meat markets. Some Christians wondered if it was right for Christians to eat meat that had been sacrificed to pagan gods. Paul said it was okay but explained that they should not eat it if it would cause weaker Christians to sin (1 Cor. 8:13).

MEASURE — when used as a noun it is a reference to dry, liquid, or area amounts; when used as a verb it is the act of determining such amounts.

MEAT OFFERING — an offering of grain presented to God to show thanks (Lev. 2).

MEDE — a person who was born in or lived in Media (Isa. 13:17, NKJV).

MEDIATOR — a person who goes between two people or groups to help them work out their differences and reach an agreement (Job 9:33, NKJV).

MEDITATION — the practice of reflection or contemplation (thinking). The word "meditation" or its verb form, "to meditate," is found mainly in the Old Testament. The "blessed man" meditates on God's law day and night (Ps. 1:2, NKJV). The psalmist also prayed that the meditation of his heart would be acceptable in God's sight (Ps. 19:14, NKJV). Joshua was instructed to meditate on the Book of the Law for the purpose of obeying all that was written in it (meditate, Josh. 1:8, NKJV).

MEEK, MEEKNESS — an attitude of humility toward God and gentleness toward people. This attitude comes from recognizing that God is in control. Many people think that meekness is the same thing as weakness. It is not. Weakness is a lack of strength or courage because of negative circumstances. Meekness is having strength and courage that comes from God.

MEET — a word that means different things including "right" (Exod. 8:26, KJV), "necessary" (Luke 15:32, KJV), and "sufficient" (Col. 1:12, KJV).

MEGIDDO [me-ghid´-do] — a walled city east of the Carmel Mountain range where many important battles were fought in Old Testament times.

MELCHISEDEC [mel-kis´-e-dek] — a form of Melchizedek.

MELCHIZEDEK [mel-kiz´-e-dek] *(king of*

righteousness) — a king of Salem (Jerusalem) and priest of the Most High God (Gen. 14:18–20; Ps. 110:4; Heb. 5:6–10; 6:20–7:28). Melchizedek gave bread and wine to Abraham and his men and then he gave Abraham a blessing in the name of El Elyon ("God Most High"), and praised God for giving Abraham a victory in battle (Gen. 14:18–20).

MEMORIAL — a monument, statue, holiday, or ceremony (ritual) that serves as a reminder of a person or an event. The Feast of the Passover was a memorial of God's sparing the firstborn of the Israelites in Egypt and of Israel's deliverance from Egyptian bondage (Exod. 12:14, NKJV).

MENE, MENE, TEKEL, PARSIN [me´-ne, me´-ne, tek´-el, far´-sin] *(numbered, numbered, weighed, and divided)* — the words that mysteriously appeared on the wall of the palace while Belshazzar, king of Babylon, was having a drunken feast (party) (Dan. 5:1–29).

Daniel was called to see if he could explain the meaning of this strange message. God let Daniel know what the message meant. Here is what Daniel said:

"Mene: God has numbered your kingdom, and finished it."

"Tekel: You have been weighed in the balances and found wanting."

"Parsin: Your kingdom has been divided, and given to the Medes and Persians."

These words meant that God had given Belshazzar a certain amount of time to rule and his time had run out. Belshazzar's character had been evaluated and his moral values were bad and spiritually, he was worthless. Because of his bad behavior, Belshazzar would die and his empire would be divided up and destroyed.

MEPHIBOSHETH [me-fib´-o-sheth] *(from the mouth of [the] shame [ful god Baal])* — a son of Jonathan and grandson of Saul. Mephibosheth was also called Merib-Baal (1 Chron. 8:34; 9:40), which meant "a striver against Baal." His name was changed because the word "Baal" was associated with idol worship.

There was another man named Mephibosheth. He was the son of King Saul and Rizpah (2 Sam. 21:8).

MERCY — the aspect of God's love that causes Him to help the miserable, just as grace is the aspect of His love that moves Him to forgive the guilty. Those who are miserable may be so either because of breaking God's law or because of circumstances beyond their control.

MERCY SEAT — the golden lid or covering on the Ark of the Covenant, regarded as the resting place of God (Exod. 25:17–22; 1 Chron. 28:11; Heb. 9:5; atonement cover, NIV).

MESHACH [me´-shak] — the Chaldean name given to Mishael, one of Daniel's companions (Dan. 1:7). Meshach would not bow down and worship the golden idols of Nebuchadnezzar. He was thrown into "the burning fiery furnace," with Shadrach and Abednego, but they were kept safe from harm by the power of God (Daniel 3).

MESOPOTAMIA [mes-o-po-ta´-me-ah] *(land between the rivers)* — a region located between the Tigris and Euphrates rivers. In the Old Testament, Mesopotamia usually means "Aram of the two rivers" and refers only to the northwestern part of Mesopotamia. In the

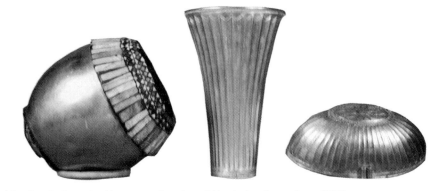

Photo by Howard Vos

Golden bowls from the Mesopotamian city of Ur, dating from about 2500 B.C.

New Testament the word "Mesopotamia" refers to the areas between and around the Tigris and Euphrates rivers, and includes ancient Syria, Accad, Babylonia, and Sumer.

MESSAGE, MESSENGER — a word or statement, the person who brings the word or statement (Judg. 3:20; 1 John 1:5).

MESSIAH [mes-si´-ah] *(anointed one)* — the one anointed by God and empowered by God's spirit to deliver His people and establish His kingdom. In Jewish thought, the Messiah would be the king of the Jews, a political leader who would defeat their enemies and bring in a golden era of peace and prosperity. In Christian thought, the term "Messiah" refers to Jesus' role as a spiritual deliverer, setting His people free from sin and death.

METHUSELAH [me-thu´-se-lah] — a son of Enoch and the grandfather of Noah. At the age of 187, Methuselah became the father of Lamech. After the birth of Lamech, Methuselah lived 782 years and died at the age of 969. He lived longer than any other human. He was an ancestor of Jesus (Luke 3:37; Mathusala, KJV).

MICAH [mi´-cah] *(Who is like the Lord)* — an Old Testament prophet and the author of the Book of Micah. Micah was from Moresheth Gath (Mic. 1:1, 14), a town in southern Judah. He learned from the great prophet Isaiah.

MICAH, BOOK OF — a short prophetic book of the Old Testament, known for scolding the rich because of their bad treatment of the poor. Micah also contains a clear prediction of the Messiah's birth in Bethlehem, written several centuries before Jesus was actually born. The book is named for its author, the prophet Micah. His name means, "Who is like the Lord?"

The Book of Micah is a message that is a mixture of judgment and promise. The passages give real insight into the character of God. We learn that even in His wrath, He remembers mercy and that He cannot stay angry forever.

MICAIAH [mi-ka-i´-ah] *(who is like the Lord?)* — the prophet who predicted the death of King Ahab in the battle against the Syrians at Ramoth Gilead (1 Kings 22:8–28; 2 Chron. 18:7–27).

MICHAEL [mi´-ka-el] *(who is like God?)* — in the Bible, Michael is usually referring to an archangel, or an angel of high rank, who served as a guardian for God's people (Dan. 10:21; 12:1).

MICHAL [mi´-kal] (*who is like God?*) — the younger daughter of King Saul. After David became a hero by killing Goliath, Saul offered to give Michal to David as his wife. Instead of a dowry, Saul asked David to kill one hundred Philistines (1 Sam. 18:25). Saul was hoping that the Philistines would kill David.

Instead of getting killed, David and his warriors killed two hundred Philistines. Then Saul had to give Michal to David to become his wife (1 Sam. 18:27–28).

MIDIAN [mid´-e-an] — a son of Abraham by his concubine Keturah (Gen. 25:1–6). Midian had four sons (1 Chron. 1:33).

Midian was also the name of the land where the Midianites (descendants of Midian) lived.

MIDIANITES [mid´-e-an-ites] — a group of people who were enemies of the Israelites in Old Testament times. The Midianites were distantly related to the Israelites, since Midian was one of the sons of Abraham.

MIDRASH [mid´-rash] *(inquiry)* — any of a group of Jewish commentaries (study guides) on the Hebrew Scriptures written between A.D. 400 and A.D. 1200. The word "Midrash" is based on a Hebrew word that means "to search out."

MIDWIFE — a person who helps deliver a baby (Gen. 35:17, NKJV).

MILLENNIUM, THE — the one thousand

Bedouin tents in the land of Midian, where Moses fled after killing an Egyptian (Exod. 2:11–15).

year period mentioned in connection with Christ's coming to reign with His saints over the earth (Rev. 20:1–9).

MILLSTONE — heavy stones used to grind grain (Matt. 18:6, NKJV).

MINISTER, MINISTRY — a biblical concept (idea) meaning "to serve" or "service" (Rom. 15:16). In the Old Testament, the word "servant" usually meant a court servant. During the period between the Old and New Testaments, it was used to describe the care given to the poor.

MIRACLES — a great thing that seemed impossible according to the laws of nature, but easily accomplished by the power of God.

MIRIAM [mir´-e-am] — a sister of Aaron and Moses (Num. 26:59; 1 Chron. 6:3). She was called "Miriam the prophetess" (Exod. 15:20, NKJV). The Bible does not specifically say it, but Miriam was probably the sister who watched over the baby Moses when he was hidden in the "ark of bulrushes" (basket) and placed in the Nile River to hide him from the king (Exod. 2:4–8). Miriam's song of victory after the Israelites' successful crossing of the Red Sea is one of the earliest known poems (Exod. 15:20–21).

Another woman named Miriam was a daughter of Ezrah of the tribe of Judah (1 Chron. 4:17).

MIRTH — joy; gladness (Isa. 24:8, NKJV).

MISHAEL [mish´-a-el] *(who is what God is?)* — the name of three men in the Old Testament:

1. A son of Uzziel and grandson of Kohath, of the tribe of Levi (Lev. 10:4).

2. An Israelite who helped Ezra (Neh. 8:4).

3. One of Daniel's friends who was cast into the fiery furnace. The Babylonians changed his name to Meshach (Dan. 1:6–7).

MIZPAH [miz´-pah] *(watchtower)* — the name of six places in the Old Testament (Gen. 31:49; Josh. 11:3, 8; Josh. 15:38; 1 Kings 15:22; Judg. 11:29, 34; 1 Sam. 22:3).

MOAB [mo´-ab] *(of my father)* — a son of Lot (Gen. 19:37). Moab became an ancestor of the Moabites. Moab was also the name of a nation.

MOABITES [mo´-ab-ites] — the people who were born in or who lived in Moab (Num. 22:4).

MOCK — to make fun of; to insult (Gal. 6:7, NKJV).

MODERATION — self-control (1 Tim. 2:9, NKJV). Although the term rarely occurs in the Bible, the concept of moderation is common. The Pharisees were not moderate. Jesus described them as those "who strain out a gnat to swallow a camel" (Matt. 23:24). They focused on tiny details of the law instead of understanding the importance of the law. As Christians, we are not supposed to act like the Pharisees. We are supposed to have self-control in all things (1 Cor. 9:25; temperate, NKJV).

MOLECH (mo´-lek) — an Ammonite god (Lev. 18:21).

MOLTEN — melted (Ezek. 24:11, KJV).

The Miracles of Jesus Christ

Miracle	Matthew	Mark	Luke	John
1. Cleansing a Leper	8:2	1:40	5:12	
2. Healing a Centurion's Servant (of paralysis)	8:5		7:1	
3. Healing Peter's Mother-in-Law	8:14	1:30	4:38	
4. Healing the Sick at Evening	8:16	1:32	4:40	
5. Stilling the Storm	8:23	4:35	8:22	
6. Demons Entering a Herd of Swine	8:28	5:1	8:26	
7. Healing a Paralytic	9:2	2:3	5:18	
8. Raising the Ruler's Daughter	9:18, 23	5:22, 35	8:40, 49	
9. Healing the Hemorrhaging Woman	9:20	5:25	8:43	
10. Healing Two Blind Men	9:27			
11. Curing a Demon-Possessed, Mute Man	9:32			
12. Healing a Man's Withered Hand	12:9	3:1	6:6	
13. Curing a Demon-Possessed, Blind, and Mute Man	12:22		11:14	
14. Feeding the Five Thousand	14:13	6:30	9:10	6:1
15. Walking on the Sea	14:25	6:48		6:19
16. Healing the Gentile Woman's Daughter	15:21	7:24		
17. Feeding the Four Thousand	15:32	8:1		
18. Healing the Epileptic Boy	17:14	9:17	9:38	
19. Temple Tax in the Fish's Mouth	17:24			
20. Healing Two Blind Men	20:30	10:46	18:35	
21. Withering the Fig Tree	21:18	11:12		
22. Casting Out an Unclean Spirit		1:23	4:33	
23. Healing a Deaf-Mute		7:31		
24. Healing a Blind Man at Bethsaida		8:22		
25. Escape from the Hostile Multitude			4:30	
26. Catch of Fish			5:1	
27. Raising of a Widow's Son at Nain			7:11	
28. Healing the Infirm, Bent Woman			13:11	
29. Healing the Man with Dropsy			14:1	
30. Cleansing the Ten Lepers			17:11	
31. Restoring a Servant's Ear			22:51	
32. Turning Water into Wine				2:1
33. Healing the Nobleman's Son (of fever)				4:46
34. Healing an Infirm Man at Bethesda				5:1
35. Healing the Man Born Blind				9:1
36. Raising of Lazarus				11:43
37. Second Catch of Fish				21:1

This silver shekel was issued by the Jewish people during their first revolt against Roman rule (A.D. 66–70). It portrayed the blossom of an almond tree on one side and a silver chalice on the other.

MONEY OF THE BIBLE — an item used to pay for merchandise or services usually made of copper, silver, or gold.

MONEYCHANGERS — the people who exchanged money for people from different countries. These people provided a service but they usually charged a really high price for their services (Matt. 21:12, KJV).

MONOGAMY — a faithful marriage to one mate.

MONTH — one of the twelve divisions of a year measured by the completed cycle of the Moon. Solomon had twelve governors over Israel. They each provided food for the king and his household for one month out of the year (1 Kings 4:7). There were also twelve military divisions of Israel, one for each month of the year, and each division consisted of fourteen thousand men (1 Chron. 27:1–15).

MORDECAI [mor´-de-cay] *(related to Marduk)* — one of the Jewish captives who returned with Zerubbabel from Babylon (Ezra 2:2; Neh. 7:7).

Another man named Mordecai was the hero of the Book of Esther. He was probably

The denarius coin was considered a day's wages for a laborer in the time of Jesus (Matt. 20:1–16). This particular denarius featured the image of the Roman Emperor Tiberius.

Michelangelo's statue of Moses, great lawgiver and leader of the Hebrew people.

Monies			
Unit	Monetary Value	Equivalents	Translations
Jewish Weights			
Talent	gold—$5,760,000[1] silver—$384,000	3,000 shekels; 6,000 bekas	talent, one hundred pounds
Shekel	gold—$1,920 silver—$128	4 days' wages; 2 bekas: 20 gerahs	shekel
Beka	gold—$960 silver—$64	1/2 shekel; 10 gerahs	beka
Gerah	gold—$96 silver—$6.40	1/20 shekel	gerahs
Persian Coins			
Daric	gold—$1,280[2] silver—$64	2 days' wages; 1/2 Jewish silver shekel	daric, drachma
Greek Coins			
Tetradrachma	$128	4 drachmas	stater
Didrachma	$64	2 drachmas	two-drachma tax
Drachma	$32	1 day's wage	coin, silver coins
Lepton	$.25	1/2 of a Roman kodrantes	cents, small copper coin
Roman Coins			
Aureus	$800	25 denarii	gold
Denarius	$32	1 day's wage	denarii
Assarius	$2	1/16 of a denarius	cent
Kodrantes	$.50	1/4 of an assarius	cent

[1] Value of gold is fifteen times the value of silver
[2] Value of gold is twenty times the value of silver

Photo by Howard Vos

A fifth-century B.C. coin from Athens, Greece, showing the sacred owl on the reverse side.

born in Babylonia during the Captivity but he lived in Susa (Shushan), the Persian capital, during the reign of Ahasuerus (Xerxes I), the king of Persia.

MORNING STAR — *(See Lucifer.)*

MORTAL — a biblical term that describes human weakness and limitation (Job 4:17, NKJV; 10:5, NKJV; Isa. 13:12, NKJV). The word means "a person who will eventually die." The apostle Paul said, "Our Savior Jesus Christ has abolished death and brought life and immortality to light through the gospel" (2 Tim. 1:10, NKJV).

MOSES [mo´-zez] — the Hebrew prophet who delivered the Israelites from Egyptian slavery and who was their leader and lawgiver during their years of wandering in the wilderness. He was the brother of Aaron and Miriam and the author of the first five books of the Bible.

MOST HIGH — a name for God that appears frequently in the Old Testament, especially in the Book of Psalms and the Books of Isaiah and Daniel (Ps. 92:1; Isa. 14:14; Dan. 4:17). The name is used to show the might and power of God.

MOST HOLY PLACE — the most sacred place inside the temple (Exod. 26:34).

MOUNT, MOUNTAIN — elevated parts of land that are larger than hills. The Hebrew words for hill and mountain basically mean the same thing.

MOUNT OF OLIVES — a ridge of hills east of Jerusalem where Jesus was betrayed on the night before His crucifixion.

MULTITUDE — a large crowd or group of people (Matt. 4:25, NKJV).

MURMUR — to grumble; to complain (Exod. 15:24, KJV).

MUSTARD SEED — the very tiny seed of a mustard plant (Matt. 13:31–32).

MUSTER — to gather (2 Kings 25:19, NKJV).

MUTE, MUTENESS — silent; unable to speak (Mark 7:37, NIV).

MUZZLE — a leather or wire covering for the mouth of an animal that prevented it from eating or biting. There is a verse in the Book of Deuteronomy that says, "You shall not muzzle an ox while it treads out the grain" (Deut. 25:4, NKJV). This verse means that the animal helping with the harvest must be allowed to eat some of the grain. The apostle Paul used this verse to show that Christian workers need to be taken care of by other Christians (1 Cor. 9:9–10, NKJV).

MYRRH — a fragrant gum (sweet-smelling sticky substance) extracted (taken) from a shrub. It had many uses (Gen. 37:25; Matt. 2:11).

MYRTLE — a shrub often used during the Feast of the Tabernacles (Neh. 8:15).

MYSTERY — the hidden, eternal plan of God that is being revealed to God's people in His time and according to His plan.

N

NAAMAN [na´-a-man] *(pleasant)* — the name of three or four men in the Old Testament:

1. A son of Benjamin (Gen. 46:21).
2. The founder of the Naamites (Num. 26:40). He may be the same Naaman who is the son of Benjamin.
3. A commander of the Syrian army who was cured of leprosy through the prophet Elisha.
4. A son of Ehud, of the tribe of Benjamin (1 Chron. 8:7).

NABAL [na´-bal] — a wealthy sheep farmer (1 Sam. 25:2–39). Nabal was "harsh and evil" and was "such a scoundrel" that no one could reason with him (1 Sam. 25:3, 17).

His wife Abigail saved him and the men in their family from being killed by David after Nabal refused to provide food for David and his men (1 Sam. 25:4–35).

NABOTH [na´-both] — an Israelite of Jezreel who owned a vineyard next to the summer palace of King Ahab (1 Kings 21:1). Ahab was jealous and wanted the property. He offered Naboth a lot of money or a better vineyard, but Naboth said no because the vineyard was a family inheritance to be passed on to his descendants.

Jezebel bribed two men to lie about Naboth and say that he blasphemed God and the king. Because of their lies, Naboth was found guilty and both he and his sons were stoned to death (2 Kings 9:26). After that, Jezebel was able to get the property for Ahab. Elijah the prophet said Ahab and his household (family) would suffer a great deal for their disgusting act of false witness (1 Kings 21:1–29; 2 Kings 9:21–26).

NADAB [na´-dab] *(liberal or willing)* — the name of four men in the Old Testament:

1. A son of Aaron and Elisheba (Exod. 6:23) and a priest at the tabernacle (Exod. 28:1).
2. The son of Jeroboam I and a king of Israel (1 Kings 14:20; 15:25).
3. A son of Shammai, of the family of Jerahmeel.
4. A Benjamite who was the son of Jeiel and Maacah (1 Chron. 8:30).

NAHUM [na´-hum] *(compassionate)* — an Old Testament prophet and the author of the Book of Nahum. He prophesied about God's judgment against Assyria.

Another man named Nahum was an ancestor of Jesus (Luke 3:25).

NAHUM, BOOK OF — a short prophetic book of the Old Testament that tells about the coming destruction of the sinful nation of Assyria and its capital city, Nineveh.

NAOMI [na´-o-mee] *(my joy)* — the mother-in-law of Ruth. After her husband and two sons died, Naomi went home to Bethlehem. Her daughter-in-law, Ruth, followed her. Naomi sent Ruth to work for a good man named Boaz (Ruth 2:1). After Boaz and Ruth got married, Naomi stayed with them and they took care of her.

NAPHTALI [naf´-ta-li] *(my wrestling)* — the sixth son of Jacob (Gen. 35:25).

NATHAN [na´-than] *(he gave)* — the name of several men in the Old Testament. The best known was a prophet during the reign of David and Solomon, who told David that he would not be the one to build the temple (1 Chron. 17:1–15).

NATHANAEL [na-than´-a-el] *(God has given)* — a native of Cana in Galilee (John 21:2) who became a disciple of Jesus (John 1:45–49). Nathanael was introduced to Jesus by his friend Philip.

Many scholars believe Nathanael is the same person as Bartholomew (Matt. 10:3), one of the twelve apostles of Christ.

NAVE — a wheel hub (1 Kings 7:33, KJV).

NAZARENE [naz-a-reen´] — a person who was born in or who lived in Nazareth. Jesus was called a "Nazarene."

NAZARETH [naz´-a-reth] *(watchtower)* — a town of lower Galilee where Jesus spent His childhood (Matt. 2:23).

NAZIRITE [naz´-a-rite] *(separated, consecrated)* — a person who made a vow (special promise) to God to live a holy life (Num. 6:1–8). Anyone could take this vow, including the poor, women, and slaves.

NEBO [ne´-bo] — the name of a mountain in Moab (Num. 33:47). Moses was on Nebo when God allowed him to see the Promised Land. He was buried in a nearby valley (Deut. 32:49).

Nebo was also the name of two towns (Num. 32:3, 38; Ezra 2:29), a man (Ezra 10:43), and a Babylonian god.

Photo by Howard Vos

Modern Nazareth, successor to the village in lower Galilee where Jesus grew up (Luke 2:39; 4:16, 31–34).

NEBUCHADNEZZAR [neb-u-kad-nez´-ar] *(O god Nabu, protect my son)* — the king of the Neo-Babylonian Empire (ruled 605–562 B.C.) who captured Jerusalem, destroyed the temple, and carried the people of Judah into captivity in Babylonia.

NECROMANCER — a person who tries to communicate with the dead (Deut. 18:10–12).

NEEDLE, EYE OF — a phrase Jesus used to explain the difficulty a rich person would have entering the kingdom of heaven (Matt. 19:24).

NEHEMIAH [ne-he-mi´-ah] *(the Lord is consolation)* — the governor of Jerusalem who helped rebuild the wall of the city (Neh. 1–12). Nehemiah had been the personal cup-bearer for Artaxerxes I Longimanus.

Another man named Nehemiah was a clan leader who returned from the Captivity with Zerubbabel (Ezra 2:2; Neh. 7:7).

NEHEMIAH, BOOK OF — a historical book of the Old Testament that describes the rebuilding of the city walls around Jerusalem. The book is named for its main character.

Nehemiah teaches an excellent lesson about good leadership and also the importance of prayer (1:5–11; 2:1–20; 4:1–14; 6:9–14).

NEPHILIM [nef´-il-im] *(fallen ones)* — the "Nephilim" were thought to be giants. They were also called "mighty warriors." (Gen. 6:4; Num. 13:33).

NETHER — under (Exod. 19:17, NKJV).

NETTLE — a thorn (Job 30:7, NKJV).

NETWORK — the grate of bronze inside the altar of burnt offering (Exod. 27:4; 38:4, NKJV). Also, the decorative bronzework on the capitals of Jachin and Boaz, which became the two great bronze pillars in Solomon's temple (1 Kings

Photo by Levant Photo Service

Excavated section of the wall built by Nehemiah in Jerusalem after the Jewish people returned from the Captivity in Babylonia.

7:18, NKJV; 2 Chron. 4:12, NKJV; Jer. 52:22–23, NKJV).

NEW JERUSALEM — *(See Jerusalem, New.)*

NEW TESTAMENT — the second major set of books (27) in the Bible. These books tell about the life and ministry of Jesus and the growth of the early church.

NICODEMUS [nic-o-de´-mus] *(conqueror of the people)* — a Pharisee and a member of the Sanhedrin who became a disciple of Jesus (John 3:1, 4, 9; 7:50). Jesus described him as "the teacher of Israel," because he was well trained in Old Testament law and tradition.

NIGER [ni´-jur] *(black)* — the Latin last name of Simeon. He was one of the Christian prophets and teachers in the church of Syrian Antioch when Barnabas and Paul were called to missionary service (Acts 13:1–3).

NIGH — near (Ps. 145:18, KJV).

NILE [nile] — a great Egyptian river that flows more than three thousand five hundred miles from central Africa to the Mediterranean Sea.

NIMROD [nim´-rod] — a son of Cush, a grandson of Ham, and a great-grandson of Noah (Gen. 10:8–12; 1 Chron. 1:10). Nimrod was a skilled hunter and warrior who became a powerful king. He is the first hero mentioned in the Bible.

NINEVEH [nin´-e-veh] — the ancient capital city of the Assyrian Empire. Ninevah is the city the prophet Jonah did not want to go to and preach. Finally Jonah went, and the people repented and turned to God (Jon. 3:5–10).

NISAN [ni´-san] — the name given to Abib, the first month of the Jewish sacred year, after the Captivity (Esther 3:7). (See Calendar.)

NOAH [no´-ah] *(rest, relief)* — a son of Lamech and the father of Shem, Ham, and Japheth. He was a hero of faith who obeyed God by building an ark (a giant boat) that was used to save mankind from total destruction by the Flood (Gen. 5:28–9:29).

There was also a woman named Noah in the Bible (Num. 26:33).

Photo by Howard Vos

The mound of Kuyunjik, one of the major mounds of the magnificent city of Nineveh in ancient Assyria.

NORTHERN KINGDOM — the northern ten tribes of Israel (1 Kings 14:19–30).

NUMBER, NUMBERS — figures, characters, or symbols used for counting and mathematics. The people of the Bible used numbers more for counting than math.

NUMBERS, BOOK OF — an Old Testament book that tells what happened to the Israelites through their long period of wandering in the wilderness as they prepared to enter the Promised Land. The book is called Numbers because of two censuses (counting) or "numberings" of the people are recorded in chapters 1 and 26.

NUN *(fish)* — the father of Joshua (pronounced *none*) and an Ephraimite (Exod. 33:11; Num. 27:18).

Nun is also the fourteenth letter of the Hebrew alphabet (pronounced *noon*). It is used in the NKJV as a heading over Psalm 119:105–112. In the original Hebrew language, each of these eight verses began with the letter nun.

O

OATH — a statement used to confirm a promise.

OBADIAH [o-ba-di-ah] *(servant of the Lord)* — the governor of Ahab's palace (1 Kings 18:3–7, 16) who was a prophet of Judah (Obad. 1). He was the fourth of the "minor" prophets. There were also twelve other men named Obadiah in the Old Testament.

OBADIAH, BOOK OF — a prophetic book of the Old Testament that tells of God's coming judgment against the Edomites. The book is the shortest book in the Old Testament, containing one chapter of only twenty-one verses.

The Book of Obadiah makes it clear that God takes His promises to His covenant people seriously, even if His people are disobedient and don't deserve it.

OBED [o´-bed] (*worshiper)* — a son of Boaz and Ruth (Ruth 4:17–22; 1 Chron. 2:12) and an ancestor of Jesus (Matt. 1:5). Obed is also the name of four other men in the Old Testament (1 Chron. 2:37–38; 1 Chron. 11:47; 1 Chron. 26:7; 2 Chron. 23:1).

OBEDIENCE — the act of doing what someone asks you to do, especially doing what God asks you to do.

OBEISANCE — an act of submission. The KJV translation of a Hebrew verb that means "to bow down." The NKJV translates the word as "bowed down to" (Gen. 37:7, Exod. 18:7), "prostrated" (2 Sam. 1:2), and "did homage" (1 Kings 1:16).

OBLATION — an offering (Jer. 14:12, KJV).

OBSERVE — to watch; to keep or practice, as in *observe the Sabbath* (Deut. 5:12, NKJV).

ODIOUS — repulsive; disgusting (1 Chron. 19:6, KJV).

ODOR, ODOUR — a fragrance; an aroma; a smell (Eccles. 10:1).

OFFENSE, OFFEND — something that causes a person to stumble (a temptation); to cause a person to stumble (give in to a temptation) (Matt. 16:23, NKJV).

OG [ahg] — an Amorite king of the land of Bashan (Num. 21:33; 32:33). Og was king over sixty cities, including Ashtaroth and Edrei. Moses and the Israelites defeated him (Deut. 3:6) and gave his kingdom to the tribes of Reuben, Gad, and the half-tribe of Manasseh.

Og was the last survivor of the race of giants. His huge iron bed frame was kept on display in Rabbah long after he died (Deut. 3:11).

OIL — a substance (usually from olive trees) that had many uses such as for food, health and beauty, and energy (Matt. 25:3). (See Ointment.)

OINTMENT — scented oil.

The term "ointment" usually means oil, particularly olive oil, mixed with aromatic ingredients such as spices, myrrh, and plant extracts. Many of these ingredients were expensive. The Egyptians were the first people known to use ointment. Ointment was often imported from Phoenicia in small alabaster boxes because the boxes helped keep the scent in the oil. Good ointments could last for hundreds of years.

OLD TESTAMENT — the first major set of books (thirty-nine) in the Bible.

These books tell the story of God's creation of the universe and the mighty acts of God in and through His people, the nation of Israel.

OLIVE — the fruit of an olive tree (Deut. 6:11; Rom. 11:17). The branch of the olive tree is also known as a symbol of peace.

OLIVET DISCOURSE — Jesus' discussion on the Mount of Olives about the destruction of Jerusalem and the end of the world (Matt. 24:1–25:46; Mark 13:1–37; Luke 21:5–36).

OMEGA [o´-me-gah] — the last letter of the Greek alphabet. The phrase "the Alpha and the Omega" is used to describe the Lord Jesus Christ as the beginning and the end (Rev. 1:8). Alpha is the first letter in the Greek alphabet.

OMEN — a sign used by magicians and fortunetellers to predict the future. God told the Israelites not to allow one who interprets omens to live among them (Deut. 18:10; an augur, NRSV).

OMER — a unit of dry measure (Exod. 16:16, NKJV). (See Weights and Measures of the Bible.)

OMNIPOTENCE [om-nip´-o-tence] — a word that means God has power over everything.

OMNIPRESENCE [om-ne-pres´-ence] — a word that means God is everywhere.

OMNISCIENCE [om-nish´-ence] — a word that means God knows everything.

OMRI [om´-ri] — the name of four men in the Old Testament:

1. The sixth king of the northern kingdom of Israel (885–874 B.C.).

Photo by Gustav Jeeninga

The temple of Apollo at Delphi. The oracle of Delphi was revered throughout the ancient world because people believed it had the power to foretell the future.

2. A member of the tribe of Benjamin and a son of Becher (1 Chron. 7:8).

3. A member of the tribe of Judah and a son of Imri (1 Chron. 9:4).

4. The son of Michael and a prince of the tribe of Issachar (1 Chron. 27:18).

ONESIMUS [o-nes´-i-mus] *(useful)* — a slave of Philemon (Col. 4:9; Philem. 10). When Onesimus ran away from his master, he went to Rome and met the apostle Paul. Paul witnessed to him, and he became a Christian. Paul sent him back to Philemon with a letter telling Philemon that Onesimus had become like a son to him, and asking Philemon to treat him as a Christian brother instead of a slave.

ONYX — a gemstone that was used on Aaron's ephod (holy vest), and also to decorate the temple (Exod. 25:7).

ORACLE [or´-i-cal] — a prophetic speech or saying. In Greek religion, an oracle was a pagan god's answer to a human's question. The most famous oracle was the Oracle at Delphi. Delphi was the shrine of Apollo. Apollo was the Greek god of the sun, prophecy, music, medicine, and poetry.

ORDAIN, ORDINATION — the process of commissioning or consecrating a priest for service or a pastor or other officer of the church. This process is rarely mentioned in the New Testament. Even though the technical sense of the term does not occur in the New Testament, there are several references that do indicate an official ordination ceremony.

ORDER — proper arrangement (1 Cor. 14:40, NKJV).

ORDINANCE — a law or a rule (Exod. 12:24, NKJV).

OTHNIEL [oth´-ne-el] — the first judge of Israel (Judg. 1:13; 3:9, 11). Othniel was a son of Kenaz and probably was a nephew of Caleb. Another man named Othniel was an ancestor of Heldai (1 Chron. 27:15).

OUTCASTS — a word used in the Old Testament that refers to refugees or exiles from the land of Israel (Ps. 147:2, NKJV; Isa. 11:12, NKJV; 56:8, NKJV). The modern idea of outcasts refers to people who are rejected by society.

OVERCOME — to prevail; to defeat; to have victory over (Num. 13:30, NKJV).

OVERLAID — covered (Exod. 26:32, NKJV; Heb. 9:4, NKJV).

OVERSEER — an administrator; a person in charge (Acts 20:28, NKJV).

OVERWHELM — taken over; covered (Ps. 55:5, NKJV).

OX, OXEN — what we think of as cattle, the Bible calls oxen. A wild ox was a massive, untamable beast (Job 39:9–10).

Cattle needed a lot of food and space because of their large size, so a person who owned many cattle probably had a lot of money.

P

PALACE — the large home of a king (2 Chron. 9:11).

PALESTINE [pal´-es-tine] — a tiny piece of land that connects the continents of Asia, Africa, and Europe (1 Sam. 13:19). The word "Palestine" (Palestina) originally meant "the land of the Philistines," but the older name, Canaan, was used more often in the Old Testament. After the Israelites took the land from the Canaanites, the entire country became known as the "land of Israel" (Matt. 2:20, NKJV) and the "land of promise" (Heb. 11:9, NKJV).

PALM TREE — a tree that grows in the Jordan Valley (1 Kings 6:29). Palm branches were considered a symbol of victory (John 12:13; Rev. 7:9).

PALSY — paralysis (Luke 5:18, KJV).

PAMPHYLIA [pam-fil´-e-ah] *(a region of every tribe)* — a Roman province on the southern coast of central Asia Minor (modern Turkey). The province consisted mainly of a plain about eighty miles long and up to about twenty miles wide. The capital of Pamphylia was its largest city, Perga (Acts 13:13–14).

PANGS — pain, especially the pain of childbirth (Isa. 26:17, NKJV).

The Hasbani Brook in northern Palestine—one of the tributaries of the Jordan River—with Mount Hermon in the background.

Palm trees in southern Palestine. The leaves of palm trees were used as tokens of peace and victory (John 12:12–13; Rev. 7:9).

PALESTINE IN CHRIST'S TIME

(1,742) Elevation, in feet

?   Exact location questionable

0   10   20
Scale of Miles

Sidon

Zarephath

MT. LEBANON (11,000)

MT. HERMON (9,200)

Damascus
33°30'

Phoenicia

Tyre

Iturea

Panias
(Caesarea Philippi)

Trachonitis

Galilee

Ptolemais

Chorazin
Capernaum *Bethsaida?*
Magdala *Sea of Cinnereth* *Gergesa*
Cana Tiberias
R. Kishon
MT. CARMEL (1,742)

R. Yarmuk

Nazareth
Nain
Esdraelon

+ MT. TABOR (1,843)
Gadara?

R. Jezreel

The Great Sea

Caesarea

MT. GILBOA (1,698)

Scythopolis

Decapolis

Samaria

Samaria
Sychar

MT. GERIZIM (2,890)

Gerasa

R. Jabbok

Antipatris
Joppa

River Jordan

Perea

Arimathea
Lydda

Ephraim

Gadara?
Philadelphia

Emmaus
Kirjath Jearim
Azotus
Beth Haccerem
Bethlehem
Herodium
Ashkelon

Jericho
Jerusalem *Bethabara*
Bethany
Qumran

Medeba

Judea
Hebron

Machaerus

Gaza

The Salt Sea
(−1,300)

R. Arnon

Idumea

Masada

Beersheba

© Thomas Nelson, Inc., 1983

PAPHOS [pa´-fos] — a city on the island of Cyprus. Paul, Barnabas, and John Mark visited Paphos during Paul's first missionary journey, about A.D. 47 or 48 (Acts 13:6–13).

PAPYRUS [pa-py´-rus] — a tall plant that grows at the edge of a body of water in southern Europe and northern Africa, especially in the Nile River valley. This plant no longer grows wild in Egypt, but it still grows in the Sudan. It can also be found growing in the marshes at the northern end of Lake Huleh in Palestine.

Papyrus is also a kind of paper made from the stems of the papyrus plant.

PARABLE — a short, simple story used as an example to explain a spiritual truth, a religious principle, or to teach a moral lesson (Luke 15).

PARACLETE [par-a-clete´] — the Holy Spirit. Paraclete is a transliteration of the Greek word *parakletos,* which means "one who speaks in favor of," as an intercessor, advocate, or legal assistant. The word, translated as "Comforter" or "Counselor," appears only in the Gospel of John. Jesus applied the term to the Holy Spirit, who would be an advocate on behalf of Jesus' followers after His ascension; the Spirit would plead their case before God (John 14:16, 26; 15:26; 16:7).

PARADISE *(park, garden)* — a place of great blessedness, complete happiness, and total delight, also another name for heaven. Originally "paradise" was a Persian word that meant "a wooded park," "an enclosed or walled orchard," or "a garden with fruit trees."

PARAMOUR — a lover in an adulterous relationship; also a mistress. The Hebrew word

Photo by Willem A. VanGemeren

Several stalks of papyrus, reedlike plants used for making a primitive type of paper in Bible times.

for paramours is usually translated as concubines. A paramour could be male or female (Ezek. 23:20, NKJV).

PARAN [pa´-ran] — a wilderness region in the central part of the Sinai Peninsula (Gen. 21:21).

PARCHED — burnt; roasted (Jer. 17:6; Ruth 2:14, NKJV).

PARCHMENT — material made from animal skins and used to write on (2 Tim. 4:13, NKJV).

PARDON — to forgive; to release a person from punishment. The Bible says God is always "ready to pardon" His people from their sins (Mic. 7:18, NKJV).

The Parables of Jesus Christ

Parable	Matthew	Mark	Luke
1. Lamp Under a Basket	5:14–16	4:21, 22	8:16, 17 11:33–36
2. A Wise Man Builds on Rock and a Foolish Man Builds on Sand	7:24–27		6:47–49
3. Unshrunk (New) Cloth on an Old Garment	9:16	2:21	5:36
4. New Wine in Old Wineskins	9:17	2:22	5:37, 38
5. The Sower	13:3–23	4:2–20	8:4–15
6. The Tares (Weeds)	13:24–30		
7. The Mustard Seed	13:31, 32	4:30–32	13:18, 19
8. The Leaven	13:33		13:20, 21
9. The Hidden Treasure	13:44		
10. The Pearl of Great Price	13:45, 46		
11. The Dragnet	13:47–50		
12. The Lost Sheep	18:12–14		15:3–7
13. The Unforgiving Servant	18:23–35		
14. The Laborers in the Vineyard	20:1–16		
15. The Two Sons	21:28–32		
16. The Wicked Vinedressers	21:33–45	12:1–12	20:9–19
17. The Wedding Feast	22:2–14		
18. The Fig Tree	24:32–44	13:28–32	21:29–33
19. The Wise and Foolish Virgins	25:1–13		
20. The Talents	25:14–30		
21. The Growing Seed		4:26–29	
22. The Absent Householder		13:33–37	
23. The Creditor and Two Debtors			7:41–43
24. The Good Samaritan			10:30–37
25. A Friend in Need			11:5–13
26. The Rich Fool			12:16–21
27. The Watchful Servants			12:35–40
28. The Faithful Servant and the Evil Servant			12:42–48
29. The Barren Fig Tree			13:6–9
30. The Great Supper			14:16–24
31. Building a Tower and a King Making War			14:25–35
32. The Lost Coin			15:8–10
33. The Lost Son			15:11–32
34. The Unjust Steward			16:1–13
35. The Rich Man and Lazarus			16:19–31
36. Unprofitable Servants			17:7–10
37. The Persistent Widow			18:1–8
38. The Pharisee and the Tax Collector			18:9–14
39. The Minas			19:11–27

PARTAKE — to join in; to participate (Heb. 3:1, NKJV).

PARTIALITY — choosing one person or group over another for the wrong reason. In the Old Testament, the Hebrew people had to be reminded not to show partiality (Lev. 19:15, NKJV; Deut. 16:19, NKJV; 2 Chron. 19:7, NKJV). The New Testament says that salvation is freely given to all who believe in Jesus Christ, whether Jew or Gentile, male or female, bondslave or free (Gal. 3:28). God does not show partiality among His children.

PASCHAL [pas´-kal] — relating to Passover (1 Cor. 5:7, RSV).

PASSAGE — the right to travel through an area. The Edomites refused to give the Israelites passage through their territory (Num. 20:21, NKJV).

A ford or river crossing is also called a passage (Jer. 51:32, NKJV).

PASSION OF CHRIST — a phrase that refers to the suffering and death of Jesus Christ by crucifixion (Acts 1:3, KJV).

PASSOVER, FEAST OF — the first of the three great feasts celebrated by the Israelites. When the people of Israel were slaves in Egypt, they were told to sacrifice a lamb and smear (paint) the blood of the lamb on their doorposts as a sign for God to "pass over" their houses when He destroyed all the firstborn of Egypt (Exod. 12:13).

Passover was celebrated on the fourteenth day of the first month, and the service began in the evening (Lev. 23:6) because it was on the evening of this day that the Israelites left Egypt.

Unleavened bread was used in the celebration because the people had no time to leaven their bread as they prepared their last meal in Egypt. The meal was eaten in a hurry so they could leave. Passover helped them to remember how God saved them when they left Egypt.

PASTOR — the feeder, protector, and guide, or shepherd, of a flock of God's people in New Testament times. In speaking of spiritual gifts, the apostle Paul wrote that Christ "gave some to be apostles, some prophets, some evangelists, and some pastors and teachers" (Eph. 4:11, NKJV). The term "pastor" at that time in church history wasn't an official title for the leader of the church. It was actually a term used to describe a person who helped and cared for God's people.

PASTORAL EPISTLES — the books of First Timothy, Second Timothy, and Titus are called the Pastoral Epistles because they are three letters written by the apostle Paul and they clearly show Paul's love and concern for them as pastor and administrator of several local churches.

PATIENCE — the ability to wait for suffering to end and the ability to stay strong when facing a problem (Rom. 5:3).

PATMOS [pat´-mos] — a small rocky island. The apostle John was banished (sent away) to Patmos. While he was there, he wrote the Book of Revelation (Rev. 1:9).

PATRIARCH [pa´-tre-ark] *(head of a father's house)* — the founder or leader of a tribe, family, or clan. "The patriarchs" usually refers to the tribal leaders of Israel who lived before the time of Moses. This included Abraham, Isaac, Jacob, and Jacob's twelve sons (Acts 7:8–9, NKJV; Heb. 7:4, NKJV).

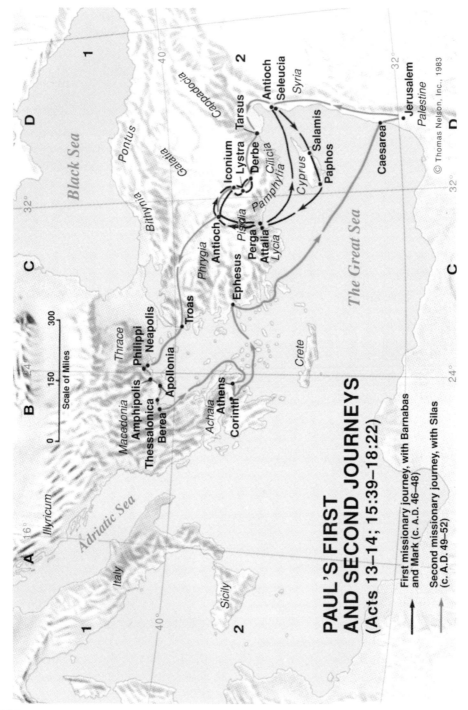

PAUL'S FIRST AND SECOND JOURNEYS
(Acts 13–14; 15:39–18:22)

→ First missionary journey, with Barnabas and Mark (c. A.D. 46–48)

→ Second missionary journey, with Silas (c. A.D. 49–52)

© Thomas Nelson, Inc., 1983

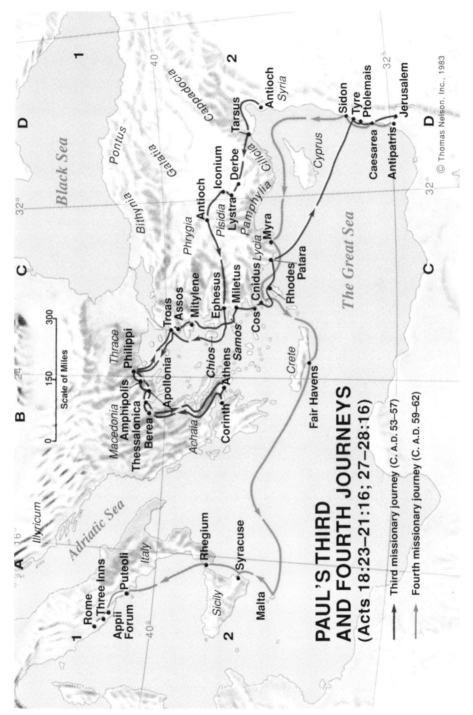

PAUL'S THIRD AND FOURTH JOURNEYS
(Acts 18:23–21:16; 27–28:16)

Third missionary journey (C. A.D. 53–57)
Fourth missionary journey (C. A.D. 59–62)

© Thomas Nelson, Inc., 1983

Scale of Miles
0   150   300

Black Sea

Pontus

Bithynia

Galatia

Cappadocia

Antioch

Syria

Tarsus

Cilicia

Phrygia

Pisidia

Antioch

Iconium

Derbe

Lystra

Pamphylia

Myra

Lycia

Cnidus

Patara

Rhodes

Cyprus

Sidon

Tyre

Ptolemais

Caesarea

Antipatris

Jerusalem

The Great Sea

Cos

Miletus

Samos

Ephesus

Chios

Mitylene

Assos

Troas

Thrace

Philippi

Apollonia

Athens

Corinth

Achaia

Berea

Thessalonica

Amphipolis

Macedonia

Crete

Fair Havens

Adriatic Sea

Illyricum

Italy

Rome

Three Inns

Puteoli

Appii Forum

Rhegium

Syracuse

Sicily

Malta

141

PAUL, THE APOSTLE — a Christian missionary in the early church. He wrote letters to several of the early Christian churches, and those letters became books in the Bible.

PAVILION — any kind of temporary shelter, such as a tent, tabernacle, or booth (2 Kings 16:18, NKJV; Ps. 27:5, NKJV; 31:20, NKJV; Jer. 43:10, NKJV).

PEACE — in the Old Testament, the meaning of peace was completeness, soundness, and the well-being of a person (Ps. 119:165; Ps. 4:8; Isa. 26:3; Ps. 122:6–7; 1 Sam. 7:14). The traditional Jewish greeting, *shalom*, means "peace" and was a wish for peace.

In the New Testament, peace usually refers to the inner peace (peace of mind) of the Christian who trusts God through Christ.

The peace that Jesus spoke of was a combination of hope, trust, and quiet in the mind and soul that comes when a person makes their relationship with God right (Luke 2:14; Matt. 5:9; John 14:27).

PEACE OFFERING — an animal sacrifice (Exod. 20:24, NKJV).

Photo by Howard Vos

Ruins of the walls and city gate at Perga, a city visited by Paul and Barnabas on their first missionary journey (Acts 13:13, 14).

PEARL — a jewel used for jewelry and decoration (1 Tim. 2:9). A pearl was also a symbol for a spiritual truth (Matt. 13:46).

PENTATEUCH [pen´-ta-tyook] — a Greek word that refers to the first five books of the Old Testament. The Jews usually call the Pentateuch "the Book of the Law," or just "the Law." Another word for the Pentateuch is "Torah." Torah means "instruction, teaching, or doctrine."

PENTECOST, FEAST OF — another name

The Pentateuch

Book	Key Idea	The Nation	The People	God's Character	God's Role	God's Command
Genesis	Beginnings	Chosen	Prepared	Powerful Sovereign	Creator	"Let there be!"
Exodus	Redemption	Delivered	Redeemed	Merciful	Deliverer	"Let my people go!"
Leviticus	Worship	Set Apart	Taught	Holy	Sanctifier	"Be holy!"
Numbers	Wandering	Directed	Tested	Just	Sustainer	"Go in!"
Deuteronomy	Renewed Covenant	Made Ready	Retaught	Loving Lord	Rewarder	"Obey!"

Chronology of Israel in the Pentateuch

Date	Event	Reference
Fifteenth day, first month, first year	Exodus	Exodus 12
Fifteenth day, second month, first year	Arrival in Wilderness of Sin	Exodus 16:1
Third month, first year	Arrival in Wilderness of Sinai	Exodus 19:1
First day, first month, second year	Erection of Tabernacle	Exodus 40:1, 17
	Dedication of Altar	Numbers 7:1
	Consecration of Levites	Numbers 8:1–26
Fourteenth day, first month, second year	Passover	Numbers 9:5
First day, second month, second year	Census	Numbers 1:1, 18
Fourteenth day, second month, second year	Supplemental Passover	Numbers 9:11
Twentieth day, second month, second year	Departure from Sinai	Numbers 10:11
First month, fortieth year	In Wilderness of Zin	Numbers 20:1, 22–29; 33:38
First day, fifth month, fortieth year	Death of Aaron	Numbers 20:22–29; 33:38
First day, eleventh month, fortieth year	Moses' Address	Deuteronomy 1:3

for the Feast of Weeks, a yearly Jewish celebration of harvest (Deut. 16:9–10). The early Christian believers, who were gathered in Jerusalem for observance of this feast, experienced the outpouring of God's Holy Spirit in a miraculous way.

PERCEIVE — to know (John 4:19, NKJV).

PERDITION — destruction, ruin, or waste, especially the eternal destruction of the wicked by God (Heb. 10:39, NKJV; 2 Pet. 3:7, NKJV).

PEREZ [pe´-res] *(breakthrough)* — Judah and Tamar had twin sons. Perez was the son born first (Gen. 38:29; Pharez, KJV). Perez was an ancestor of David and Jesus (Ruth 4:12, 18; Matt. 1:3; Luke 3:33).

PERFECT, PERFECTION — without flaw (no mistakes) or error; a state of being complete or fulfilled. God's perfection means that He is complete in Himself and He lacks nothing. He has no flaws. He is perfect in every way (Job 36:4, NKJV; Ps. 18:30, NKJV; 19:7, NKJV; Matt. 5:48).

PERFORM — to do; to complete; to confirm (Rom. 15:28, NKJV; Deut. 25:5, NKJV).

PERGA [pur´-gah] — the capital city of Pamphylia. Paul visited Perga twice (Acts 13:13–14; Acts 14:25).

The modern city of Pergamum, or Pergamos, with the ruins of the Basilica of St. John in the center.

Photo by Howard Vos

PERGAMOS [pur´-ga-mos] — the main city of Mysia, and the site of one of the seven churches of Asia (Rev. 2:12–17).

PERISH — to be lost or destroyed (Ps. 1:6, NKJV; John 3:15, NKJV).

PERIZZITES [per´-iz-ites] *(villagers)* — the people who lived in the forest country (Josh. 17:15) in the territory of the tribes of Ephraim, Manasseh, and Judah (Judg. 1:4–5).

PERPLEXED — confused (Esther 3:15, NKJV).

PERSECUTE, PERSECUTION — the hatred and suffering that tries to stop the witness and holy life of God's people (Matt. 5:10).

PERSEVERANCE — the continual effort to follow God's commands and to do His work. The New Testament makes it clear that Christians are saved by their faith. But it also makes it clear that perseverance in doing good works is the greatest sign that a person's faith is real (James 2:14–26).

PERSIA [per´-she-ah] — an ancient world empire that thrived from 539–331 B.C. The Babylonian Empire was taken over by the Persians. This was the beginning of the phase for the return of the Jews to Jerusalem in 538 B.C., after their long period of captivity by the Babylonians.

PERVERSE — improper; wrong; evil (Prov. 14:2, NKJV; Matt. 17:17, NKJV).

PERVERT — to change something and make it bad (Exod. 23:8, NKJV; Acts 13:10, NKJV).

PESTILENCE — a plague (Exod. 5:3, NKJV).

PETER, EPISTLES OF — two New Testament epistles bearing the name of "Peter, an apostle of Jesus Christ" (1 Pet. 1:1) and "Simon Peter, a servant and apostle of Jesus Christ" (2 Pet. 1:1). Except for the name, these books have nothing else in common.

First Peter is written in fine Greek and refers frequently to the Old Testament. It is an epistle for the downhearted, written to give encouragement in times of trial and disappointment. First Peter anchors the Christian's hope on the matchless sacrifice of Jesus Christ, who "suffered for you. He gave you an example to follow. So you should do as he did" (2:21).

Second Peter is shorter and written with less style. It strongly criticizes the following of false teachers, while reminding believers that they are chosen by God and assuring them that Jesus will return.

PETER, SIMON — one of Jesus' twelve apostles. The New Testament gives more information about Peter than any other disciple, except Paul.

PHARAOH [fa´-ra-o] — the title of the kings of Egypt until 323 B.C. (Gen. 40–47). In the Egyptian language, the word pharaoh means "great house." This word was originally used to describe the palace of the king. Around 1500 B.C., this term was applied to the

Photo by Willem A. VanGemeren

Jaffa, the biblical Joppa, where Peter received the heavenly vision about God's acceptance of the Gentiles (Acts 10:1–23).

Photo by Howard Vos

Entrance to the tomb of Pharaoh Tutankhamun of Egypt in the foreground with the tomb of Ramses VI just behind it.

The modern Turkish city of Alashehir, the biblical Philadelphia, on the Hermus River. John commended the Christians at Philadelphia for their faithfulness (Rev. 1:11; 3:7–13).

Photo by Gustav Jeeninga

Egyptian kings. It meant something like "his honor" or "his majesty."

PHARISEES [far´-i-sees] *(separated ones)* — a religious and political group in Palestine (Matt. 23). The Pharisees were known for insisting that the law of God be followed exactly as the scribes interpreted it and for their special commitment to keeping the laws of tithing and ritual purity.

PHILADELPHIA [fil-a-del´-fe-ah] *(brotherly love)* — a city of the province of Lydia in western Asia Minor (modern Turkey) and the site of one of the seven churches of Asia. John wrote to the Philadelphians in the Book of Revelation (Rev. 1:11).

PHILEMON [fi-le´-mon] — a wealthy Christian from Colossae who allowed the church to meet in his house. Philemon became

a Christian while listening to and learning from the apostle Paul (Philem. 19), probably when Paul was ministering in Ephesus (Acts 19:10).

He had a slave named Onesimus, who, after damaging or stealing his master's property (Philem. 11, 18), ran away to Rome. While Onesimus was in Rome, he met the apostle Paul and also became a Christian (Philem. 10).

PHILEMON, EPISTLE TO — the shortest and most personal of Paul's epistles. Philemon tells the story of a runaway slave named Onesimus. The letter is written in a warm and caring style and reminds us that the presence of Christ can change every relationship in life.

The Epistle to Philemon is a lesson in Christian relationships. There isn't a better example of "speaking the truth in love" (Eph.

4:15, NKJV). While it was Philemon's legal right to punish or even kill a runaway slave, Paul hoped (v. 19) that Philemon would accept Onesimus back as a brother in the Lord and not as a slave (v. 16). In the entire book, Paul talks to Philemon as a trusted friend rather and not an enemy (v. 22). He focuses on Philemon's good qualities (vv. 4–7, 13–14, 17, 21) and even though he encourages Philemon to forgive Onesimus, he is careful not to force Philemon to do what is right. He helps Philemon decide and choose for himself (vv. 8–9, 14).

PHILIP [fil´-ip] *(lover of horses)* — the name of four men in the New Testament:

1. A native of Bethsaida who was one of the twelve apostles (Matt. 10:3; Mark 3:18; Luke 6:14).

2. A son of Herod the Great (Matt. 14:3; Luke 3:19).

3. Philip the tetrarch, who was also a son of Herod the Great.

4. Philip the evangelist (Acts 6:5).

PHILIPPI [fil´-ip-pi] *(city of Philip)* — a city in eastern Macedonia (modern Greece) visited by the apostle Paul. Philippi was named for Philip II of Macedonia, the father of Alexander the Great.

PHILIPPIANS [fi-lip´-pe-ans] — the people who were born in or who lived in Philippi (Phil. 4:15).

PHILIPPIANS, EPISTLE TO THE — one of four shorter epistles written by the apostle Paul while he was in prison. The others are Ephesians, Colossians, and Philemon. Because Paul started the church at Philippi (Acts 16:12–40), the Philippians always held a special place in his heart. When Paul first came to Philippi, he was thrown in jail. Late at night, after he had been tied up and beaten, he sang a hymn (song) to God (Acts 16:25). Ten years later Paul was in prison again and he was still celebrating the Christians' joy even though he was suffering. He said, "Be full of joy in the Lord always. I will say again, be full of joy" (Phil. 4:4).

Photo by Howard Vos

Ruins of the agora, or marketplace, of Philippi, with the ruins of a pagan temple in the foreground.

147

PHILISTIA [fil-is´-te-ah] — the land of the Philistines mentioned in the poetry of the Book of Psalms (60:8; 108:9). This land was located between Joppa and Gaza on the coastal plain of Palestine.

PHILISTINES [fil-is´-tinz] — a strong nation that occupied part of southwest Palestine from about 1200 to 600 B.C. The name Philistine was first used by the Egyptians in reference to the people defeated by Rameses III. The Assyrians called the people Pilisti or Palastu.

PHILOSOPHY — the love of wisdom (from *phileo,* "to love," and *sophia,* "wisdom"). The philosopher Pythagoras said there were three types of people: lovers of money, lovers of fame, and lovers of wisdom.

PHINEHAS [fin´-e-has] *(the Nubian)* — the name of three men in the Old Testament:

1. A son of Eleazar and grandson of Aaron (Exod. 6:25).

2. The younger of the two sons of Eli the priest (1 Sam. 1:3).

3. The father of Eleazar (Ezra 8:33).

PHOEBE (fee´-bee) — a deaconess recommended to the Roman Christians by Paul (Rom. 16:1–2).

PHOENICIA [fo-nee´-she-ah] — the land north of Palestine on the eastern shore of the Mediterranean Sea (Acts 11:19). Phoenicia is a Greek word that means "land of purple." The area was famous from early times for its purple dyes that were produced from shellfish. In the KJV, Phoenicia is spelled Phenicia.

Phoenicia was also known for its cedar trees. The cedars of Phoenicia were cut and shipped as far away as Egypt and eastern Mesopotamia because most other nations in that part of the world had very few trees that were good for timber.

PHRYGIA [frij´-e-ah] — a large province of the mountainous region of Asia Minor (modern Turkey), visited by the apostle Paul (Acts 2:10; 16:6; 18:23).

PHYLACTERIES [fi-lack´-ter-ies] — small square leather boxes or cases that hold four strips of parchment with verses from the Pentateuch written on them (Matt. 23:5, NKJV). Every male Israelite over thirteen years of age wore phylacteries during the morning prayer service, except on the Sabbath and holidays.

PIETY — a word usually defined as religious devotion and reverence to God. It means faithfulness in taking care of one's family, especially the parents (1 Tim. 5:4, NKJV).

Photo by Gustav Jeeninga

This inscription from a theater in Caesarea mentions Pontius Pilate, prefect of Judea, who pronounced the death sentence against Jesus (Mark 15).

PILATE, PONTIUS [pi´-lut, pon´-shius] — the fifth Roman prefect (ruler) of Judea, who issued the official order sentencing Jesus to death by crucifixion (Matt. 27; Mark 15; Luke 23; John 18–19).

PILLAR — a structure that supports a roof, or a pile of stones (standing upright) with religious significance (importance). During the Exodus, God's presence was described as a "pillar of fire" and a "pillar of cloud" (Exod. 13:21).

PINE — a type of tree (Isa. 41:19). When used as a verb it means to be weary (tired and weak) or sick of heart (very sad) (Ezek. 24:23, NKJV).

PINNACLE — a part of the temple mentioned in the temptation of Jesus (Matt. 4:5, NKJV; Luke 4:9, NKJV). The pinnacle was a high place on some part of the temple. It was probably the battlement (tower or top of a castle) or the roof of Solomon's Porch.

PIPE — a musical instrument that may have been similar to a flute or bagpipes (1 Sam. 10:5, NKJV).

PISGAH [piz´-gah] — a word that refers to the rugged ridge at the top of a mountain. As a proper noun, the word "Pisgah" was sometimes identified with Mount Nebo (Deut. 34:1).

PISIDIA [pi-sid´-e-ah] — a mountainous province in central Asia Minor (modern Turkey), visited by the apostle Paul (Acts 13:14; 14:24). Pisidia was a wild, mountainous country that had many bandits (robbers).

PIT — a deep hole in the ground that can be natural (Gen. 14:10) or man-made (Gen. 37:20, NKJV).

PITCH — when used as a verb it means to set up (like set up a tent) (Heb. 8:2, KJV); when used as a noun it is a tarlike substance (Exod. 2:3, NKJV).

PITY — a feeling of sorrow for a person in a sad (unfortunate) situation (Matt. 18:33, NKJV). Pity is the emotional side of mercy. Mercy is the desire to help the person in the sad situation.

PLAGUE — an affliction (something that causes suffering) sent by God as punishment

Statue of Rameses II of Egypt. Many scholars believe he was the ruling Pharaoh at the time of the Exodus.

The Ten Plagues on Egypt

The Plague	The Effect
1. Blood (7:20)	Pharaoh hardened (7:22)
2. Frogs (8:6)	Pharaoh begs relief, promises freedom (8:8), but is hardened (8:15)
3. Lice (8:17)	Pharaoh hardened (8:19)
4. Flies (8:24)	Pharaoh bargains (8:28), but is hardened (8:32)
5. Livestock diseased (9:6)	Pharaoh hardened (9:7)
6. Boils (9:10)	Pharaoh hardened (9:12)
7. Hail (9:23)	Pharaoh begs relief (9:27), promises freedom (9:28), but is hardened (9:35)
8. Locusts (10:13)	Pharaoh bargains (10:11), begs relief (10:17), but is hardened (10:20)
9. Darkness (10:22)	Pharaoh bargains (10:24), but is hardened (10:27)
10. Death of firstborn (12:29)	Pharaoh and Egyptians beg Israel to leave Egypt (12:31–33)

God multiplied His signs and wonders in the land of Egypt that the Egyptians might know that He is the Lord.

for sin and disobedience. In the Bible, the affliction is usually a widespread disease. The Hebrew word for "plague" means a blow (hit) or a lash (whipped once), which is a reference to punishment or chastisement (Exod. 7:14–12:30, NKJV).

PLASTER — a wall covering made from clay (Deut. 27:2).

PLEDGE — an item or items given as proof of the guarantee to fulfill an obligation or keep a promise. As proof of his intention to send Tamar a young goat from his flock, Judah left his signet, cord, and staff with her as a pledge (Gen. 38:17–18, 20, NKJV).

PLEIADES [ple´-ya-dez] — a brilliant cluster of stars seen in the shoulder of Taurus (the Bull). The name Pleiades comes from the seven daughters of Atlas and Pleione in Greek mythology (Job 9:9).

PLOWSHARE — the blade of a plow used for tilling the soil. In early times plows were made of wood. Later, metal tips were placed over the wood. The prophets Micah and Isaiah spoke of making plowshares from weapons as a sign of the peace that would come during the coming reign of God (Isa. 2:4, NKJV; Mic. 4:3, NKJV).

PLUCK — to remove (John 10:28, KJV).

PLUMB LINE, PLUMMET — a small heavy weight on the end of a long cord, used to make sure a wall is standing vertically straight (2 Kings 21:13). In a vision, the prophet Amos saw the Lord measuring the nation of Israel with a plumb line. The people were not considered true and straight in their devotion to God because they worshiped false gods (Amos 7:7–8).

POLLUTE — to make something dirty or

morally impure; to defile; to profane; to corrupt. Allowing a murderer to go unpunished polluted the land of Israel (Num. 35:33, NKJV).

POLYGAMY — the practice of having several spouses, especially wives, at one time. This was a common practice in the ancient world.

POLYTHEISM — the belief in many gods.

POMEGRANATE — a round, sweet fruit about four inches across with a hard rind. It is green and turns red when ripe. Its inside is full of edible seeds. Pomegranates were used for food (Num. 20:5), drink (Song of Sol. 8:2), and decoration (Exod. 28:33–34; 39:24–26; 1 Kings 7:18, 20).

POMP — much show; large display of ceremony (Acts 25:23, NKJV).

POSSESSED — acquired, owned; also under control of (Matt. 4:24, NKJV).

POSTERITY — descendants (Dan. 11:4, NKJV).

POTIPHAR [pot´-i-far] *(dedicated to Ra)* — the Egyptian who bought Joseph as a slave (Gen. 39:1). Potiphar was a high officer of Pharaoh and a wealthy man (Gen. 37:36). In time, he put Joseph in charge of his household.

POTSHERD — a fragment (piece) of broken pottery. Job used a potsherd to scrape the sores off of his body (Job 2:8, NKJV).

POTTAGE — a soup or stew (Gen. 25:29, KJV).

POTTER'S FIELD — the field that was purchased with the thirty pieces of silver paid to

Photo by Gustav Jeeninga

A flowering pomegranate. In biblical times, pomegranates were widely cultivated in Palestine (Num. 13:23; Deut. 8:7–8). The juice of the fruit made a pleasant drink (Song of Sol. 8:2).

Judas for his betrayal of Jesus (Matt. 27:7, 10). Because the field was purchased with blood money, it wasn't good for anything but a cemetery where foreigners were buried. The potter's field was probably located at the eastern end of the Valley of Hinnom.

POUND — a weight and an amount of money (John 12:3, NKJV; Ezra 2:69, KJV; Luke 19:13, KJV). (See Money of the Bible; also see Weights and Measures of the Bible.)

POWER — the ability or strength to perform an activity or deed (Ps. 111:6).

PRAETORIUM, PRAETORIAN GUARD — a special group of Roman soldiers in New Testament times. Their job was to guard the

151

emperor of the Roman Empire (Mark 15:16). They were an elite corps (group) of soldiers and their salaries (pay), privileges (rights), and working conditions were better than the regular soldiers of the Roman Empire.

PRAISE — an act of worship or acknowledgment of goodness or kind actions of another. Human beings should seek praise from God, not from each other (Prov. 27:21; "honor" Matt. 6:1–5). We can earn praise from God by having a true servant's heart (1 Cor. 4:5; Eph. 1:3–14).

PRAYER — communication with God. Anyone can say a prayer to God, but sinners who haven't trusted Jesus for their salvation remain separated from God. So while unbelievers can pray, they aren't able to have a rewarding relationship with God.

PRECEPT — a lesson or a principle (basic truth) (Ps. 119:4, NKJV).

PREDESTINATION, PREDESTINE — the biblical teaching that clearly shows the power of God and His mighty plan but allows humans to have free will (Rom. 8:29–30, NKJV).

PREEMINENCE — top honor; superior (Col. 1:18).

PREPARATION DAY — the day immediately before the Sabbath and other Jewish festivals. Preparation Day always fell on Friday, because all religious festivals began on the Sabbath, or Saturday (Matt. 27:62; John 19:14, 31).

PRESCRIBE — to write (Isa. 10:1, NKJV).

Photo by Gustav Jeeninga

An ancient oilpress in Capernaum, used for crushing olives in Bible times (Isa. 5:2).

PRESENCE OF GOD — God's ways of making Himself known to an individual (Exod. 3:2–5; Exod. 40:34–38; John 1:14).

PRESS — when used as a noun, it is a tool used to collect juice or oil from foods (Prov. 3:10); when used as a verb, it means to strain (Phil. 3:14, NKJV).

PRESUMPTUOUS — overly bold, filled with pride (Exod. 21:14, KJV; 2 Pet. 2:10, NKJV).

PREVAIL — to conquer (Matt. 16:18, NKJV).

PREVENT — to anticipate (Ps. 119:147, KJV); to precede (come before) (Matt. 17:25, KJV; 1 Thess. 4:15). In the King James Version of the Bible, prevent does not mean "to stop from happening."

PREY — a victim (Num. 14:3, KJV).

PRIDE — arrogance; unjustified self-esteem (Prov. 29:23).

PRIEST, HIGH — the high priest was the supreme religious leader of his people. Aaron was the first to hold this position and this office would continue to be passed down through Aaron's bloodline through the first-born son of each generation. The high priest was different from other priests and this was shown by the clothes he wore, the duties he performed, and the particular requirements placed upon him (Lev. 21:10; 2 Chron. 19:11).

PRIESTS — official ministers or worship leaders in the nation of Israel who represented the people before God. The father of a family or the head of a tribe performed the job of the priest before the time of Moses and Aaron. After Aaron became the high priest, the priesthood was formed and Aaron's descendants were established as the priestly line in Israel. They performed the important duties of a priest and were known as a special group devoted to God's service.

PRINCIPALITY — a powerful ruler, or the rule of someone in authority. The word may refer to human rulers (Titus 3:1, KJV), demonic spirits (Rom. 8:38, NKJV), angels and demons in general (Eph. 3:10, NKJV), or any type of ruler other than God (Eph. 1:21, NKJV). While Christians must often wrestle against evil principalities (Eph. 6:12, NKJV), they can be victorious because Christ defeated all wicked spirits (Col. 2:15, NKJV).

PRISCILLA [pris´-sil-lah] — the wife of Aquila and a strong supporter of the Christian cause (Rom. 16:3; 1 Cor. 16:19). Aquila and Priscilla left their home in Rome for Corinth when the emperor Claudius made all the Jews leave the city (Acts 18:2). They were fellow passengers of the apostle Paul on his journey from Corinth to Ephesus (Acts 18:18). Ephesus is where they met Apollos and taught him more about the Christian faith (Acts 18:26).

PRISON, PRISONER — a place of confinement; a person held by force in a place of confinement. Most prisons of the ancient world were filthy and crude and made the prisoners feel like animals. People guilty of breaking the laws of a community were detained (held) in several different types of prisons.

PRIZE — an award (1 Cor. 9:24; Phil. 3:14).

PROCLAIM — to tell; to announce (Exod. 33:19, NKJV; Luke 12:3, NKJV).

PROCLAMATION — an official public announcement (Dan. 5:29, NKJV).

PROCONSUL [pro-con´-sul] — a title given to the governor of a senatorial province in the Roman Empire. Under the Roman system of government, the Empire was divided into senatorial provinces and imperial provinces. Imperial provinces were watched over by representatives of the emperor and the senatorial provinces were watched over by proconsuls appointed by the Roman senate. Two proconsuls are mentioned in the New Testament: Sergius Paulus (Acts 13:7–8, 12, NKJV) and Gallio (Acts 18:12, NKJV).

PROFANE — to treat anything holy with disrespect. The word "profane" is often given to a person who is foolish or irresponsible. Esau was foolish and irresponsible with his birthright and he was called a "profane" person (Heb. 12:16, NKJV).

Chronology of Old Testament Kings and Prophets

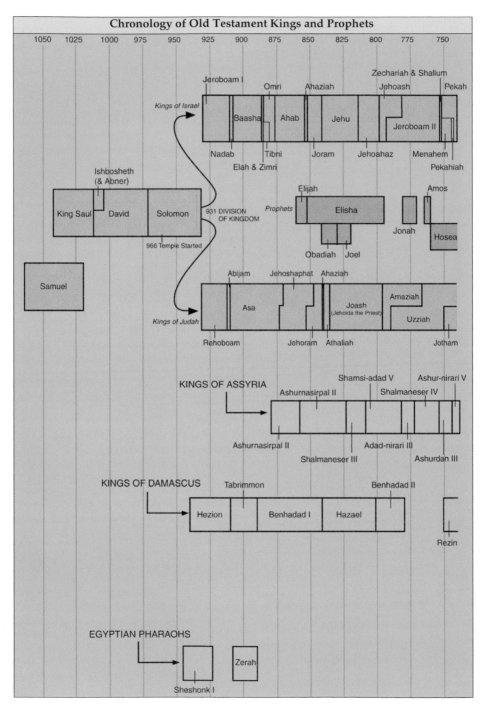

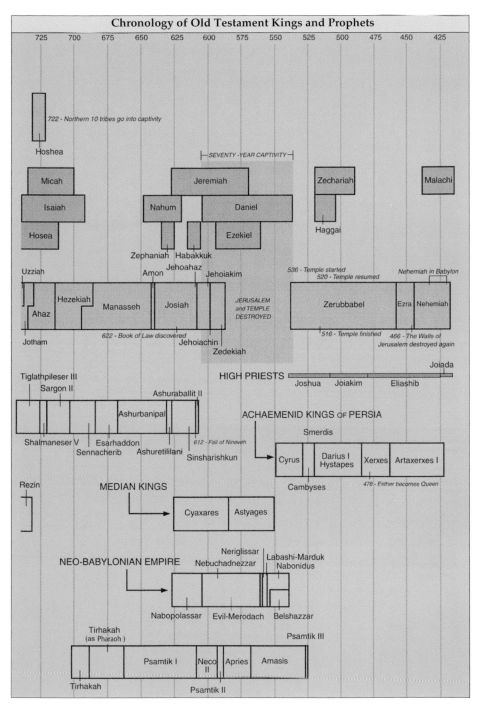

Chronology of Old Testament Kings and Prophets

| 725 | 700 | 675 | 650 | 625 | 600 | 575 | 550 | 525 | 500 | 475 | 450 | 425 |

722 - Northern 10 tribes go into captivity

Hoshea

├─ SEVENTY-YEAR CAPTIVITY ─┤

Micah

Jeremiah

Zechariah

Malachi

Isaiah

Nahum

Daniel

Hosea

Ezekiel

Haggai

Zephaniah   Habakkuk

Jehoahaz

Uzziah   Amon   Jehoiakim

536 - Temple started
520 - Temple resumed

Nehemiah in Babylon

Hezekiah

Manasseh   Josiah

JERUSALEM
and TEMPLE
DESTROYED

Zerubbabel

Ezra   Nehemiah

Ahaz

Jotham   622 - Book of Law discovered   Jehoiachin

516 - Temple finished   466 - The Walls of
Jerusalem destroyed again

Zedekiah

Joiada

Tiglathpileser III

HIGH PRIESTS

Sargon II

Joshua   Joiakim   Eliashib

Ashuraballit II

Ashurbanipal

ACHAEMENID KINGS OF PERSIA

Shalmaneser V   Esarhaddon   612 - Fall of Nineveh

Smerdis

Sennacherib   Ashuretililani

Cyrus

Darius I
Hystapes

Xerxes   Artaxerxes I

Sinsharishkun

Rezin   MEDIAN KINGS

Cambyses   478 - Esther becomes Queen

Cyaxares   Astyages

Neriglissar   Labashi-Marduk

NEO-BABYLONIAN EMPIRE   Nebuchadnezzar   Nabonidus

Nabopolassar   Evil-Merodach   Belshazzar

Tirhakah
(as Pharaoh)

Psamtik III

Psamtik I   Neco II   Apries   Amasis

Tirhakah

Psamtik II

Fulfilled Prophecies from Isaiah

The Prophecy	The Fulfillment
The Messiah . . .	Jesus Christ . . .
will be born of a virgin (Isa. 7:14).	was born of a virgin named Mary (Luke 1:26–31).
will have a Galilean ministry (Isa. 9:1, 2).	ministered in Galilee of the Gentiles (Matt. 4:13–16).
will be an heir to the throne of David (Isa. 9:7).	was given the throne of His father David (Luke 1:32, 33).
will have His way prepared (Isa. 40:3–5).	was announced by John the Baptist (John 1:19–28).
will be spat on and struck (Isa. 50:6).	was spat on and beaten (Matt. 26:67).
will be exalted (Isa. 52:13).	was highly exalted by God and the people (Phil. 2:9, 10).
will be disfigured by suffering (Isa. 52:14; 53:2).	was scourged by the soldiers who gave Him a crown of thorns (Mark 15:15–19).
will make a blood atonement (Isa. 53:5).	shed His blood to atone for our sins (1 Pet. 1:2).
will be widely rejected (Isa. 53:1, 3).	was not accepted by many (John 12:37, 38).
will bear our sins and sorrows (Isa. 53:4, 5).	died because of our sins (Rom. 4:25; 1 Pet. 2:24, 25).
will be our substitute (Isa. 53:6, 8).	died in our place (Rom. 5:6, 8; 2 Cor. 5:21).
will voluntarily accept our guilt and punishment (Isa. 53:7, 8).	was silent about our sin (Mark 15:4, 5; John 10:11; 19:30).
will be buried in a rich man's tomb (Isa. 53:9).	was buried in the tomb of Joseph, a rich man from Arimathea (Matt. 27:57–60; John 19:38–42).
will save us who believe in Him (Isa. 53:10, 11).	provided salvation for all who believe (John 3:16; Acts 16:31).
will die with transgressors (Isa. 53:12).	was numbered with the transgressors (Mark 15:27, 28; Luke 22:37).
will heal the brokenhearted (Isa. 61:1, 2).	healed the brokenhearted (Luke 4:18, 19).

PROMISE — a pledge to do or give something.

PRONOUNCE — to say or speak (Jer. 11:17, NKJV).

PROPHECY, PROPHESY — predictions about the future and the end times, or special messages from God, often delivered through a human spokesman (Mark 7:6).

PROPHET — a person who spoke for God and gave His message to God's chosen people—the nation of Israel (Mic. 1:1; Judg. 4:4; Acts 21:9).

PROPHETESS — a female prophet.

PROPITIATION [pro-pish´-e-a-shun] — the act of Jesus dying on the cross to pay the price for sin demanded by a holy God (1 John 2:2, NKJV; 4:10, NKJV).

PROSELYTE — a convert from one religious belief to another. In the New Testament, the term is used to describe Gentile converts who had committed themselves to the teachings of the Jewish faith (Matt. 23:15, NKJV; Acts 2:10, NKJV).

PROSTITUTE, PROSTITUTION — the act of having sexual relations outside of marriage, especially for money. Several words are used for a woman who participates in this type of activity, including harlot and whore (Hosea 3:3).

PROVE — to try; to test (Ps. 17:3, KJV; Luke 14:19, KJV).

PROVENDER — a grass-based animal food (Judg. 19:21, KJV).

PROVERB — a short, meaningful statement about human nature and life. In the Bible Solomon is known for his use of proverbs (1 Kings 4:32). His wisdom was shown by his ability to make clear, true statements about the nature of things. Proverbs are designed to make God's truth accessible to all people, so they can live their lives according to His will.

PROVERBS, BOOK OF — one of the "wisdom books" of the Old Testament, containing instructions on many of the practical matters of daily life. The Book of Proverbs points the believer to God with instructions on how to live a holy, upright life.

PROVIDENCE — the continuous activity of God in His creation by which He preserves and governs (Acts 24:2, KJV). The doctrine of providence affirms God's absolute lordship over His creation and confirms the dependence of all creation on the Creator. It is the denial of the idea that the universe is governed by chance or fate.

PROVINCE — an administrative district of the government or civil ruling authority. The word "province" is used only four times for rulers in Israel. All these occurrences come from the time of King Ahab (1 Kings 20:14–15, 17, 19, NKJV).

The other occurrences of the word refer to the administrative districts during the Babylonian and Persian rules (Ezra 2:1; 4:15; Neh. 1:3). The term occurs only twice in the New Testament (Acts 23:34, NKJV; 25:1, NKJV).

PROVOCATION — anything that provokes, excites, incites, or stimulates. The reference in Hebrews 3:8, 15 to "the provocation" (KJV), or "the rebellion" (NKJV, NIV), is a quotation from Psalm 95:7–11. This passage points back to a specific time when the Israelites provoked God by their rebellion against Moses during the Exodus (Exod. 17:1–7).

PRUDENT — smart; wise (Prov. 18:15, NKJV; Matt. 11:25, NKJV).

PRUNING HOOKS — small knives with curved blades used for pruning grapevines. The prophets Isaiah, Joel, and Micah spoke of pruning hooks in a way that allowed these knives to become symbols of peace (Isa. 2:4; Joel 3:10; Mic. 4:3).

PSALM — a song (Col. 3:16).

PSALMS, BOOK OF — a collection of prayers, poems, and hymns that focus the worshiper's thoughts on God in praise and adoration. Parts of this book were used as a hymnal in the worship services of ancient Israel.

PSEUDEPIGRAPHA [su-de-pig´-graph-ah] — a collection of Jewish books containing different kinds of literature that used the names of famous people in Israel's history for the titles of the books. The real authors are unknown.

PUBLICAN — a word for a tax collector (Matt. 9:10, KJV).

PUBLISH — to proclaim; to tell (Mark 1:45, KJV).

PUFFED UP — full of false pride (1 Cor. 4:6, NKJV).

PULPIT — a raised platform that could only be reached by steps, or a desk used for preaching and teaching in a worship service (Neh. 8:4; platform, ICB).

PURE — (See Chaste.)

PURGE — to remove the undesirable; to refine or free from impurities (Dan. 11:35, KJV; 1 Cor. 5:7, NKJV; Heb. 9:14, KJV).

PURIFICATION — the act of making clean and pure before God and people. The Mosaic Law gave instructions for both physical and spiritual purification.

PURIM [pur´-im] *(lots)* — a Jewish holiday observed on the fourteenth and fifteenth days of the month of Adar. This holiday happened a month before Passover to remind the Jews how Esther and Mordecai saved the Jewish people from being killed by Haman (Pur, Esther 3:7; 9:24–32).

PURPLE — a color that is a symbol for royalty (Acts 16:14).

Q

Q — the letter Q (from the German word *Quelle*, meaning "source") refers to a hypothetical document containing material that Matthew and Luke used as they wrote certain sections of their gospels. This document supposedly contained many sayings of Jesus. Not all scholars accept the existence of Q as an information source for these gospels.

QUAIL — a small bird. The Hebrew people probably ate dried, salted quail while they were slaves to the Egyptians. When they were hungry for meat in the Sinai desert, God promised He would provide enough meat for a month. He sent thousands of quail to their camp and the birds fell to the ground from exhaustion (Num. 11:31–34; Exod. 16:13; Ps. 105:40).

QUARRY — a huge opening in the ground where stone is cut, usually for building purposes. Archaeologists have discovered quarries throughout Palestine. In Old Testament times, there were quarries near Megiddo, Samaria, Jerusalem, and Ramat Rahel.

QUEEN — a female member of the royal house, either the wife of a king or a woman who ruled by her own power. The word usually means an actual ruler, like the queen of Sheba (1 Kings 10) or Candace, the queen of the

Photo by Howard Vos

This massive cut stone was never removed from an ancient quarry at the Phoenician city of Baalbek, perhaps because of its weight and size.

Cave Four at Qumran, where hundreds of Dead Sea Scrolls were discovered, is visible at the upper right. The Dead Sea looms in the background.

Ethiopians (Acts 8:27). Sometimes the word is used as a reference to the king's favorite wife, like with both Queen Vashti and Queen Esther (Esther 1–2).

QUICK, QUICKEN — the KJV translation of several Hebrew and Greek words translated by the NKJV as "alive" (Ps. 55:15), "living" (Acts 10:42), "revive" (Ps. 119:25), and "gives life to" (John 5:21).

QUIRINIUS [kwy-ren´-e-us] — a Roman governor of Syria at the time of Jesus' birth (Luke 2:1–5; Cyrenius, KJV).

QUIVER — when used as a noun it is a pouch for carrying arrows (Lam. 3:13, NKJV); when used as a verb it means to tremble or shake (Hab. 3:16, NKJV).

QUMRAN, KHIRBET [koom´-rahn, kir´-bet] — an ancient ruin on the northwestern shore of the Dead Sea. In 1947 a wandering goatherder looking for his goats in the caves above the dry riverbed of Qumran found several large jars. The jars contained the ancient scrolls that are now known as the Dead Sea Scrolls.

R

RABBI [rab´-bi], RABBONI [rab-bo´-ni] *(my teacher)* — a title of honor and respect given by the Jews to a doctor (teacher) of the Law (John 1:38; 20:16). Today rabbi means a Jew trained for professional religious leadership.

RABSHAKEH, THE [rab´-sha-keh] *(chief cupbearer)* — the title of an Assyrian military official under Sennacherib, king of Assyria (2 Kings 18:17–37, NKJV; Isa. 36:2–22, NKJV).

RACA [ra´-cah] *(stupid)* — a disrespectful comment (Matt. 5:22, NKJV). The word appears often in the writings of the Jewish rabbis with the meaning of "ignorant, senseless, or empty-headed." To say "Raca" to a person was like saying, "You idiot!"

RACHEL [ra´-chel] *(lamb)* — the younger daughter of Laban. Rachel was the second wife of Jacob and the mother of Joseph and Benjamin.

RAHAB [ra´-hab] — a harlot of Jericho who hid two Hebrew spies and helped them escape. She became an ancestor of David and Jesus (Josh. 2:1–21; 6:17–25; Matt. 1:5).

RAHAB THE DRAGON [ra´-hab] — a mythological sea monster or dragon that represented the evil forces of chaos that God subdued by His creative power. The name Rahab as it occurs in Job 9:13, Job 26:12, Isaiah 30:7, and Isaiah 51:9 has no connection with the personal name of Rahab, the harlot of Jericho (Josh. 2:1–21). The references to Rahab in the books of Job, Psalms, and Isaiah, refer to an evil power overcome by God.

Ancient tomb near Bethlehem, traditionally identified as the burial place of Rachel (Gen. 48:2, 7).

Photo by Howard Vos

RAIL — to criticize; to scold. Also, "revile" (2 Chron. 32:17, NKJV; 1 Sam. 25:14, NKJV), "blasphemed" (Mark 15:29, NKJV; Luke 23:39, NKJV), "reviling" (1 Tim. 6:4, NKJV; 1 Pet. 3:9, NKJV), and "reviler" (1 Cor. 5:11, NKJV).

RAIMENT — clothing (Gen. 24:53, KJV; Matt. 3:4, KJV).

RAINBOW — a colorful arch in the sky. A rainbow happens when light passes through moisture in the air. The most important reference to the rainbow in the Bible occurs in Genesis 9:13–17, where the rainbow serves as a sign of God's covenant with Noah.

RAM [ramm] *(high, exalted)* — a male goat used in sacrifices (Gen. 15:9, NKJV). A ram is also a weapon and the name of three men in the Bible.

RAMA [ra´-mah], **RAMAH** [ra´-mah] (*height*) — the name of six cities in the Old Testament. The two most important cities were:
1. Ramah of Benjamin, a city given to the tribe of Benjamin (Josh. 18:25).
2. Ramah of Ephraim, a city where the prophet Samuel was born, lived, and was buried (1 Sam. 7:17; 19:18–23; 28:3).

RAMESES, RAAMSES [ram´-ah-seez, ram´-seez] *(the god Ra has fathered a son)* — the royal city of the Egyptian kings of the 19th and 20th dynasties (about 1300–1100 B.C.) located in the northeastern section of the Nile Delta. While the people of Israel were slaves in Egypt, they were forced to build the cities of Pithom and Raamses (Exod. 1:11).

RAMPART — a fortification consisting of an elevation or embankment often provided with a wall to protect soldiers. A rampart was used as a protective barrier against an attacking army. The Hebrew word translated as rampart (Lam. 2:8, NKJV; Nah. 3:8, NKJV) means encirclement.

RAPTURE — a reference to the concept of Christians joining Christ upon His glorious return (Mark 13:26–27; 1 Thess. 4:16–17).

RASH — impulsive; a quick thoughtless act (Eccles. 5:2, NKJV).

Photo by Howard Vos

The modern village of Ramah, successor to the Old Testament city where the prophet Samuel was born and buried.

REAP, REAPING — the practice of harvesting grain.

REAR — to raise, like to raise a child (2 Kings 10;1, NKJV).

REBECCA [re-bek´-kah], **REBEKAH** [re-bek´-kah] — the wife of Isaac and the mother of Esau and Jacob.

REBUKE — strong disapproval (Isa. 25:8, NKJV).

RECHAB, RECAB [re´-kab] *(charioteer)* — the name of three men in the Old Testament:

1. A son of Rimmon, a Benjamite from Beeroth (2 Sam. 4:2, 5, 9).

2. The father of Jehonadab (2 Kings 10:15, 23). Jehonadab helped Jehu in his fight against Baal worshipers.

3. The father of Malchijah (Neh. 3:14). Malchijah helped Nehemiah rebuild the wall of Jerusalem.

RECKON — to consider; to count (Rom. 4:4, KJV).

RECOMPENSE — a payback or reward (Ruth 2:12, KJV; Luke 14:14, KJV).

RECONCILE, RECONCILIATION — the Bible teaches that God and mankind are separated from one another because of God's holiness and human sinfulness. The process by which God and people are brought together again is called reconciliation. God loves the sinner (Rom. 5:8, KJV), but it is impossible for Him not to judge sin (Heb. 10:27, KJV).

RECORD — witness (John 1:19, KJV).

RECOUNT — to call; to summon (Nah. 2:5, KJV).

RED HEIFER — a young cow "without blemish" that was slaughtered outside the camp of the Israelites and then burned in the fire. Its

A rocky shore along the Red Sea, at a point north of where the Israelites crossed during the Exodus (Exod. 14).

ashes were to be used in the water for the purification ceremony for uncleanness. The need for purification from uncleanness would arise when a person touched a corpse, a human bone, or a grave (Num. 19:2–17, NKJV).

RED SEA — a narrow body of water that stretches in a southeasterly direction from Suez to the Gulf of Aden for about thirteen hundred miles.

REDEEM — to buy back; to pay for (Gal. 3:13).

REDEMPTION — deliverance by payment of a price. In the New Testament, redemption refers to salvation from sin, death, and the wrath of God by Christ's sacrifice. In the Old Testament, redemption refers to redemption by a kinsman (Lev. 25:24, 51–52, NKJV), rescue or deliverance (Num. 3:49, NKJV), and ransom (Ps. 111:9, NKJV).

REED — a plant used to make baskets and paper (Matt. 27:30, NKJV).

REEL — to wobble like a drunken person (Isa. 24:20, NKJV).

REFINE — to separate pure metal from the impurities in the ore in the smelting process. This procedure is spoken of in the Old Testament as a symbol of God's purification of the nation of Israel when he sent hardship and affliction upon them as punishment for their sins (Jer. 9:7, NKJV; Zech. 13:9, NKJV).

REFRAIN — to keep from doing; to stay away from (Acts 5:38, KJV).

REFUGE — a safe place (Ps. 46:1, NKJV).

REGENERATION — the spiritual change that happens in a person's life because of an act of God. A person's sinful nature is changed, and they are able to respond to God in faith.

REGISTER — a written record (Ezra 2:62, NKJV).

REHOBOAM [re-ho-bo´-am] *(the people is enlarged)* — the son of Solomon and the last king of the united monarchy and first king of the southern kingdom, Judah (reigned about 931–913 B.C.). His mother was Naamah, a woman of Ammon (1 Kings 14:31).

REIGN — to rule (Matt. 2:22, NKJV).

RELIEF — aid; help; assistance (Acts 11:29, NKJV).

RELIGION, RELIGIOUS — belief in and reverence for God or some supernatural power that is recognized as the creator and ruler of the universe; an organized system of doctrine with an approved pattern of behavior and a proper form of worship.

REMISSION — release from sin (Acts 2:38, NKJV; Heb. 9:22, NKJV).

REMNANT — the part of a community or nation that remains after a dreadful judgment or devastating calamity and forms a new community (Isa. 10:20–23, NKJV).

REND, RENT — to tear or pull apart. In the ancient world, rending one's garments was a sign of grief, despair, or sorrow. To "rend your heart" (Joel 2:13, NKJV) signified inward, spiritual repentance and sorrow for sin. God's pri-

The Preservation of the Remnant

In the eighth century B.C., Amos prophesied Israel's doom (8:1, 2), but he also declared the possibility of deliverance for the "remnant of Joseph" (5:15). Throughout history God has always preserved a remnant of His people, as the following chart shows.

People or Group	Reference
Noah and family in the Flood	Gen. 7:1
Joseph in Egypt during the famine	Gen. 45:7
Israel to their homeland	Deut. 4:27–31
7,000 who had not worshiped Baal	1 Kings 19:18
Portion of Judah after captivity	Isa. 10:20–23
Remnant to Zion	Mic. 2:12, 13
The church—both Jews and Gentiles	Rom. 9:22–27

mary requirement from sinners is "a broken and a contrite heart" (Ps. 51:17, KJV).

RENDER — to pay; to return (Matt. 22:21).

RENOWN — fame (Ezek. 16:14).

REPENTANCE — a turning away from sin, disobedience, or rebellion and a turning back to God. Generally, repentance means a change of mind or a feeling of sorrow or regret for past behavior. True repentance is a "godly sorrow" for sin. It is an act of turning around and going in the opposite direction. This type of repentance leads a person to a closer relationship to God (Matt. 3:2; 4:17; Mark 1:15; Luke 15:7, 10).

REPHIDIM [ref´-i-dim] — an Israelite camp in the wilderness (Exod. 17:1–7). The Amalekites attacked the Israelites at Rephidim (Exod. 17:8–16). During the battle, Moses stood on a hill and held the rod of God high up in the air. Aaron and Hur helped him by holding his arms up until sundown. The Israelites won the battle at Rephidim.

REPORT — testimony (Acts 6:3, KJV).

REPROACH — to scorn; to rebuke; to shame (1 Tim. 3:7, NKJV).

REPROBATE — a person who fails to pass a test and is rejected. While the word "reprobate" only appears in the KJV, it speaks strongly against the people who God has rejected and left to their own corruption (Rom. 1:28).

REPROVE — convict (John 16:8, KJV).

REQUITE — repay (1 Tim. 5:4, KJV).

RESIDUE — that which remains; left over (Acts 15:17, KJV).

165

RESOLVED — figured out (Luke 16:4, NKJV).

RESPECT OF PERSONS — showing favoritism or partiality toward certain people (Acts 10:34, KJV; James 2:1, KJV).

RESPITE — relief; rest (Exod. 8:15).

RESTITUTION — the act of restoring to the rightful owner something that has been taken away, stolen, lost, or surrendered. Leviticus 6:1–7 gives the Mosaic Law of restitution. This law tells the rules to be followed in restoring stolen property.

RESURRECTION — being raised from the dead. Resurrection refers to individuals who have been brought back to life (resuscitated) in this present world (Matt. 22:23).

RESURRECTION OF JESUS CHRIST — a central doctrine of Christianity that affirms that God raised Jesus from the dead on the third day. Without the resurrection, the apostle Paul declared, Christian preaching and belief are meaningless (1 Cor. 15:14). The resurrection is the point at which God's intention for Jesus becomes clear (Rom. 1:4), and believers are assured that Jesus is the Christ.

REUBEN [ru´-ben] *(behold a son)* — the firstborn son of Jacob and Leah (Gen. 29:31–32; 35:23).

The Seven Churches of Revelation

	Commendation	Criticism	Instruction	Promise
Ephesus (2:1–7)	Rejects evil, perseveres, has patience	Love for Christ no longer fervent	Do the works you did at first	The tree of life
Smyrna (2:8–11)	Gracefully bears suffering	None	Be faithful until death	The crown of life
Pergamos (2:12–17)	Keeps the faith of Christ	Tolerates immorality, idolatry, and heresies	Repent	Hidden manna and a stone with a new name
Thyatira (2:18–29)	Love, service, faith, patience is greater than at first	Tolerates cult of idolatry and immorality	Judgment coming; keep the faith	Rule over nations and receive morning star
Sardis (3:1–6)	Some have kept the faith	A dead church	Repent; strengthen what remains	Faithful honored and clothed in white
Philadelphia (3:7–13)	Perseveres in the faith	None	Keep the faith	A place in God's presence, a new name, and the New Jerusalem
Laodicea (3:14–22)	None	Indifferent	Be zealous and repent	Share Christ's throne

Photo by Howard Vos

St. Paul's Harbor at Rhodes where Paul's ship landed on its way back to Palestine after his third missionary journey (Acts 21:1).

REVELATION — God's communication to people concerning Himself, His moral standards, and His plan of salvation (Rom. 1:1–3).

REVELATION OF JOHN — the last book of the Bible.

The whole theme of the Book of Revelation is that God will have the ultimate victory in the fight between Him and Satan. God and Satan are not equal. God is stronger than Satan. Satan only continues his plans to make trouble because God allows him to do so. At the final battle, Satan and his followers will be completely destroyed by fire from heaven (20:7–10).

REVERENCE — a strong feeling of awe and respect. God's majesty and holiness cause a feeling of reverence in those who worship and serve Him (Heb. 12:28–29, NKJV).

REVILE — to insult; despise (John 9:28, NKJV).

REVIVE — to bring back to life (Neh. 4:2, NKJV; Rom. 14:9, NKJV).

REVOLT — to rebel against (2 Kings 8:20, NKJV).

REWARD — something offered in return for a service. In the Bible, a reward can refer to something given for either a good or bad act. The psalmist writes about "a reward for the righteous" (Ps. 58:11) as well as "the reward of the wicked" (Ps. 91:8, NKJV). When the Son of Man returns in glory, "He will reward each according to his works" (Matt. 16:27).

REZIN [re´-zin] — the last king of Syria who was killed by Tiglath–Pileser III, king of Assyria, in 732 B.C.

A man who started the family of Nethinim, or temple servants was also named Rezin. His descendants returned from the Captivity with Zerubbabel (Ezra 2:48).

RHODA [ro´-dah] *(rose)* — a servant girl in the home of Mary (John Mark's mother) (Acts 12:13). When the apostle Peter was released from prison, he went to Mary's house. Rhoda answered the door and was so surprised and excited, that instead of letting him in, she ran to tell the others in the house. Peter had to keep knocking on the door until someone finally let him in (Acts 12:16).

RHODES [rodes] *(a rose)* — a city on a large island in the Aegean Sea visited by the apostle Paul (Acts 21:1). The city of Rhodes was an important commercial (business), cultural (art), and tourist center for the Greeks as well as the Romans.

RIGHTEOUS — right with God (Mal. 3:18, NKJV).

RIGHTEOUSNESS — holy and upright living, in accordance with God's standard. The word "righteousness" comes from a root word that means "straightness." It refers to a state that conforms to an authoritative standard. Righteousness is a moral concept. God's character is the definition and source of all righteousness (Gen. 18:25, NKJV; Deut. 32:4, NKJV). Therefore, the righteousness of human beings is defined in terms of God's.

RIMMONO [rim´-mon-o] *(pomegranate)* — the name of two towns (Josh. 19:7; Josh. 19:13; 1 Chron. 6:77), a large rock (Judg. 20:45, 47), a man (2 Sam. 4:1–12).

RIZPAH [riz´-pah] — a daughter of Aiah who became a concubine of King Saul (2 Sam.

Photo by Gustav Jeeninga

Ruins of the Forum in the city of Rome. The Forum was the meetingplace, marketplace, and religious and political center of the Roman Empire's capital city.

3:7; 21:8, 10–11). She had two sons named Armoni and Mephibosheth.

ROBE — a cloak (John 19:2).

ROD — a staff, pole, or stick with many uses (Exod. 4:2, NKJV; Exod. 21:20, NKJV; 1 Sam. 14:27, NKJV).

ROE, ROEBUCK — a small deer (Deut. 12:15, KJV).

ROMANS, EPISTLE TO THE — the most formal of Paul's letters. The main theme of Romans is that righteousness comes as a free gift from God and is received by faith alone.

ROME, CITY OF — the capital city of the ancient Roman Empire. Rome is also the capital of modern Italy.

ROOT — the part of a plant that provides stability and nourishment (food) for the plant. Most of the references to roots in the Bible are symbolic. As a metaphor, to be rooted means to be established; to be uprooted means to be displaced.

RUDDY — a healthy, reddish color. In two places in the Bible the word refers to the rosy complexion of vigorous health (Song of Sol. 5:10, NKJV; Lam. 4:7, NKJV). As a boy, David was also described as ruddy (1 Sam. 16:12, NKJV; 17:42, NKJV). Some scholars believe this meant that David had red hair.

RUSH — a plant (Isa. 9:14, KJV). (See Bulrush.)

RUTH [rooth] *(friendship)* — the mother of Obed and great-grandmother of David. Ruth was from the country of Moab. She married Mahlon, a son of Elimelech and Naomi. Elimelech, his wife, and sons had migrated to Moab to escape a famine in the land of Israel. When Elimelech and both of his sons died, they left three widows: Naomi, Ruth, and Orpah (Ruth's sister-in-law). When Naomi decided to return home to Bethlehem, Ruth chose to go with her.

RUTH, BOOK OF — a short Old Testament book about Ruth of Moab. She was a devoted Gentile woman who became an ancestor of King David.

Ruth's life is a beautiful example of the providence of God. The name Ruth means "friendship," and this book gives one of the most touching examples of friendship in the Bible.

Ruth's words to her mother-in-law are quoted often as a pledge of love and devotion. "Don't ask me to leave you! Don't beg me not to follow you! Every place you go, I will go. Every place you live, I will live. Your people will be my people. Your God will be my God" (1:16).

S

SABBATH [sab´-bath] — the practice of observing one day in seven as a time for rest and worship. This practice apparently started in creation, because God created the universe in six days and rested on the seventh (Gen. 1–2:1–3).

SACKCLOTH — a rough, coarse cloth, or a baglike garment made of this cloth and worn as a symbol of mourning or repentance (Gen. 37:34, NKJV; Joel 1:8, NKJV; Esther 4:1–4, NKJV; Job 16:15, NKJV; 1 Kings 21:27, NKJV).

SACRIFICE — the ritual through which the Hebrew people offered the blood or the flesh of an animal to God as a substitute payment for their sin. Sacrifice and sacrificing started in the Garden of Eden soon after the first sin (fall of man).

SADDUCEES [sad´-du-sees] — the members of a Jewish faction (group) that opposed (was against) Jesus. The Sadducees did not believe in bodily resurrection. They came from the leading families of the nation—the priests, merchants, and aristocrats. The high priests and the most powerful members of the priesthood were mainly Sadducees (Acts 5:17).

SAINTS — the people who have been separated from the world and consecrated (set apart) to the worship and service of God.

Sacrificial altar for wine and fruit at the Nabatean city of Petra in southern Canaan.

Believers are called "saints" (Rom. 1:7, NKJV) and "saints in Christ Jesus" (Phil. 1:1, NKJV) because they belong to the One who provided their sanctification.

SALVATION — deliverance from the power of sin; redemption.

In the Old Testament, the word "salvation" sometimes refers to deliverance from danger (Jer. 15:20, NKJV), deliverance of the weak from an oppressor (Ps. 35:9–10, NKJV), the healing of sickness (Isa. 38:20, NKJV), and deliverance from bloodguiltiness and its consequences (Ps. 51:14, NKJV). It may also refer to national deliverance from a military threat (Exod. 14:13, NKJV) or release from captivity (Ps. 14:7, NKJV). But salvation finds its deepest meaning in the spiritual realm of life. Our need for salvation is one of the clearest teachings of the Bible.

SAMARIA, CITY OF [sa-ma´-re-ah] *(lookout)* — the capital city of the northern kingdom of Israel built about 880 B.C. by Omri, the sixth king of Israel (1 Kings 16:24).

SAMARITANS [sa-mar´-i-tans] — the people who were born in or who lived in Samaria, a territory in central Canaan.

SAMUEL [sam´-u-el] *(name of God)* — a great Hebrew prophet and the last judge of Israel. Samuel led his people against the Philistines. When he was an old man, Samuel anointed Saul as the first king of Israel and later anointed David to be king after Saul. Samuel is recognized as one of the greatest leaders of Israel (Jer. 15:1; Heb. 11:32).

SAMUEL, BOOKS OF — two historical books of the Old Testament that tell about the nation of Israel's transition (change) from a tribal form of government to a united kingship under Saul and David. The books are named for the prophet Samuel, who anointed Saul and David.

SANCTIFICATION — the process of God's grace by which the believer is separated from sin and becomes dedicated to God's righteousness. Holiness, or purification from the guilt and power of sin, happen when sanctification is accomplished by the Word of God (John 17:7) and the Holy Spirit (Rom. 8:3–4).

SANCTIFY — to set apart (Gen. 2:3, NKJV); to dedicate for God's use (Exod. 13:2, NKJV).

SANHEDRIN [san´-he-drin] — the highest ruling body and court of justice for the Jewish people during the time of Jesus.

SAPPHIRA [saf-fi´-rah] — a dishonest woman who was married to Ananias. She

Photo by Howard Vos

A fragment of 1 Samuel 23:9–16 discovered at Qumran. It dates from the third century B.C.

Photo by Howard Vos

These copper scrolls were discovered among the Dead Sea Scrolls at Qumran. Most scrolls in ancient times were written on papyrus, parchment, or leather.

and her husband agreed to share everything with the early Christian community, but they didn't honor their agreement and lied about keeping some of the things they were supposed to share. They died because of their bad behavior (Acts 5:1–11). Death may seem like a severe punishment, but it clearly shows the need and importance for absolute honesty in all our dealings with God.

SARAH, SARAI [sa´-rah, sa´-rahee] *(noble lady)* — the wife of Abraham, and the mother of Isaac. Sarah's name was originally Sarai, but God changed it to Sarah at the same time he changed Abram's name to Abraham. Asher also had a daughter named Sarah (Num. 26:46, KJV; Serah, ICB).

SATAN [sa´-tun] *(adversary)* — the great adversary of God and humankind. Satan is the name of the devil.

SAUL [sawl] *(asked [of God])* — the name of three men in the Bible:

1. The sixth of the ancient kings of Edom (Gen. 36:36–38; 1 Chron. 1:48–49).

2. The first king of Israel (1 Sam. 9:2–31:12; 1 Chron. 5:10–26:28).

3. The original name of Paul, a persecutor of the church, who became an apostle of Christ and a missionary of the early church (Acts 7:58–9:26; 11:25–13:9).

SAVIOR — a person who rescues others from evil, danger, or destruction. In the Old Testament, people saw God as the Savior (Isa. 45:21).

In the New Testament the word for "savior" describes both God the Father (1 Tim. 1:1; Jude 25) and Jesus Christ the Son (Acts 5:31; Phil. 3:20). The apostles rejoiced that in Christ, God had become the "Savior of all people" (1 Tim. 4:10). He was the Savior of Gentiles as well as Jews. As Christians, we are taught to "grow in the grace and knowledge of our Lord and Savior Jesus Christ" (2 Pet. 3:18).

SCAPEGOAT — a live goat over whose head Aaron confessed all the sins of the people of Israel. The goat was then sent into the wilderness on the Day of Atonement, symbolically taking away their sins (Lev. 16:8, 10, 26, NKJV; Azazel, NRSV).

SCROLL — a roll of papyrus, leather, or parchment that ancient documents were written on (Ezra 6:2). Rolled up on a stick, a scroll was usually about thirty-five feet long. The Book of Luke or the Book of Acts would have fit on one scroll; longer books of the Bible would have needed two or more scrolls.

SECURITY OF THE BELIEVER — the "once saved, always saved" concept taught from the Bible (Rom. 8:38–39; Phil. 1:6). Denominations have different opinions about this subject.

SELAH [se´-lah] — a word found seventy-one times in the Book of Psalms. Scholars agree that the word is a musical direction of some sort, but they do not agree on what the direction is. It may mean: (1) an interlude—a pause in the singing while the orchestra continues; (2) the equivalent of today's "Amen"; as such it would separate psalms or sections of psalms which have different liturgical purposes; or (3) an acrostic that means "a change of voices" or "repeat."

SEMITES — the descendants of Noah's son, Shem. This included the people of Assyria (Gen. 5:32; Luke 3:36).

SEPTUAGINT — a Bible translation where the Old Testament was translated from Hebrew into Greek for the benefit of the Greek-speaking Jews in Alexandria, Egypt. These Jews had used the Greek language for so long, they forgot their Palestinian language (Hebrew).

This translation (version) is called the Septuagint, from the Latin word for seventy because of the seventy elders of Israel who were brought to Alexandria specifically for the purpose of translating the Pentateuch into Greek.

SEPULCHER, SEPULCHRE — a tomb (Matt. 27:61, KJV).

SERAPHIM [ser´-a-fim] *(fiery, burning ones)* — angelic or heavenly beings associated with Isaiah's vision of God in the temple when he was called to his ministry (Isa. 6:1–7, NKJV).

Names of Satan		
1. Accuser	Opposes believers before God	Rev. 12:10
2. Adversary	Against God	1 Pet. 5:8
3. Beelzebub	Lord of the fly	Matt. 12:24
4. Belial	Worthless	2 Cor. 6:15
5. Devil	Slanderer	Matt. 4:1
6. Dragon	Destructive	Rev. 12:3, 7, 9
7. Enemy	Opponent	Matt. 13:28
8. Evil one	Intrinsically evil	John 17:15
9. God of this age	Influences wordly thinking	2 Cor. 4:4
10. Liar	Distorts the truth	John 8:44
11. Murderer	Leads people to eternal death	John 8:44
12. Prince of the power of the air	Control of unbelievers	Eph. 2:2
13. Roaring lion	One who destroys	1 Pet. 5:8
14. Ruler of demons	Leader of fallen angels	Mark 3:22
15. Ruler of this world	Rules in world system	John 12:31
16. Satan	Adversary	1 Tim. 5:15
17. Serpent of old	Deceiver in garden	Rev. 12:9; 20:2
18. Tempter	Encourages people to sin	1 Thess. 3:5

SERPENT — a crawling reptile, or snake, often associated in the Bible with temptation, sin, and evil. A serpent is the Bible's first—and last—animal villain (Gen. 3, NKJV; Rev. 20:2, NKJV).

SERVANT — a slave (Rom. 1:1).

SETH [seth] *(appoint, compensate)* — the third son of Adam and Eve, born after Cain murdered Abel (Gen. 4:25–26; 5:3–8; Sheth, KJV). Seth was the father of Enosh (or Enos) and an ancestor of Jesus Christ (Luke 3:38). He died at the age of 912.

SHADRACH [sha´-drak] *(command of [the god] Aku)* — the name that Ashpenaz gave to Hananiah (Dan. 1:7; 3:12–30).

Shadrach was one of the three faithful Jews who refused to bow down and worship the golden idols of King Nebuchadnezzar (Dan. 3:1). Along with his two friends, Meshach and Abednego, he was thrown into "the burning fiery furnace," but they were kept safe from harm by the power of God (Dan. 3).

SHEKEL — a unit of measure (Exod. 30:23–24, NKJV). (See Weights and Measures of the Bible.)

SHEKINAH [she-ki´-nah] *(dwelling)* — a visible manifestation of the presence of God (also spelled Shechinah and Shekhinah). Although the word is not found in the Bible, it occurs frequently in later Jewish writings.

SHEMA, THE [she-mah´] *(hear thou)* — the Jewish confession of faith that begins, "Hear, O Israel: The Lord our God, the LORD is one!" (Deut. 6:4, KJV). The complete Shema is found in three passages from the Old Testament: Numbers 15:37–41, Deuteronomy 6:4–9 and 11:13–21.

SHEOL [she´-ol] — the abode (place) of the dead. Sheol is the Hebrew equivalent of the Greek *Hades,* which means "the unseen world."

SHOWBREAD — holy or consecrated (blessed) bread placed in the sanctuary of the tabernacle or temple every Sabbath as a symbol of God's presence and provision for the people. The ritual always involved twelve loaves of bread, representing the twelve tribes of the nation of Israel.

SIN — lawlessness (1 John 3:4) or transgression of God's will, either by omitting to do what God's law requires or by doing what it forbids. The transgression can occur in thought (1 John 3:15), word (Matt. 5:22), or deed (Rom. 1:32).

SIN OFFERING — an offering given out of repentance (Lev. 4:2–35).

SINAI [si´-nai] — the name of a peninsula, a wilderness, and a mountain in the Bible.

SOLEMN ASSEMBLY — a day during a festival (feast) set aside to devote one's self to God and be humble (Lev. 23:36). It is different from the Sabbath.

SOLOMON [sol´-o-mon] *(peaceful)* — the first king of Israel to trade commercial goods with other nations to make money. He was also the builder of the temple in Jerusalem and the author of most of the Book of Proverbs. He is

Solomon's Empire

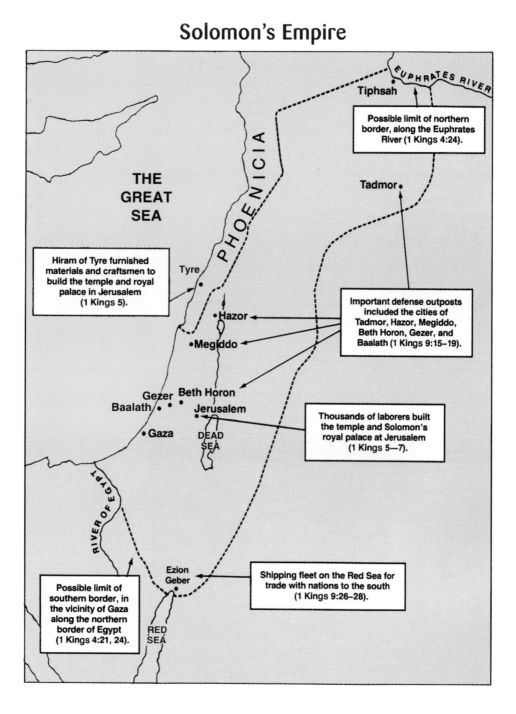

THE GREAT SEA

PHOENICIA

EUPHRATES RIVER

Tiphsah

Possible limit of northern border, along the Euphrates River (1 Kings 4:24).

Tadmor

Hiram of Tyre furnished materials and craftsmen to build the temple and royal palace in Jerusalem (1 Kings 5).

Tyre

Hazor

Megiddo

Important defense outposts included the cities of Tadmor, Hazor, Megiddo, Beth Horon, Gezer, and Baalath (1 Kings 9:15–19).

Gezer   Beth Horon
Baalath   Jerusalem

Thousands of laborers built the temple and Solomon's royal palace at Jerusalem (1 Kings 5—7).

Gaza

DEAD SEA

RIVER OF EGYPT

Ezion Geber

Shipping fleet on the Red Sea for trade with nations to the south (1 Kings 9:26–28).

Possible limit of southern border, in the vicinity of Gaza along the northern border of Egypt (1 Kings 4:21, 24).

RED SEA

Solomon's Twelve Districts

King Solomon set up a greatly improved administrative plan for Israel. This was needed because he maintained a large standing army, carried out many large building projects, and had a great number of helpers in his palace. He added some official positions to those established by King David. One of these new positions was the "chief of the prefects," who presided over **twelve districts** that Solomon had created. The district governors, or prefects, collected taxes and the temple tithe, supplied the royal court with food for one month of the year, and helped with the building **projects** and with the army (1 Kings 4:1–19).

Thus, our modern management principles of delegation of **authority** and responsibility were used by early rulers of Judah and Israel.

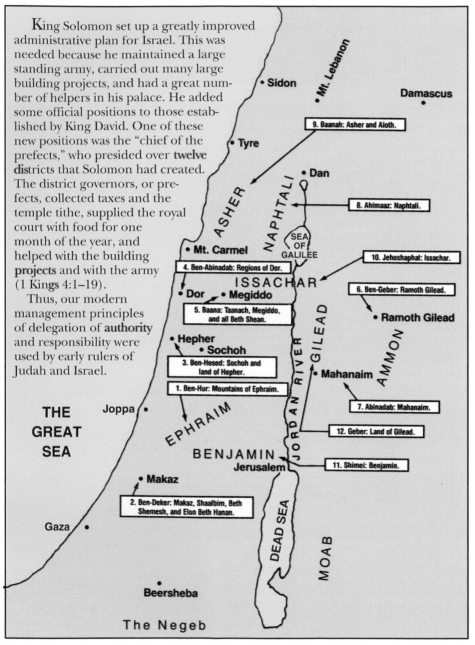

- Sidon

Mt. Lebanon

Damascus

9. Baanah: Asher and Aloth.

- Tyre

- Dan

ASHER

NAPHTALI

8. Ahimaaz: Naphtali.

SEA OF GALILEE

- Mt. Carmel

4. Ben-Abinadab: Regions of Dor.

ISSACHAR

10. Jehoshaphat: Issachar.

- Dor   - Megiddo

6. Ben-Geber: Ramoth Gilead.

5. Baana: Taanach, Megiddo, and all Beth Shean.

GILEAD

- Ramoth Gilead

- Hepher
  - Sochoh

AMMON

3. Ben-Hesed: Sochoh and land of Hepher.

JORDAN RIVER

- Mahanaim

1. Ben-Hur: Mountains of Ephraim.

7. Abinadab: Mahanaim.

THE GREAT SEA

Joppa -

EPHRAIM

12. Geber: Land of Gilead.

BENJAMIN

11. Shimei: Benjamin.

Jerusalem

- Makaz

DEAD SEA

MOAB

2. Ben-Deker: Makaz, Shaalbim, Beth Shemesh, and Elon Beth Hanan.

Gaza -

- Beersheba

The Negeb

also believed to be the author of the Song of Solomon and the Book of Ecclesiastes.

SONG OF SOLOMON, THE — an Old Testament book written in the form of a love song. Some people believe this song is speaking symbolically about the love of God for the nation of Israel. Other people say it is an example of romantic love between a man and a woman.

The message of the Song of Solomon is the beauty of love between a man and a woman as experienced in the relationship of marriage. The song praises the mutual love that a husband and wife feel toward each other in this highest of all human relationships.

The physical side of marriage is a natural and proper part of God's plan. God's plan didn't change—this is the same truth presented at the beginning of time. God created man and woman and brought them together to share their lives with one another and start a family (Gen. 2:24).

SOUTHERN KINGDOM — the tribes of Judah and Benjamin (1 Kings 14:19–30).

SOVEREIGNTY OF GOD — a term that refers to the unlimited power of God (Isa. 45:9–19; Rom. 8:18–39).

SPAN — the distance between the extended thumb and the little finger (Exod. 28:16, NKJV). (See Weights and Measures of the Bible.)

SPIRIT — a word with three distinct meanings in the Bible:

1. A general reference to the spirit of human beings (Matt. 5:3; Rom. 8:16; Heb. 4:12).

2. Good and evil spirits—a reference to beings other than God and humans. An example of a good spirit is an angel; an example of an evil spirit is a demon (Mark 9:25; Acts 19:12–17; Rev. 18:2).

3. The word "spirit" also refers to the Spirit of God, known as the Holy Spirit.

SPIRITUAL — of the spirit, not physical. The word "spiritual" refers to nonmaterial things, including a spiritual body (1 Cor. 15:44–46) and spiritual things as distinct from earthly things (Rom. 15:27; 1 Cor. 9:11). But the most

New Testament Lists of Spiritual Gifts

Rom. 12:6–8	1 Cor. 12:8–10	1 Cor. 12:28–30	Eph. 4:11	1 Pet. 4:9–11
Prophecy	Word of Wisdom	Apostleship	Apostleship	Speaking
Serving	Word of Knowledge	Prophecy	Prophecy	Serving
Teaching	Faith	Teaching	Evangelism	
Exhortation	Healings	Miracles	Pastor/Teacher	
Giving	Miracles	Healing		
Leading	Prophecy	Helping		
Showing Mercy	Discerning of Spirits	Administrating		
	Tongues	Tongues		
	Interpretation of Tongues	Interpretation of Tongues		

important use of the word is in reference to the Holy Spirit. The Spirit gave the law (Rom. 7:14) and supplied Israel with water and food (1 Cor. 10:3–4).

SPIRITUAL GIFTS — special gifts given to Christians by the Holy Spirit for the purpose of building up the church. The list of spiritual gifts in 1 Corinthians 12:8–10 includes wisdom, knowledge, faith, healing, miracles, prophecy, discerning of spirits, speaking in tongues, and interpretation of tongues.

STATUTE — a decree or law issued by a ruler or governing body, especially by God who is the supreme ruler (Gen. 26:5, NKJV; Ps. 18:22, NKJV; Ezek. 5:6, NKJV).

STEPHEN [ste´-ven] — one of the first seven deacons of the early church and the first Christian martyr. The story of Stephen is found in Acts 6:7–7:60.

STEWARD, STEWARDSHIP — a person who manages money or property for another; the management of another person's property, finances, or household affairs. For a Christian, stewardship involves the responsibility of managing God's work through the church (1 Cor. 9:17, NKJV).

SUBJECT — obedient to (Luke 2:51, NKJV); under control of (Heb. 2:15, NKJV).

SUBMISSION, SUBMIT — to yield or give in; can be by force or voluntary (Eph. 5:21, NKJV; James 4:7, NKJV).

SUFFER, SUFFERING — agony; affliction; distress; intense pain or sorrow. Suffering has been part of the human experience since people fell into sin (Gen. 3).

SUPPLICATION — to request (ask) humbly and earnestly (sincerely), usually in the form of prayer (Job 8:5, NKJV).

SWADDLE — to wrap in swaddling clothes.

Photo by Gustav Jeeninga

A synagogue at Masada. The synagogue was a place of worship, instruction, teaching of Scripture, and prayer for the Jewish people (Acts 13:13–15).

Photo by Gustav Jeeninga

Remains of a synagogue at Capernaum. It was probably built during the third or fourth century A.D.

These were long, narrow strips of cloth wrapped around a newborn infant. This was believed to help the child properly develop. Swaddling was a mark of parental love and care, while the need for swaddling was a symbol for the humble, dependent position of the newborn child (Job 38:9, NKJV; Ezek. 16:4, NKJV; Luke 2:7, 12, NKJV).

SYCAMORE — a large tree good for climbing (Luke 19:4) but probably not the same as a modern-day sycamore tree.

SYNAGOGUE [syn´-a-gog] — a congregation of Jews for worship or religious study. The word "synagogue" comes from the Greek *synagoge* (literally, "a leading or bringing together"), which refers to any assembly or gathering of people for secular or religious purposes. Eventually the term came to refer exclusively to an assembly of Jewish people.

The synagogue was a place where local groups of Jews in cities and villages could gather for the reading and explanation of the Jewish sacred Scriptures and for prayer. The original emphasis was not on preaching but on teaching the Law of Moses.

SYRIA [sihr´-e-ah] — a major nation northeast of Palestine that served as a political threat to the nations of Judah and Israel during much of their history.

T

TABERNACLE [tab´-er-nack-el] — the tent that was used as a place of worship for the nation of Israel during their early history.

TABERNACLES, FEAST OF — a festival observed on the fifteenth day of the seventh month to celebrate the completion of the autumn harvest. Also called the "Feast of Tents" or "feast of Shelters." There were special prayers said on the first and eighth days, and there were also special offerings (animal sacrifices) made. During this celebration, the Israelites lived in small booths (huts made of palm and willow trees) to remind them of the time they spent wandering in the wilderness and living in temporary shelters (Exod. 23:16; Lev. 23:34–36; Num. 29:12–32; Deut. 16:13–16).

TABITHA [tab´-ith-ah] — a follower of Jesus (Acts 9:36–42). Tabitha is another name for Dorcas.

TABLE — a piece of furniture used to set things on for ceremonies, eating meals, and

The Plan of the Tabernacle

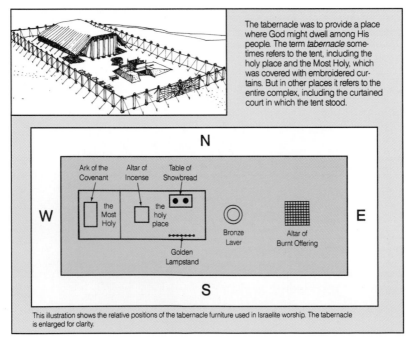

The tabernacle was to provide a place where God might dwell among His people. The term *tabernacle* sometimes refers to the tent, including the holy place and the Most Holy, which was covered with embroidered curtains. But in other places it refers to the entire complex, including the curtained court in which the tent stood.

This illustration shows the relative positions of the tabernacle furniture used in Israelite worship. The tabernacle is enlarged for clarity.

money changing. The tabernacle had a table of acacia wood decorated with gold. The showbread was placed on it (Exod. 25:23; Num. 3:31; Heb. 9:2). A table of gold was in the temple (1 Kings 7:48). Ezekiel's temple had tables for burnt offerings (Ezek. 40:39–43).

TABLET — a word used to describe material used for writing on like the stone tablets given to Moses at Mount Sinai (Exod. 24:12; Deut. 10:1–5). There were also writing tablets made of clay and wood (Ezek. 4:1, NKJV; Luke 1:63, NKJV).

The Bible also uses the word "tablet" as a symbol of God's law written on the heart (Prov. 3:3; Cor. 3:3).

TALENT — a unit of weight and also money (Exod. 25:39, NKJV; Rev. 16:21, NKJV). (See Weights and Measures of the Bible; also see Money of the Bible.)

TAMAR [ta´-mar] *(palm)* — the lovely daughter of David. Her mother was Maacah and her brother was Absalom (2 Sam. 13:1–22, 32; 1 Chron. 3:9). Tamar's half-brother Amnon

The Furniture of the Tabernacle

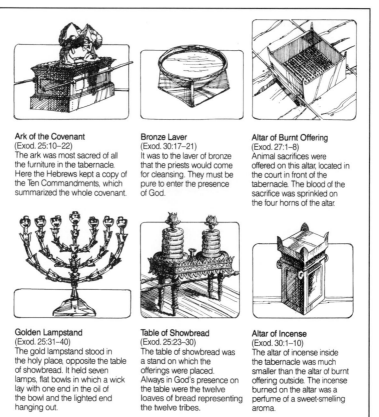

Ark of the Covenant
(Exod. 25:10–22)
The ark was most sacred of all the furniture in the tabernacle. Here the Hebrews kept a copy of the Ten Commandments, which summarized the whole covenant.

Bronze Laver
(Exod. 30:17–21)
It was to the laver of bronze that the priests would come for cleansing. They must be pure to enter the presence of God.

Altar of Burnt Offering
(Exod. 27:1–8)
Animal sacrifices were offered on this altar, located in the court in front of the tabernacle. The blood of the sacrifice was sprinkled on the four horns of the altar.

Golden Lampstand
(Exod. 25:31–40)
The gold lampstand stood in the holy place, opposite the table of showbread. It held seven lamps, flat bowls in which a wick lay with one end in the oil of the bowl and the lighted end hanging out.

Table of Showbread
(Exod. 25:23–30)
The table of showbread was a stand on which the offerings were placed. Always in God's presence on the table were the twelve loaves of bread representing the twelve tribes.

Altar of Incense
(Exod. 30:1–10)
The altar of incense inside the tabernacle was much smaller than the altar of burnt offering outside. The incense burned on the altar was a perfume of a sweet-smelling aroma.

attacked her. She went to Absalom and told him what happened. He was very upset and angry and wanted Amnon to suffer for the terrible thing that he did. Two years later Absalom got his revenge for Tamar by arranging for Amnon to be killed.

Tamar was also the name of two other women and a city in the Bible.

TANNER — a person who makes leather from animal skins (Acts 9:43, NKJV).

TARRY — to wait; to delay (Heb. 10:37, NKJV).

TARSHISH [tar´-shish] *(jasper)* — the name of several items in the Old Testament:

1. The Hebrew name for a type of cargo ship used for long voyages (trips across the sea) (1 Kings 10:22, NKJV; Tharshish, KJV).

2. A city or territory where the Phoenicians traded (2 Chron. 9:21, NKJV; Ps. 72:10).

3. One of seven princes of Persia and Media "who had access to the king's presence" (Esther 1:14).

4. The Hebrew name of a precious stone.

TARSUS [tar´-sus] — the birthplace of Saul (Acts 9:11) who later became the apostle Paul (Acts 21:39; 22:3). Tarsus was the main city of Cilicia, a province of southeast Asia Minor (modern Turkey).

TASKMASTER — a harsh supervisor (Exod. 1:11, NKJV).

TASSEL — a decorative ornament around the hems of the clothes of the Hebrew people. Tassels were worn to remind them of God's commandments in the Law (Deut. 22:12) and to encourage them to do His will.

TAX, TAXES — a fee or financial contribution (usually mandatory) for the maintenance of government. Taxes probably started as a

Photo by Howard Vos

St. Paul's Gate at Tarsus. The chief city of Cilicia in eastern Asia Minor, Tarsus was the birthplace of the apostle Paul (Acts 21:39).

custom of giving presents for protection from harm (Gen. 32:13–21; 33:10; 43:11).

When Joseph told the Pharaoh that there would be seven years of famine after seven years of abundance, Pharaoh put him in charge of raising money. Joseph collected a 20 percent tax to buy and store food, and to buy land for Pharaoh (Gen. 47:20–26). This tax was collected during the years of abundance and the years of famine.

TEACH, TEACHING — to cause a person to understand (John 3:2), the act of instructing students or giving knowledge and information. In the New Testament, the concept (idea) of teaching usually means religious instruction.

TEKOA [te-ko´-ah] **TEKOAH** (*trumpet blast*) — the birthplace of the prophet Amos, located in Judah (1 Chron. 2:24; 4:5).

TEMPERANCE — control over worldly desires. The meaning of the word "temperate" is more than the kind of self-control a person shows by not drinking alcoholic beverages.

The temperance of the Bible is a self-control that masters all kinds of desires and allows the Christian to work toward their spiritual reward (1 Cor. 9:24–27, NKJV).

TEMPEST — a violent storm (Matt. 8:24, NKJV).

TEMPLE — a building for worship. Temples were used to worship all kinds of false gods as well as the one true God. The place where the temple was located was considered holy, or sacred.

TEMPTATION — an invitation to sin with the promise of a better outcome from following the way of disobedience. God does not tempt people, nor can He be tempted (James 1:13). The supreme tempter is Satan (Matt. 4:3; 1 Cor. 7:5; 1 Thess. 3:5). He uses peoples' weaknesses against them (James 1:14) and leads them to destruction.

TEMPTATION OF CHRIST — the forty-day period in the wilderness when Jesus was

Photo by Levant Photo Service

The mound of Tekoa south of Jerusalem—home of the prophet Amos (Amos 1:1).

The Temples of the Bible

The Temple	Date	Description	Reference
The Tabernacle (Mobile Temple)	about 1444 B.C.	Detailed plan received by Moses from the Lord Constructed by divinely appointed artisans Desecrated by Nadab and Abihu	Exod. 25–30; Exod. 35:30–40:38; Lev. 10:1–7
Solomon's Temple	966–586 B.C.	Planned by David Constructed by Solomon Destroyed by Nebuchadnezzar	2 Sam. 7:1–29; 1 Kings 8:1–66; Jer. 32:28–44
Zerubbabel's Temple	516–169 B.C.	Envisioned by Zerubbabel Constructed by Zerubbabel and the elders of the Jews Desecrated by Antiochus Epiphanes	Ezra 6:1–22; Ezra 3:1–8; 4:1–14; Matt. 24:15
Herod's Temple	19 B.C.–A.D. 70	Zerubbabel's temple restored by Herod the Great Destroyed by the Romans	Mark 13:2, 14–23; Luke 1:11–20; 2:22–38; 2:42–51; 4:21–24; Acts 21:27–33
The Present Temple	Present Age	Found in the heart of the believer The body of the believer is the Lord's only temple until the Messiah returns	1 Cor. 6:19, 20; 2 Cor. 6:16–18
The Temple of Revelation 11	Tribulation Period	To be constructed during the Tribulation by the Antichrist To be desecrated and destroyed	Dan. 9:2; Matt. 24:15; 2 Thess. 2:4; Rev. 17:18
Ezekiel's (Millennial) Temple	Millennium	Envisioned by the prophet Ezekiel To be built by the Messiah during His millennial reign	Ezek. 40:1–42:20; Zech. 6:12, 13
The Eternal Temple of His Presence	The Eternal Kingdom	The greatest temple of all ("The Lord God Almighty and the Lamb are its temple") A spiritual temple	Rev. 21:22; Rev. 22:1–21

The temple (Gk. *hieron*) is a place of worship, a sacred or holy space built primarily for the national worship of God.

Photo by Howard Vos

The temple of Hephaestus (Vulcan) in Athens is one of the best-preserved Greek temples from ancient times.

tempted by the devil (Matt. 4:1–13; Mark 1:12–13). Jesus' first temptation (to turn stones to bread) was to use His divine power to satisfy His own physical needs. The second (to jump off the temple) was to perform a miracle so the people would follow Him. The third was to gain possession of the world by worshiping Satan.

The only reason Satan tempted Jesus was to try to stop Jesus from completing His mission. Satan knew that Jesus' death would destroy his (Satan's) power and he needed that power to make people worship him instead of God.

TEN COMMANDMENTS — the rules for living given to the Israelites by God through Moses (Exod. 20:1–17).

TENDER EYED — timid; eye weakness (Gen. 29:17, KJV).

TERAH [te´-rah] — the father of Abraham (Gen. 11:26–27; Luke 3:34; Thara, KJV). Terah

was also the name of an Israelite camp in the wilderness (Num. 33:27–28; Tarah, KJV).

TERAPHIM [ter´-ra-fim] — figurines or images in human form used in the ancient world as household gods.

TERRESTRIAL — of the earth (1 Cor. 15:40).

TERRIBLE — horrible; scary (Heb. 12:21, NKJV).

TESTAMENT — a written document that explains what is to happen to a person's personal property after they die. In the Bible, the word "testament" is used to mean "covenant" or "agreement" (promise) (Matt. 26:28; 2 Cor. 3:6; Rev. 11:19).

TESTIFY — to tell as a witness (Acts 2:40, KJV).

TESTIMONY — witness (John 3:32, NKJV); the Law (Exod. 25:21, NKJV).

185

TETRARCH [tet´-rark] *(ruler of a fourth part)* — the ruler or governor of a fourth part of a country. Many countries were divided into parts for efficient government, especially under the Roman Empire. (Luke 3:1, NKJV).

THADDAEUS [that-de´-us] — one of the twelve apostles of Jesus (Matt. 10:3; Mark 3:18). Also called Lebbaeus (Matt. 10:3) and Judas the son of James (Luke 6:16; Acts 1:13). But he is not Judas Iscariot (John 14:22). Not much is known about this apostle, but some scholars believe he wrote the Epistle of Jude.

THANK OFFERING — an offering (sacrifice) made when a person received a blessing from God without having asked for it (2 Chron. 29:31; 33:16).

THANKSGIVING — giving thanks to God for what He does for us (1 Thess. 5:18).

THENCE — from there (Gen. 11:8, KJV).

THEOPHILUS [the-off´-i-lus] *(lover of God)* — Luke dedicated the Gospel of Luke and the Book of Acts to a Christian man named Theophilus (Luke 1:1; Acts 1:1).

THESSALONIANS, EPISTLES TO THE — two letters written by the apostle Paul. The major theme of 1 and 2 Thessalonians is the return of Christ to earth. Another important theme is the believers' responsibilities of the present. In other words, they were to stay focused on their daily life and not worry about the future. Both epistles are written to help establish and strengthen a young church during difficult times (1 Thess. 3:2, 13; 2 Thess. 2:17; 3:3).

Photo by Howard Vos

The ancient walls of Thessalonica, a city in Macedonia where Paul founded a church (Acts 17:1–4; 1 Thess. 1:1).

THESSALONICA [thes-sa-lo-ni´-cah] — a city in Macedonia visited by the apostle Paul (Acts 17:1, 11, 13; 27:2; Phil. 4:16).

THISTLES, THORNS — a sticker plant, these words are also used as symbols for trouble (Matt. 7:16; 2 Kings 14:9).

THITHER — there (1 Sam. 10:22, KJV).

THOMAS [tom´-us] *(twin)* — one of the twelve apostles of Jesus; also called Didymus, the Greek word for "twin" (Matt. 10:3; Mark 3:18; Luke 6:15). Thomas is probably best known for his inability to believe that Jesus had indeed risen from the dead. Because of his inability to believe, he earned the name "doubting Thomas."

A threshing floor in Samaria. The oxen are dragging a weighted sled over the harvest to separate the grain from the stalks.

THONGS — straps (Acts 22:25, NKJV).

THORN IN THE FLESH — a reference to some extreme difficulty "in the flesh" that the apostle Paul encountered in his ministry (2 Cor. 12:7, NKJV).

THRESH, THRESHING — removing the kernel of grain from its stalk. Some farmers would beat the stalks to remove the grain; other farmers would walk their animals over the grain to thresh it.

THRESHING FLOOR — a flat surface prepared for threshing grain. The threshing floor was usually located at the edge of a village on a large flat rock. When no flat rock was available, the threshing floor would be prepared by clearing an area of ground and pounding the earth to create a hard surface.

THRONG — a crowd (Mark 5:31, NKJV).

THYATIRA [thi-a-ti´-rah] — a city of the province of Lydia in western Asia Minor (modern Turkey). Thyatira wasn't a large city, but it was a busy city in New Testament times.

The apostle Paul's first convert in Europe was "a certain woman named Lydia . . . a seller of purple from the city of Thyatira" (Acts 16:14).

TIBERIAS, SEA OF — a body of water also known as Chinnereth and the Sea of Galilee (Num. 34:11, NKJV; John 6:1, NKJV).

TIDINGS — news, information (Luke 2:10, NKJV; Rom. 10:15, NKJV).

TIGLATH-PILESER [tig´-lath-pi-le´-zur] *(the firstborn of [the god] Esharra is my*

A stone carving of Tiglath-Pileser III of Assyria, from his excavated palace at Nimrud.

confidence) — a king of Assyria (ruled 745–727 B.C.) and a king of Babylonia (729–727 B.C.). When he was the king of Babylonia, he used the name Pul (2 Kings 15:19). He is also called Tilgath-Pilneser (1 Chron. 5:6, 26; 2 Chron. 28:20).

TIGRIS [ti´-gris] — a major river of southwest Asia. The Tigris joins the Euphrates River north of Basra. The Tigris and Euphrates flow beside each other for hundreds of miles in the "Land of the Two Rivers," or Mesopotamia. The Tigris is the same as Hiddekel (Gen. 2:14, KJV, NKJV), one of the four branches of the river that flowed from the Garden of Eden.

TILL — to plow (Gen. 2:5, NKJV).

TIMBREL — a musical instrument kind of like a tambourine (Ps. 81:2, NKJV).

TIME — a measurable period during which an action or condition exists or continues. Among the Hebrew people, units of time were measured in hours, days, weeks, months, and years.

TIMOTHY [tim´-o-thy] *(honored by God)* — a friend and coworker of the apostle Paul. He is mentioned as joint sender in six of Paul's epistles (letters) (2 Cor. 1:1; Phil. 1:1; Col. 1:1; 1 Thess. 1:1; 2 Thess. 1:1; Philem. 1).

TIMOTHY, EPISTLES TO — two letters written by the apostle Paul. These letters, along with the Epistle to Titus, form a trilogy called the Pastoral Epistles. These letters are called Pastoral Epistles because they deal with matters affecting pastors and congregations. In these letters to Timothy, Paul's main concern is

to teach his young associate to guard the spiritual heritage that he has received (1 Tim. 6:20; 2 Tim. 1:12–14; 2:2) by establishing sound doctrine in the church.

TISHBITE, TISHBE [tish´-bite] — a name given to Elijah the prophet (1 Kings 17:1; 21:17; 2 Kings 9:36).

TITHE — the act of giving a tenth of one's income or property as an offering to God (Mal. 3:8–10, NKJV).

TITTLE — a decorative stroke on the letters of the Hebrew alphabet (Matt. 5:18; Luke 16:17; stroke, NRSV; the smallest stroke, NASB; the least stroke of a pen, NIV). The word "tittle" comes from a Greek word that means "little horn." Jesus meant that even the smallest detail of the law of Moses would never fail or pass away.

TITUS [ti´-tus] — a "partner and fellow worker" (2 Cor. 8:23) of the apostle Paul. He is the author of the Book of Titus in the New Testament.

TITUS, EPISTLE TO — one of three Pastoral Epistles written by the apostle Paul. The others are 1 and 2 Timothy. They are the only letters of Paul addressed to individuals (Philemon is addressed "to the church in your house," 2). The purpose of the epistle to Titus was to warn against false teaching and to provide guidance for one of Paul's younger associates on sound doctrine and good works.

TOIL — strenuous labor; hard work (Gen. 5:29, NKJV; Matt. 6:28, NKJV).

TOKEN — a sign or symbol. Rahab the harlot begged the two spies to give her a "true token" that her family would be spared when Joshua attacked Jericho (Josh. 2:12, NKJV).

TOLERABLE, TOLERATE — able to bear (Matt. 10:15, NKJV).

TOLL — a tax (Ezra 4:13, KJV).

TOMB — a special burial place for the dead. In Palestine, ordinary people were buried in shallow graves covered by stones or a stone slab. Important or wealthy people were placed in tombs.

TONGUES, GIFT OF — the power to speak in an unknown language. The Holy Spirit is the giver of this power (Isa. 28:11, NKJV; Mark 16:17, NKJV; Acts 2:4, NKJV; 1 Cor. 12 and 14, NKJV).

TORAH [tor-rah'] — guidance or direction from God to His people. In earlier times, the term "Torah" referred directly to the five books of Moses, or the Pentateuch.

TORMENT — to inflict physical pain or mental agony. Job cried out to his three friends, "How long will you torment my soul?" (Job 19:2, NKJV). The rich man in Jesus' story of the rich man and Lazarus used the words "place of torment" to describe hell (Luke 16:28, NKJV).

TOW — a word for the leftover product of flax used to make linen (Judg. 16:9, KJV; yarn, NKJV; Isa. 1:31, KJV; tinder, NKJV, NIV).

TOWER — a tall building used for protection. Some landowners used watchtowers to look over their crops (Isa. 5:2; Matt. 21:33; Mark 12:1). In the wilderness, towers were used to watch for bandits or robbers (2 Kings 17:9; 2 Chron. 26:10). In cities, towers were part of the walls that were built to keep out enemies (2 Chron. 14:7; Neh. 3:1).

TRADITION — the customs and practices from the past that are passed on as accepted standards of behavior for the present. Jesus criticized the Pharisees for slavishly following their traditions and making them more authoritative than the Scripture (Matt. 15:2, NKJV; Mark 7:3, NKJV).

TRAIN — the lowest hem on the back of an outer garment (Isa. 6:1, NKJV). The outer garment worn by the Hebrew people was a long, loosely fitting robe without any sleeves. The back of the robe was pulled up between the legs

This massive stone tower was part of the defense system of the ancient city of Jericho. It dates back to about 6000 B.C., long before Joshua and his army destroyed the city.

of the person wearing it and tied around their waist by a belt or girdle when they were working. When the back of the robe was pulled up and tied like this it was called "girded." When the back of the robe was hanging down it was called a "train." A person with a long train on their robe or cloak was probably wealthy.

TRANSFIGURATION — a display of God's glory in the person of His Son, Jesus Christ (Matt. 17:1–8).

TRANSFIGURED — changed (Mark 9:2, NKJV).

TRANSFORM, TRANSFORMED — to completely change. In Romans 12:2 the apostle Paul told Christians, "Do not be conformed to this world, but be transformed by the renewing of your mind" (NKJV). Followers of Christ should not behave like the people in the world. Believers should always be praying and studying God's Word, so the power of the Holy Spirit can change them and help them be more like Jesus (2 Cor. 3:18, NKJV).

TRANSGRESS, TRANSGRESSION — the breaking of a law or a rule, not following a command, or failing to perform a duty (job). In the Old Testament, a transgression could be accidental (Ps. 32:1, NKJV). In the New Testament, a transgression was always done on purpose (Rom. 4:15, NKJV; 1 Tim. 2:14, NKJV; Heb. 2:2, NKJV).

TRANSLATE, TRANSLATION — to take a person out of a situation or place and put them in a different situation or place. In the Bible, the word "translation" or the idea of translation is used in three different ways: (1)

the physical translation of Enoch (Gen. 5:24; Heb. 11:5, KJV) and Elijah (2 Kings 2:11) to heaven without them dying; (2) the spiritual translation of Christians from "the power of darkness" into "the kingdom of God" (Col. 1:13, KJV); and (3) the future physical translation and transformation of Christians at the Second Coming of Christ, or "the rapture" (1 Cor. 15:51–57; Phil. 3:21; 1 Thess. 4:13–18).

Translation is a special act of God. It is a permanent action that happens because of a person's faith.

TRAVAIL — to suffer great physical or mental pain. Rachel travailed in childbirth and she died while giving birth to Benjamin (Gen. 35:16–19, KJV).

TREACHEROUS — tricky; deceitful (Hos. 6:7, NKJV).

TREAD — to trample (trodden, Lam. 1:15, KJV).

TREASON — a conspiracy; a plan to go against a person or group like a king or government (1 Kings 16:20, NKJV).

TREASURE, TREASURY — something of value; a place for storing valuables (Gen. 43:23, NKJV; Deut. 32:34, NKJV; Esther 3:9; 4:7; Ezra 5:17, NKJV).

TREE OF KNOWLEDGE — one of two special trees planted by God in the Garden of Eden. The "tree of knowledge of good and evil" was a symbol for all of the knowledge of God. God knew that Adam and Eve wouldn't understand all of this knowledge and that they wouldn't be able to handle the power that comes from having all of that knowledge, so He told Adam and Eve not to eat the fruit of that tree (Gen. 2:17). The other tree in the garden was the tree of life and they were allowed to eat all they wanted from it (Gen. 2:9). But the tempter (Satan) tricked them by making them think that if they ate the fruit of the tree of knowledge, it would make them exactly like God (Gen. 3:5). They decided to disobey God and eat the fruit. Instead of knowing everything and being equal to God, they only received knowledge of their guilt and shame and condemnation. This act of disobeying God was the first sin in the world.

TREE OF LIFE — the tree in the Garden of Eden that provided life (Gen. 2:9, 17; 3:1–24). Before Adam and Eve sinned, they were allowed to eat the fruit from this tree. After they sinned, they had to leave the Garden of Eden and no longer had access to the tree of life.

TRESPASS — the violation of a law (Gen. 31:36, NKJV; Exod. 22:9, NKJV; Mark 11:25–26, NKJV; Eph. 2:1, 5, NKJV; 2 Cor. 5:19, NKJV).

TRIAL — a test or temptation. If a person passed the test or worked through the temptation, it proved that the person had real faith. Since good things can happen when a person gets through a trial, Christians are told to be happy about their trials (James 1:2, NKJV; 1 Pet. 4:12–13, NKJV). Christ gave us the example of how trials should be handled when He didn't give in to Satan's temptations. He was able to remain strong because He knew the Word of God (scripture) and what God expected Him to do (God's will) (Luke 4:1–13).

TRIBE — a social group made up of many clans and families. People became part of a tribe through covenant, marriage, adoption, or slavery. The nation of Israel was a tribal society (Num. 1; 2; 26; Josh. 13–21; Judg. 19–21) and there were also many tribes in the nations next to Israel (Gen. 25:13–16).

TRIBULATION — great difficulty and suffering; also persecution. Tribulation is part of God's process for making the world right again. His Son went through great suffering, and His people have to go through a great deal of tribulation from the world (Rom. 5:3, NKJV; Acts 14:22, NKJV). This tribulation happens because of a conflict (fight) between God and the devil (Gen. 3:15). The Bible tells us that this fight will end with the devil being thrown into the lake of fire to suffer eternal tribulation (Rev. 20:10).

TRIBULATION, THE GREAT — a short but intense period of distress and suffering at the end of time. The exact phrase, "the great tribulation," is found only once in the Bible (Rev. 7:14, NKJV). The great tribulation is not the same as the general tribulation a believer faces in the world (Matt. 13:21, NKJV; John 16:33, NKJV; Acts 14:22, NKJV). It is also different from God's wrath (anger and punishment) on the unbelievers of the world at the end of time (Mark 13:24, NKJV; Rom. 2:5–10, NKJV; 2 Thess. 1:6, NKJV).

The great tribulation is the fulfillment of Daniel's prophecies (Dan. 7–12). It will be a time of evil. There will be people claiming to be "Jesus Christ" and there will be many false prophets (Mark 13:22). Natural disasters will happen all over the world.

TRIBUTE — a fee or financial contribution

levied on (charged to) a person by a ruler or a country. A tribute is also the same as a tax (Ezra 4:20, NKJV).

TRINITY — the Father, the Son, and the Holy Spirit in the unity of the Godhead. The doctrine of the trinity means that there is one God who operates as three different persons: Father, Son, and Holy Spirit. Although the word "trinity" does not appear in the Bible, the concept (idea) is mentioned in the Great Commission (Matt. 28:19) and in the benediction (closing or end) of the apostle Paul's Second Epistle (letter) to the Corinthians (2 Cor. 13:14).

TRIUMPH — the joy felt over a victory (Ps. 47:1, NKJV).

TRIUMPHAL ENTRY — Jesus' entrance into Jerusalem on the Sunday (Palm Sunday) before His crucifixion (Matt. 21:1–9, NKJV; Mark 11:1–10, NKJV; Luke 19:29–38, NKJV; John 12:12–16, NKJV).

TROAS [tro´-as] — an important city on the coast of Mysia, in northwest Asia Minor (modern Turkey), visited at least three times by the apostle Paul (Acts 16:8, 11; 20:5–6; 2 Cor. 2:12; 2 Tim. 4:13).

TROPHIMUS [trof´-ih-mus] — a Gentile Christian who lived in Ephesus. He traveled with Paul to Jerusalem at the end of Paul's third missionary journey (Acts 20:4).

TROUGH — a place that holds food or water for animals (Exod. 2:16).

TRUE, TRUTH — an actual fact; faithfulness to a rule or standard. God said that He is "merciful and gracious, longsuffering, and abounding in goodness and truth" (Exod. 34:6, NKJV).

Photo by Howard Vos

Ruins of Roman baths at Troas—the city where Paul received a vision to evangelize Macedonia (Acts 16:6–10).

Roman ruins at the ancient city of Tyre, with buildings of the modern city in the background.

TRUMPETS, FEAST OF — a Hebrew festival that celebrated the new civil year (Num. 29:1).

TUMULT — a riot (Matt. 27:24, NKJV).

TUNIC — a loose-fitting garment; a piece of clothing sort of like a short dress or long shirt (Mark 6:9, NIV).

TURBAN — a long piece of linen cloth wound around the head and fastened in the back to form a type of headdress worn by men in Bible times (Job 29:14). The headdress worn by the priests of the nation of Israel was not a turban (Exod. 28:39).

TURTLEDOVE — another name for dove. Poor people used turtledoves for their sacrifices because they could not afford lambs or other more expensive animals (Lev. 12:6–8, NKJV).

TWELVE, THE — a phrase that identified the group of twelve disciples that had close relationships with Jesus (Mark 4:10). Early in His ministry, Jesus picked twelve of His followers and called them "apostles" (Luke 6:12–16). They are also called the "twelve disciples" (Matt. 10:1). Jesus appointed (chose) them to travel with Him, to preach, to heal, and to cast out demons (Mark 3:14–15).

TWO-EDGED — sharp on both sides, like a sword (Heb. 4:12, NKJV).

TYCHICUS [tik´-ik-us] — a faithful friend, coworker, and messenger of the apostle Paul (Eph. 6:21–22; Col. 4:7–8). Tychicus traveled with other disciples from Macedonia to Troas, where he waited for the apostle Paul's arrival (Acts 20:4).

TYRE [tire] *(rock)* — an ancient city of the Phoenicians located north of Israel. Tyre was the principal seaport of the Phoenician coast.

U

UNBELIEF — a lack of belief or faith in God. Unbelief doesn't prevent God from being faithful (Rom. 3:3, NKJV), but it does affect the person's ability to receive the benefits of that faithfulness (Mark 9:23–24, NKJV).

UNCIRCUMCISED — a man who has not gone through the Jewish rite of circumcision. This word is also used to describe a person who is not Jewish (Gentile) (Exod. 12:48), or a person who is spiritually impure because they refuse to listen to and obey God (Acts 7:51). The real issue isn't about actual circumcision; it is about having faith in Christ (1 Cor. 7:18–19).

UNCLEAN, UNCLEANNESS — defiled; foul; unfit; dirty. "Unclean" refers to foods that are unfit to eat and to a person's spiritual impurity. The Old Testament says an item is either clean and helpful or unclean and unacceptable (not useful) (Lev. 10:10; 11:47). The priest was supposed to teach the people the difference (Ezek. 44:23).

UNDEFILED — unstained; unsoiled; not tainted with evil; also clean; pure; faultless. The word "undefiled" is used to describe Christ as sinless (Heb. 7:26, NKJV). It is also used in reference to sex between a man and his wife (Heb. 13:4, NKJV).

UNFAITHFUL — deceitful; a person who acts like they are doing what they should, but they really aren't (Prov. 25:19).

UNGODLY — wicked; lost (from God) (Rom. 5:6, NKJV).

UNHOLY — wicked; evil (2 Tim. 3:2, NKJV).

UNITY — oneness; harmony; agreement. The church experienced unity on the day of Pentecost (Acts 2:1). The church is a group of many different people; the combination of faith, hope, and love that forms a bond between them is unity (Eph. 4:3, 13, NKJV).

UNLEAVENED BREAD — bread baked from unfermented dough, or dough without yeast (Gen. 19:3; Josh. 5:11; 1 Sam. 28:24). Unleavened bread was the flat bread used in the Passover celebration and the priestly rituals (Lev. 23:4–8). The tradition of eating unleavened bread goes back to the time of the Exodus, when the Hebrews left Egypt in such a hurry that they had no time to wait for the dough to rise before baking it (Exod. 12:8, 15–20, 34, 39; 13:6–7).

UNLEAVENED BREAD, FEAST OF — also called Passover. This feast was celebrated to remind the Israelites of their deliverance (Exod. 12).

UNPARDONABLE SIN — blasphemy against the Holy Spirit (Matt. 12:31–32, NKJV; Mark 3:29, NKJV).

UNRIGHTEOUS — unacceptable to God (Isa. 55:7, NKJV).

UNSEARCHABLE — beyond understanding; unable to find an answer (Job 5:9, NKJV).

UNWITTINGLY — unknowingly (Heb. 13:2, NKJV); by accident (Josh. 20:3, KJV).

UPPER ROOM — a place where Jesus met with His disciples before the crucifixion (Mark 14:15, NKJV). (See Lord's Supper.)

UR — a large city in southern Mesopotamia where Abraham was from. This city is now the country of Iraq.

URIAH [u-ri´-ah] *(the Lord is my light)* — the name of three men in the Old Testament:

1. A Hittite married to Bathsheba and one of David's best soldiers (2 Sam. 11:3–26; 12:9–10, 15; 1 Kings 15:5; Matt. 1:6; Urias, KJV).

2. The son of Koz, the father of Meremoth and a priest who helped rebuild the wall of Jerusalem under Nehemiah.

3. A priest who was one of two faithful witnesses to a scroll written by the prophet Isaiah (Isa. 8:2).

URIM AND THUMMIM [u´-rim, thum´-mem] — stones carried by the high priests that were used to help them make important decisions.

USURY — the interest paid on borrowed money.

UTTER — when used as a verb, it means to speak (Matt. 13:35, NKJV); when used as an adjective, it means complete or total (1 Kings 20:42, NKJV).

UTTERANCE — spoken words (Acts 2:4, NKJV).

UZZA, UZZAH [uz´-zah] *(strength)* — the name of five men in the Old Testament:

1. A man who died because he touched the Ark of the Covenant (2 Sam. 6:3–8; 1 Chron. 13:7–11).

2. A person who allowed Manasseh and Amon (Manasseh's son), who were both kings of Judah, to be buried in his garden (2 Kings 21:18, 26).

3. A Levite of the family of Merari (1 Chron. 6:29).

4. A descendant of Ehud mentioned in the family tree of King Saul (1 Chron. 8:7).

5. An ancestor of a family of Nethinim (temple servants) who returned with Zerubbabel from the Captivity (Ezra 2:49; Neh. 7:51).

UZZIAH [uz-zi´-ah] *(the Lord is my strength)* — the son of Amaziah and Jecholiah, the ninth king of Judah, and the father of Jotham (2 Chron. 26). He was also called Azariah (2 Kings 14:21; 15:1–7). Uzziah became king at the age of sixteen and was king for fifty-two years. That was longer than any other king before him. In the beginning, he was a good king and did what God wanted him to do. After he stopped obeying God, he got leprosy (a skin disease) and died.

Ruins of ancient Ur on the Euphrates River in Mesopotamia—the city from which Abraham migrated (Gen. 11:31).

V

VAGABOND — a person who moves from place to place without a permanent home; also an aimless wanderer (Ps. 109:10, NKJV).

VAIN — empty; useless; for nothing (Ps. 73:13, NKJV; 1 Cor. 15:14, KJV).

VALIANT — brave (Jer. 46:15, NKJV).

VANITY — emptiness; worthlessness; uselessness. The word is found more than thirty times in the Old Testament (NKJV), mostly in the Book of Ecclesiastes. When the word "vanity" is used in the Bible in reference to a person, it describes the emptiness or worthlessness of human life (Job 7:3, KJV; Eccles. 1:2, NKJV; 2:1, NKJV; 5:10, NKJV).

When the word is used in reference to things, it is usually describing an idol (Isa. 41:29, KJV). Believers are taught to stay away from vain (empty) things and to focus on a fulfilling relationship with Christ. The act of a person trusting anything but God to meet their needs is vanity (Eph. 4:17–24, KJV).

VARIANCE — separate (Matt. 10:35, KJV); turmoil (Gal. 5:20, KJV).

VASHTI [vash´-ti] — the beautiful queen of King Ahasuerus. She was sent away because she refused to let the king show her off during a drunken feast (party) (Esther 1:11). After she was gone, Esther became Ahasuerus's new queen, and God used her to save the Jewish people from being killed.

VASSAL — a slave or a person who has an unimportant place in society. Hoshea, king of Israel, became the vassal of Shalmaneser, the king of Assyria, and had to pay him tribute money (taxes) (2 Kings 17:3, NKJV). Jehoiakim, king of Judah, became the vassal of Nebuchadnezzar, king of Babylon, for three years (2 Kings 24:1, NKJV).

VEIL — a woman's head covering (Gen. 24:65; 38:14). A veil was also a curtain in the tabernacle or temple that separated the Holy Place from the Holy of Holies (or Most Holy Place).

VENGEANCE — a harmful action taken by one person against another person who did something wrong or caused harm to them. Only God is qualified to take vengeance because His actions are based on His holiness, righteousness, and justice (Deut. 32:35, NKJV; Rom. 12:19, NKJV).

VESSEL — any kind of container used to hold things. The vessels of the Hebrew people were usually made of clay, but vessels of glass, metal, leather, wicker, and stone were also used. Vessels were used to hold all kinds of things including documents (Jer. 32:14, NKJV), wine, fruits, and oil (Jer. 40:10, NKJV).

Sometimes ships are called vessels (Isa. 18:2) because they "hold" people and goods. A vessel can also be a person who "holds" within them the knowledge of God (2 Cor. 4:6–7, NKJV).

Just like a clay vessel reflects the craftsmanship of its potter, people reflect the craftsmanship of God. In God's hands we are molded and formed according to His plan (Rom. 9:21–23, NKJV).

VESTMENT, VESTURE — robe (2 Kings 10:22); clothes (Matt. 27:35).

VEXATION — wrong (Eccles. 1:14, KJV); trouble (2 Chron. 15:5, KJV); sadness (Isa. 65:14, KJV).

VILE — disgusting; despised (Ps. 12:8, NKJV).

VINE, VINEYARD — a wandering plant that produces fruit. It usually means grapes and grapevines (Matt. 26:29).

VINEGAR — a drink made from wine that had been soured or overfermented.

VINTAGE — a harvest (Lev. 26:5).

VIOLATE — to commit violence against a person or group (Ezek. 22:26, NKJV).

VIOLENCE — the use of physical force to hurt or destroy. Violence is against the rules of God's perfect order.

VIPER — a poisonous snake (Acts 28:3, NKJV); a symbol for evil leaders (Matt. 3:7, NKJV; 12:34, NKJV).

VIRGIN — a person who has not had sexual intercourse. A priest was only allowed to marry a virgin (Gen. 24:16; Deut. 22:15–28; Isa. 7:14).

VIRGIN BIRTH — the phrase "virgin birth" is the explanation of how Jesus became human; it means that Mary did not have sexual relations with any man when she became pregnant with Jesus (Matt. 1:18–25). Her pregnancy was a miracle from God.

VIRTUE — moral excellence or goodness

Photo by Willem A. VanGemeren

A modern vineyard at the foot of the mound of ancient Lachish. As in biblical times, winemaking is still an important industry in Israel.

(Phil. 4:8, NKJV). Virtue is considered a necessary ingredient in the exercise of faith (2 Pet. 1:3, 5, NKJV). The Greek word for virtue is sometimes used to show the idea of power or strength (Luke 6:19, KJV).

VISAGE — face (Dan. 3:19, KJV); representation (Isa. 52:14, NKJV).

VISION — a revelation from God (Acts 9:10).

VISIONS — sort of like dreams where supernatural insight (wisdom) or awareness (knowledge) is given by revelation. The difference between a dream and a vision is that dreams happen only during sleep and visions can happen while a person is awake (Dan. 10:7).

VOCATION — a calling or an invitation to a profession (job), or way of life. In religious thoughts or ideas, the word "vocation" is not used in reference to a person's job. It refers to the invitation God has given to all people to become His children through Christ's work. This vocation, or calling, does not come to people because they deserve it; it comes strictly as a result of God's grace (2 Tim. 1:9). People are free to decide whether or not they will accept this invitation.

VOID — emptiness; without; lifeless. When the earth was first created, it was void and without form (Gen. 1:2, NKJV). This means it was an empty place without any life. God had not yet filled it with the plants and creatures that He later created.

VOW — a promise or pledge to perform a specific act or to behave in a certain manner. The first mention of a vow in the Bible is of Jacob at Bethel (Gen. 28:20–22; 31:13, NKJV).

W

WAGES — payment for performing work or service. In Bible times, wages were often paid in the form of property or privileges instead of money.

The term "wages" is also used in reference to the consequences (results) of a person's actions or deeds. The apostle Paul said, "The wages of sin is death" (Rom. 6:23, NKJV).

WAIL — a mournful cry of grief, sorrow, or lamentation (Jer. 9:17, NKJV).

WALK — to move at a pace slower than a run; also the way a person lives their life (conduct or behavior) (Gen. 5:24; 6:9; Eccles. 11:9, NKJV).

WALL — a thick, high, continuous structure of stones or brick that formed a defensive barricade around an ancient city. Interior walls of houses in Palestine were also made of bricks or stones, but these were usually plastered over to give them a smooth surface (1 Kings 6:5).

WANTONNESS — acting without restraint or inhibition (Rom. 13:13, KJV; 2 Pet. 2:18, KJV).

WARD — a prison; a hospital; or other place of confinement (Gen. 42:16–19, KJV).

WARE — goods; utensils (Neh. 13:16, KJV).

WASTE — trash or garbage; to make desolate (Lev. 26:31, NKJV).

WATCH — a group of soldiers or others who are posted to keep guard (Neh. 4:9, NKJV; 7:3, NKJV; 12:25, NKJV). A watch is also one of the units of time that a night was divided into (Ps. 63:6, NKJV; Lam. 2:19, NKJV; Luke 12:38, NKJV).

WATCHMAN — a guard or lookout person (2 Kings 9:17, NKJV).

WATCHTOWER — an observation tower where a guard or lookout was stationed to keep watch. A tall structure that allowed a person to see far away in all directions (2 Kings 17:9; 18:8; Isa. 21:8).

WAX — a sticky substance secreted by bees to build the honeycomb, also called beeswax. The wicked melt like wax before God's judgment (Ps. 68:2).

WEAN — to make independent of, usually in reference to a child and mother (1 Sam. 1:23, NKJV).

WEAVING — the skill of making cloth from threads. The Hebrews practiced weaving probably as early as Abraham's time, about 2000 B.C. The great skill required to weave the tabernacle curtains (Exod. 26, NKJV) and priestly garments (35:35, NKJV) was probably learned in Egypt.

WEDDING — a marriage ceremony (Luke 12:36; 14:8). An Israelite wedding was a festive

A mosaic of the wedding procession of the virgins (Matt. 25:1–13) in an ancient church in Ravenna, Italy.

occasion that lasted for a few days and the whole community participated.

WEEK — any seven consecutive days, also the time that passes between two Sabbaths (Lev. 12:5; Jer. 5:24; Luke 18:12). The Hebrew people observed the seventh day of the week, from Friday evening (beginning at sunset) to Saturday evening, as their Sabbath or day of rest and worship (Exod. 16:23–27).

In memory and celebration of the resurrection of Christ, early Christians did not worship on the old Jewish Sabbath. They chose to worship on the Lord's Day (the first day of the week, or Sunday), which became the new Christian "Sabbath" (Mark 16:2, 9; Acts 20:7; 1 Cor. 16:2).

WEEKS, FEAST OF — a feast that was observed early in the third month on the fiftieth day after the offering of the barley sheaf at the

Feast of Passover. It included a holy convocation with the usual restriction on manual labor. Numbers 28:26–31 describes the number and nature of offerings and Deuteronomy 16:9–12 describes those who were to be invited. This feast was also known as the Feast of Harvest as well as Pentecost (a Greek word meaning "fifty").

WEIGHTS AND MEASURES OF THE BIBLE — weighing (pounds) and measuring (volume, length, and area) are two important functions in the Bible.

Weights
The balance was an early method of determining weight. It consisted of a beam supported in the middle and pans hanging from cords on each end. A known quantity of weight would be placed in the pan on one side of the balance and the object to be weighed on

the other side. By adding or removing known weights until each side was equal (balanced), the weight of the object could be determined. These ancient weights were sometimes used as money.

Measures

The Bible uses three types of measurement: (1) volume, which measured the amount of dry goods (like flour) or liquids (like oil) that could be held in a vessel; (2) length, which measured height, width, and depth of an object or person; and (3) total area, which measured the size of a building, a field, or a city.

WELFARE — a person's state of being; also completeness and prosperity (Neh. 2:10, KJV).

WELL — a pit or hole dug into the earth to provide water. The words "well," "natural spring," and "cistern" mean different things. A well was usually a pit or hole dug by man to provide water (John 4:11–12). God made natural springs (fountain) (Ps. 84:6; Neh. 2:13), and a cistern was usually a container placed in a hole in the ground to store water (Gen. 16:14; 2 Sam. 17:18).

WHEAT — the grain used to make flour.

Weights			
Unit	Weight	Equivalents	Translations
Jewish Weights			
Talent	ca. 75 pounds for common talent, ca. 150 pounds for royal talent	60 minas; 3000 shekels	talent, one hundred pounds
Mina	1.25 pounds	50 shekels	maneh, mina
Shekel	ca. .4 ounce (11.4 grams) for common shekel	2 bekas; 20 gerahs	shekel
	ca. .8 ounce for royal shekel		
Beka	ca. .2 ounce (5.7 grams)	1/2 shekel; 10 gerahs	half-shekel
Gerah	ca. .02 ounce (.57 grams)	1/20 shekel	gerah
Roman Weight			
Litra	12 ounces		pound, pint

Measures of Length			
Unit	Length	Equivalents	Translations
Day's journey	ca. 20 miles		day's journey, day's walk
Roman mile	4,854 feet	8 stadia	mile
Sabbath day's journey	3,637 feet	6 stadia	a Sabbath day's journey
Stadion	606 feet	1/8 Roman mile	mile, stadion
Rod	9 feet (10.5 feet in Ezekiel)	3 paces; 6 cubits	measuring rod
Fathom	6 feet	4 cubits	fathom
Pace	3 feet	1/3 rod; 2 cubits	pace
Cubit	18 inches	1/2 pace; 2 spans	cubit, yards
Span	9 inches	1/2 cubit; 3 handbreadths	span
Handbreadth	3 inches	1/3 span; 4 fingers	handbreadth
Finger	.75 inches	1/4 handbreadth	finger

Dry Measures			
Unit	Measures	Equivalents	Translations
Homer	6.52 bushels	10 ephahs	homer
Kor	6.52 bushels	1 homer; 10 ephahs	kor, measure
Lethech	3.26 bushels	$^{1}/_{2}$ kor	a homer and a half
Ephah	.65 bushel, 20.8 quarts	$^{1}/_{10}$ homer	ephah
Modius	7.68 quarts		peck-measure
Seah	7 quarts	$^{1}/_{3}$ ephah	measure, pecks
Omer	2.08 quarts	$^{1}/_{10}$ ephah; $1^{4}/_{5}$ kab	omer
Kab	1.16 quarts	4 logs	kab
Choenix	1 quart		quart
Xestes	$1^{1}/_{16}$ pints		pitcher
Log	.58 pint	$^{1}/_{4}$ kab	log

Liquid Measures			
Unit	Measures	Equivalents	Translations
Kor	60 gallons	10 baths	kor
Metretes	10.2 gallons		gallon
Bath	6 gallons	6 hins	measure, bath
Hin	1 gallon	2 kabs	hin
Kab	2 quarts	4 logs	kab
Log	1 pint	$^{1}/_{4}$ kab	log

Wheat is also used as a symbol for commitment to God (John 12:24; Matt. 3:12; Luke 3:17).

WHELP — the baby of a dog, wolf, or lion (a pup or a cub). In the Bible the word "whelp" always refers to a lion cub (Gen. 49:9, NKJV; Deut. 33:22, NKJV).

WHENCE — from where (Phil. 3:20, KJV).

WHEREAS — since; because (James 4:14, KJV).

WHIRLWIND — any violent storm or destructive wind (Isa. 66:15, NKJV).

WHITEWASHED — covered with white paint to hide corruption or uncleanness (flaws) (Matt. 23:27, NKJV).

WHITHER — where (Gen. 28:15, KJV).

WHOLE, WHOLESOME — well; complete; healthy; all; entire (Prov. 15:4, NKJV).

WHORE, WHOREDOM — a prostitute; the crime of prostitution. These words are also used as symbols for idolatry (Hosea 1:2, KJV).

WICKED — evil; wrong; malicious (Ps. 9:16; 2 Thess. 3:2, NKJV).

WIDOW — a woman whose husband has died and who has not remarried.

Photo by Gustav Jeeninga

Ancient weights were frequently cast in the shapes of animals such as turtles, ducks, and lions to make them easily recognizable and easy to handle.

WIFE — a term for a woman who is a man's partner in marriage (Gen. 2:18; Gen. 2:24).

WILDERNESS — a land not good for farming. Wilderness land was too dry, rough, or rocky to grow crops, but it was okay for grazing animals (Gen. 14:6, NKJV; Exod. 3:18, NKJV). Occasionally the word "wilderness" is used to mean "desert."

WILL — wishing; wanting; choosing especially in reference to God's will. A will is also a legal document that explains what is to happen to a person's property after they die.

WIMPLE — a covering made of cloth and wound around the head. It framed the face, and was drawn into folds beneath the chin (Isa. 3:22, KJV). Other translations are veil (KJV), mantle (NRSV), and shawl (NKJV, NIV).

WIND — the natural movement of air as a part of the weather pattern.

WINE — the fermented juice of grapes. Wine was common in Hebrew life and had many uses. It was used for trade purposes and sometimes as payment for a fine (Amos 2:8). Wine was also used in worship (Exod. 29:40; Num. 28:7; Lev. 23:13; Num. 15:5), as a common drink, and as medicine (2 Sam. 16:2; Prov. 31:6; Luke 10:34; 1 Tim. 5:23).

Even though wine was used for many different purposes, the Bible also clearly warns of the dangers of drunkenness (Prov. 20:1; 23:29–35; Hosea 4:11). The prophets accused the Hebrew people of drinking too much (Isa. 28:1; Amos 6:6), and of wanting prophets who would say it was okay (Mic. 2:11). The prophets said that the nation's leaders were too interested in drinking to notice what was happening to their country (Isa. 5:11–12; 22:13).

In New Testament times, people still used wine but the apostle Paul told them to be filled with the Holy Spirit instead of wine (Eph. 5:18).

WINEBIBBERS — people who drink too much wine. The Bible says we should not spend our time with these people (Prov. 23:20, NKJV).

WINEPRESS — a container where juice is pressed from grapes before it is made into wine (Deut. 16:13; Judg. 6:11).

WINESKIN — a bag made from the skin of a goat or another animal that was used to store and serve wine (Job 32:19, NKJV).

Jesus refers to wineskins to show how the Jewish legalism of the Old Testament was inflexible and outdated. He said, "No one puts new wine into old wineskins; or else the new wine bursts the wineskins, the wine is spilled, and the wineskins are ruined" (Mark 2:22, NKJV). The "old wineskins" were Judaism, and the "new wine" was the dynamic (powerful) new faith of Christianity.

WINNOWING — the process of separating the kernels of threshed grain (like wheat or barley) from the chaff (the husks or seed coverings). The grain and chaff were thrown into the air. The kernels of wheat or barley would fall into a pile on the threshing floor and the chaff would be blown away by the wind (Ps. 1:4).

WISDOM — the ability to know and do the right thing (1 Kings 4:29–34).

WISE — a person who understands and makes good decisions based on what they know (Prov. 10:5).

WISE MEN — the men from the East who were led by a star to come to Palestine to worship the baby Jesus (Matt. 2:1, 7, 16).

WIT, WIST, WOT — to know (Luke 2:49, KJV).

WIT, TO — specifically (Rom. 8:23, KJV).

WITHER — to deplete; to dry up; to become ineffective (useless) (Ps. 102:4, NKJV; 1 Pet. 1:24, NKJV).

WITHSTAND — to stand up against (Eph. 6:13, NKJV).

WITNESS, WITNESSING — a person who

Old Testament Women

Name	Description	Biblical Reference
Bathsheba	Wife of David; mother of Solomon	2 Sam. 11:3, 27
Deborah	Judge who defeated the Canaanites	Judg. 4:4
Delilah	Philistine who tricked Samson	Judg. 16:4, 5
Dinah	Only daughter of Jacob	Gen. 30:21
Eve	First woman	Gen. 3:20
Gomer	Prophet Hosea's unfaithful wife	Hosea 1:2, 3
Hagar	Sarah's maid; mother of Ishmael	Gen. 16:3–16
Hannah	Mother of Samuel	1 Sam. 1
Jezebel	Wicked wife of King Ahab	1 Kings 16:30, 31
Jochebed	Mother of Moses	Exod. 6:20
Miriam	Sister of Moses; a prophetess	Exod. 15:20
Naomi	Ruth's mother-in-law	Ruth 1:2, 4
Orpah	Ruth's sister-in-law	Ruth 1:4
Rachel	Wife of Jacob	Gen. 29:28
Rahab	Harlot who harbored Israel's spies; ancestor of Jesus	Josh. 2:3–1; Matt. 1:5
Ruth	Wife of Boaz; mother of Obed; ancestor of Jesus	Ruth 4:13, 17; Matt. 1:5
Sarah	Wife of Abraham; mother of Isaac	Gen. 11:29; 21:2, 3
Tamar	A daughter of David	2 Sam. 13:1
Zipporah	Wife of Moses	Exod. 2:21

gives testimony or a testimony given for or against another person. Witnessing is also telling what you know, especially the gospel (Acts 1:8, 22; 2:32; 22:14, 15).

WIZARD — magician; sorcerer; person who speaks with the dead (Isa. 8:19, NKJV).

WOE — deep sorrow, grief, or affliction. Old Testament prophets often used the word to describe great feelings of despair or misfortune (Isa. 3:9, 11, NKJV; Jer. 10:19, NKJV; Amos 5:18, NKJV). In the New Testament Jesus pronounced woes on the cities of Chorazin and Bethsaida (Matt. 11:21, NKJV), on the scribes, the Pharisees, and lawyers (Luke 11:42–44, NKJV), and on the one who betrayed Him (Judas Iscariot) (Mark 14:21, NKJV).

WOMAN — an adult female (Gen. 36:12).

WOMB — a woman's uterus (Gen. 25:24, NKJV).

WONDER — something amazing; a miracle.

New Testament Women

Mary, the virgin mother of Jesus, has a place of honor among the women of the New Testament. She is an enduring example of faith, humility, and service (Luke 1:26–56). Other notable women of the New Testament include the following:

Name	Description	Biblical Reference
Anna	Recognized Jesus as the long-awaited Messiah	Luke 2:36–38
Bernice	Sister of Agrippa before whom Paul made his defense	Acts 25:13
Candace	A queen of Ethiopia	Acts 8:27
Chloe	Woman who knew of divisions in the church at Corinth	1 Cor. 1:11
Claudia	Christian of Rome	2 Tim. 4:21
Damaris	Woman of Athens converted under Paul's ministry	Acts 17:34
Dorcas (Tabitha)	Christian in Joppa who was raised from the dead by Peter	Acts 9:36–41
Drusilla	Wife of Felix, governor of Judea	Acts 24:24
Elizabeth	Mother of John the Baptist	Luke 1:5, 13
Eunice	Mother of Timothy	2 Tim. 1:5
Herodias	Queen who demanded the execution of John the Baptist	Matt. 14:3–10
Joanna	Provided for the material needs of Jesus	Luke 8:3
Lois	Grandmother of Timothy	2 Tim. 1:5
Lydia	Converted under Paul's ministry in Philippi	Acts 16:14
Martha and Mary	Sisters of Lazarus; friends of Jesus	Luke 10:38–42
Mary Magdalene	Woman from whom Jesus cast out demons	Matt. 27:56–61; Mark 16:9
Phoebe	A servant, perhaps a deaconess, in the church at Cenchrea	Rom. 16:1, 2
Priscilla	Wife of Aquila; laborer with Paul at Corinth and Ephesus	Acts 18:2, 18, 19
Salome	Mother of Jesus' disciples James and John	Matt. 20:20–24
Sapphira	Hold back goods from the early Christian community	Acts 5:1
Susanna	Provided for the material needs of Jesus	Luke 8:3

The feeling you feel after seeing something amazing or a miracle (Matt. 24:24, NKJV; Acts 3:10, NKJV).

WONT — used to; established; habit (Luke 22:39, KJV).

WORD, THE — a religious phrase that describes the absolute, eternal, and ultimate being (person) of Jesus Christ (John 1:1–14; 1 John 1:1; Rev. 19:13).

WORD OF GOD — how God makes Himself known, tells His will, and fulfills His purposes. Phrases such as "word of God" and "word of the Lord" are names for the power of God (Gen. 1), an announcement of God (Exod. 9:20–21; 1 Kings 2:27), the commitment and promises of God (Gen. 15:1, 4), and a particular instruction from God (Josh. 8:27).

WORK — physical or mental activity. Man was created to work and to enjoy it. One of his primary tasks in the Garden of Eden was to "till [work] the ground" (Gen. 2:5, NKJV). God meant for work to be a blessing, but it became a curse after sin entered the world (Gen. 3:17–19).

WORLD — the heavens and the earth that form the universe and the place where people and animals live. The Hebrew people and the Greeks use both of the terms "world" and "earth" to mean the created universe. In Psalm 24:1, the words are used as a reference to all of creation.

The word "world" is also a reference to humankind. Christ called His disciples "the light of the world" (Matt. 5:14).

The word "world" can also be used to describe the seeking of riches and pleasures and the foolishness of making them the most important thing in life (Matt. 16:26).

WORM, WORMS — a small crawling creature that is often used as a symbol of weakness (Job 17:14; Isa. 41:14).

WORMWOOD — any of several aromatic (strong-smelling) plants that yield a bitter, dark green oil (Deut. 29:18, NKJV; Rev. 8:11).

WORSHIP — the reverent devotion and allegiance pledged to God; the rituals or ceremonies performed to show this reverence (John 4:23). The English word "worship" comes from the Old English word "worthship," a word that refers to the worthiness of the one receiving the special honor or devotion.

WRATH — God's holy anger directed against sin (Rom. 1:18, NKJV). Wrath is not irrational or out of control like a fit of anger, and it is not vindictive or malicious.

WREST — to change; manipulate (2 Pet. 3:16, KJV).

WROTH — angry (Gen. 4:5, KJV; Rev. 12:17, KJV).

XYZ

XERXES [zurk´-sees] — the Greek name of Ahasuerus, the king mentioned in the Book of Esther (Esther 1:1; 2:1; 3:1, NIV). He was also known as Xerxes the Great. He was the king of Persia from 486 to 465 B.C.

YAHWEH, YAHWEH ELOHIM [yah´-way, el-oh-heem´] — name for God; pronunciation of the Hebrew consonants YHWH, usually translated "the Lord" (Exod. 3:15).

YEA — yes; indeed; truly (Ps. 23:4, NKJV).

YEAR — the period of time required for the earth to complete a single revolution around the sun. The year of the Hebrew people consisted of twelve months (1 Kings 4:7; 1 Chron. 27:1–5). These months were based on the changing cycles of the moon. A year would usually have about 354 days, but periodically a thirteenth month had to be added to the Hebrew calendar to balance out the time.

YEAR OF JUBILEE — the Year of Jubilee took place every fifty years. It was a special year for families because a man who was a slave or working off a debt was set free and allowed to return home to his family. If any members of his family were also slaves or working off a debt, the entire family was set free and allowed to go home. Houses and lands could also be redeemed in the Year of Jubilee (Lev. 25:9–14).

YEARN — to feel strongly about (1 Kings 3:26, NKJV).

YHWH — the Hebrew name of the God of Israel, originally pronounced Yahweh. Eventually the Jews quit pronouncing it because they thought the name was too holy for human mouths. Instead they said *Adonai* or "Lord."

YOKE — a device that harnesses animals together (Deut. 21:3). The word "yoke" is also used as a symbol for slavery or a burden.

YONDER — there (Matt. 26:36, KJV).

ZACCHAEUS [zak-ke´-us] *(pure)* — a tax collector of Jericho who made a lot of money by overtaxing the people. When Jesus visited Jericho, Zacchaeus climbed a tree in order to see him (Luke 19:3). Jesus asked Zacchaeus to come down from the tree and then went to his house to visit. During the visit, Zacchaeus became a follower of Jesus. He repented of his sins and tried to make up for the things he had done wrong. He gave half of what he owned to the poor and gave back four times the money to the people he had cheated.

ZACHARIAH [zak-a-ri´-ah] — a form of Zechariah.

ZACHARIAS [zak´-a-ri´-as] *(the Lord has remembered)* — the prophet who was killed by the Jews because he scolded them for breaking God's commandments; another form of Zechariah (Matt. 23:35, KJV; Luke 11:51, KJV).

Another man named Zacharias was the father of John the Baptist (Luke 1:13; 3:2).

ZADOK [za´-dok] *(just, righteous)* — a high priest in the time of David. Zadok was a son of Ahitub (2 Sam. 8:17) and a descendant of Aaron (1 Chron. 24:3). Zadok served as high priest with Abiathar (2 Sam. 8:17).

ZEAL, ZEALOUS — enthusiastic devotion; eager desire; true allegiance (support) (2 Sam. 21:2, NKJV; 2 Kings 10:16, NKJV; 19:31, NKJV).

ZEALOT [zel´-ot] *(devoted supporter)* — a Zealot was a member of a strict Jewish sect (group) that fought against the Roman domination (control) of Palestine during the first century A.D.

The Zealots were devoted to the Jewish law and religion just like the Pharisees. But the Zealots thought it was treason against God to pay taxes to the Roman emperor because God alone was Israel's king. They were willing to fight to the death for Jewish independence.

Zealot was also a nickname given to Simon, one of Jesus' twelve apostles (Luke 6:15; Acts 1:13).

ZEBEDEE [zeb´-e-dee] *(gift [of the Lord])* — the father of James and John (Matt. 4:21–22; Mark 1:19–20). He was a fisherman on the Sea of Galilee. He most likely lived in Capernaum or Bethsaida and was probably wealthy (Mark 1:20).

ZEBULUN [zeb´-u-lun] — the tenth son of Jacob and the sixth and last son of Leah (Gen. 30:19–20; 35:23; 1 Chron. 2:1). Zebulun had three sons: Sered, Elon, and Jahleel (Gen. 46:14;

The mound of New Testament Jericho, the home of Zacchaeus the tax collector who became a disciple of Jesus (Luke 19:1–10).

Num. 26:26–27). This is the only information about Zebulun in the Bible.

The territory where the tribe of Zebulun lived was also called Zebulun.

ZEBULUN, TRIBE OF — the tribe (family group) that began with Zebulun (Num. 1:9; Deut. 27:13; Josh. 19:10, 16; Judg. 1:30). The tribe was divided into three large families. Zebulun's three sons were the leaders of these families (Num. 26:26–27).

ZECHARIAH [zec-a-ri´-ah] *(the Lord remembers)* — the name of about thirty men in the Bible. A few of these are:

1. The fifteenth king of Israel (2 Kings 14:29; 15:8, 11; Zachariah, KJV). The son of Jeroboam II, Zechariah became king when his father died. Shallum killed (assassinated) him only six months after he became king.

2. A son of Meshelemiah (1 Chron. 9:21; 26:2, 14) and a Levite doorkeeper in the days of David.

3. A Levite who helped cleanse the temple during the reign of King Hezekiah of Judah (2 Chron. 29:13).

4. A prophet in the days of Ezra (Ezra 5:1; 6:14; Zech. 1:1, 7; 7:1, 8) and the author of the Book of Zechariah. He was a leader in the rebuilding of the nation of Israel after the Captivity.

5. A Levite who led a group of musicians at the dedication of the rebuilt wall of Jerusalem (Neh. 12:35–36).

ZECHARIAH, BOOK OF — a prophetic book in the Old Testament that tells about the coming of the Messiah.

Zechariah is naturally divided into two major sections: Chapters 1–8 are the prophet's encouragement to the people to finish the work of rebuilding the temple. Chapters 9–14 are Zechariah's description of Israel's glorious future and the coming of the Messiah.

ZEDEKIAH [zed-e-ki´-ah] *(the Lord my righteousness)* — a son of Chenaanah and a false prophet who told King Ahab to attack the Syrian army at Ramoth Gilead (1 Kings 22:11).

Another man named Zedekiah was the last king of Judah (597–586 B.C.). He was the son of Josiah. He became king after Jehoiachin (2 Kings 24:17–20; 25:1–7; 2 Chron. 36:10–13). Zedekiah's original name was Mattaniah, but Nebuchadnezzar renamed him to show that he had power over him and that he controlled him (2 Kings 24:17). He was king for eleven years but the people of Judah never fully accepted him as king.

ZEPHANIAH [zef-a-ni´-ah] *(the Lord has*

A painting of the prophet Zechariah by Michelangelo, in the Sistine Chapel in Rome.

hidden) — the name of four men in the Old Testament:

1. A son of Maaseiah (2 Kings 25:18; Jer. 21:1; 29:25, 29; 37:3).

2. A Levite of the family of Kohath (1 Chron. 6:36).

3. An Old Testament prophet who wrote the Book of Zephaniah (Zeph. 1:1). He began his ministry about 627 B.C., the same year as the great prophet Jeremiah.

4. Father of Josiah (Zech. 6:10).

ZEPHANIAH, BOOK OF — a short prophetic book of the Old Testament. This book reminds us that even though God's judgment is certain, He will always see to it that His chosen people will survive and continue to serve Him throughout the world.

Even though there is a lot written about judgment and punishment, the Book of Zephaniah ends with a glorious promise for the future (3:17).

ZERAH [ze´-rah] *(sprout)* — the name of seven men in the Old Testament, but the best known was probably one of the twins born to Judah by Tamar (his daughter-in-law) (Gen. 38:30; 46:12, Zarah, KJV; Matt. 1:3, Zara, KJV). Zerah started a tribal family called the Zarhites (Num. 26:20).

ZERUBBABEL [ze-rub´-ba-bel] *(offspring of Babylon)* — he led the first group of cap-tives back to Jerusalem and started rebuilding the temple on its old site. For twenty years or so, he worked closely with the prophets, priests, and kings until the new temple was dedicated and the Jewish sacrificial system was reestablished (Ezra 3:2–4:4; 5:2).

ZEUS [zoose] — the main god of the ancient Greeks. They believed that he ruled the heavens and that he was the father of other gods. The temple of Zeus at Athens was the largest temple in Greece and his statue at Olympia was one of the seven wonders of the ancient world.

ZILPAH [zil´-pah] — a female slave of Laban (the father of Leah and Rachel) and the mother of Gad and Asher (Gen. 30:9–13; 35:26). When Leah married Jacob, Laban gave her Zilpah to serve as her maid (Gen. 29:24; 46:18). Later, Leah gave Zilpah to Jacob as a concubine (Gen. 30:9).

ZION [zi´-un] — the city of David and the city of God.

In the New Testament, Zion is used as a reference to God's spiritual kingdom, the church of God, and the heavenly Jerusalem (Heb. 12:22; Rev. 14:1).

ZIPPORAH [zip-po´-rah] *(female bird)* — a daughter of Jethro who was a Midianite priest and Moses' wife (Exod. 2:21–22; 4:25; 18:2–4). She had two sons named Gershom and Eliezer.